MCKAY: A COACH'S STORY

McKay:

NEW YORK

ATHENEUM

1974

A COACH'S STORY

John McKay

OF THE USC TROJANS

with Jim Perry

To Corky and my four wonderful children,
whose dedication to football is as great as mine.

ACKNOWLEDGMENTS

SUCCESS IS A product of many men, and I want to thank all the coaches who have spent so many days and nights working with me the last fourteen years, particularly, on our current staff, Willie Brown, Dick Beam, Wayne Fontes, Marv Goux, Skip Husbands, Dave Levy, Don Lindsey and John Robinson. A special nod of appreciation also goes to a close friend and former assistant, Craig Fertig, who is now in pro football.

All of us, of course, are indebted to the hundreds of USC players who have actually gone out and won the games.

Special thanks, too, go to Norman Topping, the USC president who hired me; Nick Pappas, who helped persuade me to come to the university; and Bonnie Waite, the world's greatest secretary.

INTRODUCTION

"I told you not to fumble"

I'LL NEVER be hung in effigy. Before every season I send my men out to buy up all the rope in Los Angeles.

But I'm John McKay, a college football coach, and every fall Saturday I do stick my neck out. I have one of the few jobs in America that calls for displaying your work before thousands of people—or millions if we're on television—while everybody out there knows who the dumb guy is running this show.

A football coach today stands naked on the sideline while the television camera zooms right in and focuses on his face. Even if he's not on television, there are 80,000 other people in the stands who can find him easily enough with their binoculars. It could make a man self-conscious. But I've got enough problems of my own without worrying about the people who check me out.

I remember standing on the Rose Bowl sideline the first day of January in 1963, basking in the glow of a 42–14 lead over Wisconsin. There were only 12 minutes left in the game, and I was on my way to coaching USC to its first unbeaten, untied season in 30 years. A spectacular victory seemed inevitable.

A speedy Wisconsin halfback suddenly escaped for a touchdown to cut our lead to 42–21. Realizing how quickly games can turn around, I decided to be conservative. As our offensive unit returned to the field, I put my arm around Ben Wilson, our powerful fullback.

"Ben," I said, "go in there and tell the quarterback to run you up the middle three straight times. And Ben, for God's sake, don't fumble."

On the very first play they hit old Ben, the ball popped from his arms and rolled back to our 29, and Wisconsin recovered. Ben slumped off the field.

"Ben!" I yelled. "Damn it, I told you not to fumble!"

"Coach," he said. "I didn't hear you."

Angry and frustrated as I was, I couldn't help laughing. Before that day was over, I needed my sense of humor, because Wisconsin assumed the momentum we had lost. With a barrage of passes, they scored two more touchdowns, added a safety and just missed scoring again. We walked out with a 42–37 victory.

When I was growing up, I hardly expected to be squirming nervously on the sideline of the Rose Bowl. Until I was 25, my goal was to become football and basketball coach at my old high school in Shinnston, West Virginia—which had to be better than working in a coal mine. Most of the men in Shinnston went to the mines.

But as I joke today, I guess I failed in my ambition. I'm now in my second decade as head coach at the University of Southern California with no plans to leave. Instead of working in a town of 3,000, I operate out of the Los Angeles Coliseum. Shinnston would get lost in the Coliseum. And there's a little more pressure here. Can you imagine what it's like to be booed by 80,000 people all at once? Whenever that happens—and it's inevitable —I may look calm, but I'm so tense inside that I feel sick. I sweat on the coldest days.

I get nervous before games, too. There are times I sit alone in my dressing cubicle just before kickoff and think, "Boy, this is really gonna be something today. It would be a hell of a lot quieter, drinking a vodka and tonic somewhere and watching this game on TV."

But pressure or not, I love football, and particularly college football. I've turned down half a dozen lucrative offers to coach in the pros, because I enjoy my job so much. And don't tell me pro football is more challenging. That's nonsense. I'd like to see some of those pro coaches come in our game and win, like in South Bend against Notre Dame.

I like the atmosphere of a university and find what I do very rewarding. I originally got into coaching to work with young men, to see them grow and maybe help them develop, not just as players but also as people. You greet a boy as a freshman and four years later you see him move on with maturity and poise—a deeper person. That's one of the real joys of this business.

It's also a profession that changes daily. It's never the same team on Tuesday as it is on Wednesday, and certainly it's not the same on Saturday afternoon. There's an air of mystery. You'll write out a lineup, but some of the kids won't be able to play, and so you wonder what will happen when the new ones get in. There are always surprises.

Every week of the season is a new challenge to see if you're better than another man. In so many jobs you don't have that challenge. Football is one of the greatest sports in the world, because it's so much like a chess match. It's more a coach's game than most. There's more that can be planned and less that is improvised on the field than in other sports. One of the great pleasures is doing someing another coach doesn't expect.

I admit the season itself with all those 16-hour days is an ordeal—and the off-season with recruiting can be just as aggravating—but any coach who moans about the agony of his job ought to quit and become a fry cook. Boredom is what scares me, and as a coach I've never been bored. When I wake up in the morning I look forward to going to work. I doubt most people do. I'm 51, and I've never even thought of quitting.

There are enormous surges of emotion. There's great joy when you win and despair when you lose. One interception or fumble can ruin a month's work. Or a season's. And there have been days I felt like the greatest living teacher of the goal-line fumble.

Football may be very physical, but it's also mental and emotional, and the longer I'm in it the less I can figure the players out. You hear, for example, a lot about how players are "up" for certain games. Yet you look at them in the dressing room, at how they're acting, and there's no way of knowing if they're up or down. I'm the last to know. Even so, it's a coach's responsibility to keep them from getting too excited and panicking or from getting lazy and not concentrating.

Playing Nebraska in the first game of 1969, we were breezing along with a comfortable lead in the fourth quarter when the Cornhuskers started a comeback. After a Nebraska touchdown, everybody in the stadium knew what was coming next—an onside kick. Everybody knew, that is, except our 11 people on the field. We warned them to watch for the onside kick, and that's exactly what they did. They watched Nebraska get it. When our kickoff team returned to the bench, one of the players said, "You were right, coach. It was an onside kick."

Coaches make stupid statements, too. In my first year

as head coach, we were a big underdog to Washington in a game played in driving rain. But if we could win, we could go to the Rose Bowl. They took a 7–0 lead, but we came right back, drove inside their ten, made a first down on the five, and then ran a play to the two or three. However, our quarterback, Billy Nelsen, dislocated his finger on the last play and had to leave the game. His finger was a mess. The bone was sticking out, and it was covered with blood. I looked at his hand and asked, "Does it hurt?"

On the next play our new quarterback lost the ball on a fumble, and I said to myself, "Boy, now it really hurts." The pain was compounded when we lost the game.

But when you win a big game, it can be bedlam. After the 1963 Rose Bowl, I had my coat half torn off as I approached the dressing room and then was drenched with champagne.

I remember another bath. After we upset Notre Dame, the nation's top-ranked team, in 1964, my team, which is usually very much in awe of their old coach, threw me in the shower. Everything got wet, including my victory cigar, and I had to borrow an old practice jersey and pair of pants to sneak out of the Coliseum.

The degree of bedlam often depends on how narrowly and how late we win. In 1968 and 1969, the players were always streaming down to the end zone for on-the-field celebrations. We won ten games in the fourth quarter.

In 1972, the celebrating was less exuberant, but how could a coach and his staff feel any better than we did that season? We not only won our third national title, but were so good that we never trailed in any second half. For the first time I watched almost everything we planned work just like it was drawn.

But there are the other days in a coach's life—when

he loses and all his work has gained him nothing. I'll never rub out the frustration of 1965, when UCLA rallied to beat us in the last two and a half minutes and steal the Rose Bowl, 20 to 16.

Throughout most of the game I felt there was no way they could win. UCLA was good, but our kids were playing super football, particularly on defense. Although our offense squandered several opportunities and couldn't put UCLA away, the Bruins couldn't move at all. Nothing they tried worked. With four minutes left, we had outgained them by 250 yards, had twice as many first downs, a ten-point lead, possession of the ball—and wound up losing. A fumble, an onside kick recovery and two long touchdown passes beat us.

After the game I sipped a few drinks with friends of mine and finally fell asleep. About four in the morning I woke up and reality hit me like a slap in the face.

"My God," I thought, "this is unbelievable. We beat their damned ears back, and we lost. And they're in the Rose Bowl."

It just killed me, because I knew we had planned as well as we could, that the kids had played about as well as they could, and the result was that another coach won the big game. He was the toast of the town and I was the goat.

But the worst occurrence of my life—far worse than anything that ever happened off a football field—was losing to Notre Dame, 51–0, in 1966. USC has been playing football for 85 years, and I directed the worst defeat in Trojan history. As I stood there in the fourth quarter, I heard the public address announcer remind the crowd of that fact 14 times.

Nothing is worse to a coach than losing badly. To get beat is one thing. To get beat badly means your team is not playing anywhere near its ability. It's a giant blow to your ego. It took a year—until we beat Notre Dame in 1967—before I could go to sleep without thinking of that game. But it still sticks in my mind and will for a long time. After that, we didn't lose to Notre Dame again for six straight years. I guarantee we'll never lose to anyone 51–0 again, if I have to run 87 quarterback sneaks.

The games are easier on the players. I remember, because I played for three years at Purdue and Oregon. Players have their lives in front of them. They lose and they can still go to a dance afterward. For the coaches there is no dance. When coaches lose, they feel old.

But though I know what it's like to lose, I'm never negative. I always think we're going to move the ball, and I always think we're going to win. Of course, there have been days when I've looked out there in the first quarter and thought, "Son of a bitch, I was wrong again."

But usually we win. Starting with my third season at USC, we've won 81 percent of our games, and the winning percentage is .757 for all 14 seasons. We've captured three national titles, had three unbeaten years, gone to seven Rose Bowls and taken eight league championships. I've never seen anyone that could beat our 1972 team. It did not have a weakness.

The trouble with winning, however, is that you never take time to enjoy it. As soon as one game is over, you begin to worry about the next one. As soon as one season is over, the same thing happens. If you win a national championship, you're not successful with the public unless you win another.

After we had finished 12-0 and number one in 1972, a reporter asked me if I feared a letdown in 1973, like the one we had after winning the national title back in 1967. What letdown was that? In 1968 we lost one game and in 1969 we didn't lose any. But we ended up ranked fourth and third, instead of first, so I guess we had a letdown.

Success, I'll admit, makes me paranoid. The more I win, the more I can't stand the thought of losing. My worst extremes of emotion are when I'm consistently winning or consistently losing. If I have a winning streak going, the fear of defeat crawls at me and I catch myself thinking I must not lose. It makes me irritable.

But a coach will never escape this pressure. No matter how dazzling your record is, when you lose a game or two you hear about it from the fans. In 1969 we were undefeated, but they growled that we didn't win easily enough.

After our perfect regular season in 1972, I was in a restaurant celebrating the final victory over Notre Dame. A man walked over to our table—about an hour after we'd left the locker room—and said:

"Boy, you better be ready for Ohio State in the Rose Bowl." The Rose Bowl was a month away.

But I'm lucky, I guess, because not that many people recognize me. Don't get the idea I hide, however. I like my privacy, but my phone number's in the book. My wife, Corky, insists on it. People can call me. I figure if an old grad ever phones and says, "Drop dead, McKay," I can fall over on my own rug.

There's one woman who has called for many years to pray for our football team. She prayed so long once that Corky cooked a whole dinner while she was on the phone. But we never hang up. We need all the fans and all the prayers we can get.

CONTENTS

ILLUSTRATIONS

Following page 151

MC KAY: A COACH'S STORY

WHAT COACHING DEMANDS

"It's a very lonely job"

I'VE OFTEN BEEN ASKED how one becomes a successful big-time coach and often answered that it's simple. Get an O. J. Simpson and order him to "Run fast," "Catch the ball," and "Head for the goal line."

What a coach really has to do is work like hell. I've never worried—and know very few coaches who worry —about taking a vacation. I mean, I take them, but I don't think a vacation is crucial in my life. I work until the job is done. I know I'm going to relax sometime— of course, it might be after I die or just before I do— but right now it's enough for me to take a couple of days off and play golf or go to the beach. And that fits my nature. I couldn't sit still long enough for a two- or three-week vacation.

Corky complains, however, that my work never seems done. Even when we go to the beach for a few days in midsummer, I'll get restless after a day or two and start phoning my assistants. There have been days Corky returned from a day in the sun to find our beach house full of USC coaches.

"What are they doing here in July?" she asks.

There always seems to be a stack of work to finish, no matter what the month. We spend the winter recruiting. Then we spend spring and summer preparing for fall, and I personally warm up for the season by traveling up and down California, speaking to seven USC booster clubs in seven nights.

During the season every moment I'm awake is devoted to football. Everything else I enjoy—my family, golf, movies—is out. The team itself is the only important part of my life and I lose myself in it. I imagine the same total immersion happens to people who write novels.

So, if you want to be a good coach, the first question you must answer is not how much you know about football, but how much you like it. The game is continually evolving, and you have to keep abreast of the changes. You must like it a lot to do that.

Then, how much do you like people? Can you be around people all the time without letting them constantly irritate you? Coaching involves a tremendous number of speaking engagements, social functions and discussions with the news media. The questions about the team never end.

Next, can you accept criticism? Nobody likes it, and quite often the criticism against coaches is unjust, because people attack without knowing all the facts. Some situations are more delicate than others, and often the coach can't give the whole story.

For example, in an important game a few years ago, I played one of my stars only a few minutes and we lost. I really caught it in the press. What the sportswriters didn't know and I didn't feel I could say was that the young man had received a call from his wife three hours before the game, and she said she was leaving him. I knew it wouldn't be fair to play him with that on his mind.

A successful coach must also have strong confidence in himself. We're all consumed with self-doubt. Nobody becomes great without struggling with it. But you can't let it control you. One of the traits that makes coaches unsuccessful is jumping from one offensive or defensive trend to another, always trying to find new answers. Once I have formulated a plan, checked the alternatives and concluded what is best, I must believe in it and stick with it.

How about the pressure? It's tremendous.

Internal pressure is the toughest. Coaching is very lonely, because one man alone is responsible for the team. There's not a man who takes his first head coaching job and isn't scared. You really don't know how the players and assistants are going to react to you, and the number of problems that hit all at once is shocking. I remember realizing decisions were not as apparent as I thought when I was a bright young assistant.

Nobody knows what it's like to be a head football coach, unless he is one. An assistant only worries about his segment of the team. Of course, he cares about the rest of the players, but if his are performing well, he can sleep at night.

But the pressure on a head coach surrounds him. He has to decide everything: What is the starting lineup? What formations are we going to use? How do we practice? Whom do we recruit? What group should I speak to next?

"Damn," I thought one day early in my career, "just once I'd like to be an assistant coach again, handle the offensive backs and to hell with the rest of them."

Today no decision scares me. I'll make all the big ones, on and off the field. I'll call the play on the goal line in the fourth quarter. I've seen coaches turn and walk away from the sideline and let someone else call the crucial play. I don't want anyone else to be responsible. If it doesn't work, I'll take the blame. You need that courage to be a good coach.

Several years ago, Mel Hein, the Hall of Fame center who was in a crouch so long I think it took him 15 years to see the sun, surfaced to make a remark that still amuses me. Hein was an assistant of mine at the time, even though I was several years younger than he was.

"That kid McKay," said Mel, "is so cool about things that he can walk by your table and ice your drinks."

Best call icy McKay ever made was against Stanford in 1969, with one of our unbeaten teams. The lead changed hands seven times that night, and it looked as if it had changed for good when Stanford kicked a field goal with a minute and three seconds left for a 24–23 lead.

After the kickoff, we began from our 15. A five-yard gain and two incomplete passes later, it was fourth and five on the 20. There were 41 seconds left, and our chance for the Rose Bowl was slipping away.

Stanford had been playing in a pass prevent defense, which was logical, but I called a blast play, which would send our tailback, Clarence Davis, running off tackle. It's one of our standard plays, one we've practiced and used several thousand times.. But my assistants were stunned when I called it with 41 seconds left.

However, I thought that was the best call. I've always believed that when you get behind you should do what you know best. Most big errors come on wild plays when you're trying to catch up.

Davis took the handoff, ran off tackle and made seven yards for a first down.

Three completed passes later, we were on the Stanford 17. As the clock blinked down to zero, Ron Ayala kicked a field goal, and we won by two points, 26 to 24.

In some ways a successful coach must be aloof, at times to the point of arrogance. Not only must he make the big decisions, but he must ignore what people think of him and those decisions. A desire to be liked can kill a coach. You decide on something and then think, "Hmm, wonder what the assistants thought of that? The players? The alumni? The school president?" Pretty soon you're trying to appease everybody all the time. Everyone cares about being liked, but you can care and not let it bother you if they don't like you.

Another requisite for being a successful coach is a sense of humor. It helps you survive. At times, such as after a tough loss, my jokes are sort of a defense mechanism. If I give the reporters a fast line, it helps them and bails me out. For the players, a quip can help ease their suffering. Life will always go on if we lose. You can't tell your team the games are matters of life and death.

In the midnight gloom of our dressing room—after that horrible 51–0 loss to Notre Dame—I gathered my players and talked to them for a few moments. No one felt worse than I did. But before sending them to the showers, I said:

"Forget it, guys. Do you realize there are 700 million Chinese who didn't even know the game was played?"

The next week I got three letters from China complaining about the loss.

Now, if an aspiring young coach has all these qualities I have recounted, the last and most important question for him is: Who did you marry? I don't think any coach has much chance to be successful unless he has a super wife.

She hears the abuse and has to learn to live with it, adjust to it and not let it get too personal. She has to learn to raise a family with the father away much of the time. If your wife wants you home at night—and most nights you aren't going to be there—then she's going to be mad, and you'll have a terrible existence. There are so many wives that can't handle the life.

I can phone Corky, say I'm on my way home, ask her to have some drinks and a steak ready, and suddenly I get a call from one of my assistants. "That kid in Long Beach we're recruiting is ready to sign with us," he says, "if you'll go right down and see him." Let's say this kid runs 9.3 in the 100, is 6 foot 2, weighs 227 pounds. No way I'm going home. This is something wives have to understand.

I've always felt that if a man's wife demands where he's been when he's late, he's got to think, "Damn, I lost a mother and just inherited another one."

But, oh God, Corky is the greatest football wife in the country. Luckily we got married in 1950, the first year I went into this business, so she learned immediately that a coach's wife never sees her husband during the season.

I do take her on a lot of trips, such as to all the road games, but there are many, many nights when she's home alone with the kids. I'd say I'm out about 280 nights a year.

But I think this life is very good for us. Since I'm not around very often, Corky and I have little time to get on each other's nerves. I'm too restless to be home all the time anyway.

"And I couldn't stand you here, either," Corky says. "If you came home for lunch and worked eight to five, we'd both go crazy."

In many ways she likes the life. She enjoys the travel, enjoys meeting people—much more than I do—and even likes the big banquets we have to attend, although she does kid about them.

"How exciting," she says, "another night out with 400 of our most intimate friends."

Of course, the games often shake her up. For many years, when she sat in the stands in the Coliseum, she often left her seat and retreated to one of the tunnels which lead in and out of the stadium. From there, she would peek out to watch the game, and then duck back in—sort of like putting your hands over your eyes during a horror film. Once, she says, another fan asked an usher why she was standing back there. "Oh, that's Mrs. Mc-Kay," the usher replied. "She's spent ten years in this tunnel."

Now Mrs. McKay has even more to worry about at games, because our oldest son, Johnny, starts at split end for USC. As she points out:

"John, when I used to go to games, people around me would point angrily at you and say, 'There's that idiot coach McKay.' Now they point and say, 'There's that idiot coach McKay using his idiot son.' "

Although we've been married 24 years, Corky and I do have problems during the season. There is strain. Because of the nature of my work, for example, when I'm preparing for a game I start concentrating so hard that I don't see people. That's my personality. I won't bother myself with a person or some incidental problem.

Many people don't understand this at all. Some of them think John McKay is an arrogant horse's ass. I'll be friendly one day and ignore them the next. But on Friday nights before games, and on Saturday mornings, I don't want to talk to anyone. I hardly talk to Corky.

No matter how hard I try and explain this to my wife, she doesn't always understand, because she's never had the experience. A typical conversation the night before a game—we'll be in a hotel—might go like this:

"Well, you didn't even talk to our friend," she'll say. "You just went right to bed."

"Yes, that's always what I'm going to do."

"But we went out with him last year and had such a good time."

"Yeah, we did have a good time, but we were in Palm Springs. We weren't about to play Notre Dame."

I'll never forget a night about 20 years ago, when I was an assistant at Oregon. Another coach and I went to a cocktail party and mingled with the alumni. The next day our team lost to Washington in Seattle. "No wonder they lost," people said. "They were out drinking all night."

That really hurt me—that someone would insinuate I wasn't doing my job. I determined then I would never go out again.

Other coaches are more gregarious. They're out that night or in the hotel lobby the next morning mingling with alumni and sportswriters, patting people on the back. Inevitably, since their minds are everywhere but on football, they're going to turn to some assistant coach during the game and ask what to do.

This is not my style. Kickoff begins for me when I get up Saturday morning. The staff meets me at eight, and we'll have coffee and doughnuts and review all our plans. We won't tolerate interruptions.

But there was one exception to even that rule. It was 1967, a cold morning when we were getting ready to play Notre Dame in South Bend—one of the most important games of my life. There was a knock at the door, so one of my assistants looked out, and standing in the hallway was my mother. She had come over from West Virginia to watch the game.

Mom came in and met the staff, wished us luck and then turned to leave. She paused at the door.

"Jack," she said—my family always called me Jack—"did you eat your breakfast? If you didn't, don't forget."

I don't remember if I ate, but we did win the game.

On the bus going to the stadium I'm very quiet. I used to sit with our first-string quarterback, but in the past few years I began to feel I was making them nervous. So now I sit with the assistant who coaches the quarterbacks. I want to write down the final details while we're still on the bus, no matter how trivial. Besides the game strategy, I want to know exactly when we're going on the field, who the captains are for this game, what their numbers are, who's going to lead the team prayer. Maybe 28 or 30 items go down on that pad. By the time we reach the stadium I'm almost ready.

When I talk to the players before the game, I don't talk off the top of my head. I review again what the game means to us and what happened last year against this team. I tell them, this is what we believe we'll do this time. This is the defense our opponents will probably use, but they're underdogs and might switch to another one to fool us, so don't bet on the first one. We'll start with these plays, and if they start changing defenses, don't panic. We'll change the plays. We'll get you out of any mess you get into. Just relax and play our kind of game and you'll win. So go out and have some fun.

For a while before the kickoff I'll sit alone, smoke a cigar and review the technical details again. I'll study all my offensive and defensive cards outlining our plan, but I want the information in my head. I don't want to stare at the cards like a dummy all afternoon.

You see, I'm about to take an examination: the game. Actors say they shut themselves in a trailer to think about their scene before going out to perform, and that's what I do—for almost 24 hours. There will be a lot of decisions made in that game and I'm going to be able to make them. I better be sure that I'm mentally alert—that I've thought out every situation.

I would hate to think to myself after the game, "Damn, if I had only thought ahead a little more, maybe we could have won."

So I'll know what the other team might do in every case and how we should react. What happens on the field isn't automatic. It has to come from one strong source.

Many losing coaches, however, fail to think ahead. They figure they'll adjust when something happens. And they get whipped, because they wait too long to react.

When I'm coaching I concentrate so hard that I wouldn't be embarrassed if my pants fell down. I wouldn't have time to be embarrassed. In fact, one day, when we were playing UCLA on national TV, I was wearing my lucky pants, and right before halftime I squatted down and they split. At the half I just went in and changed.

I don't think most people pay attention as well as they should. I remember a recent example of a friend of mine, who wasn't a coach. He said to me one day, "I can always tell when you're nervous on the sideline."

"How do you know when I'm nervous?"

"Because you're running up and down really puffing on that cigar."

Well, I've been smoking cigars since I was in the service, 30 years ago, but I have never smoked on the sideline of a football field.

While I'm concentrating, I try to keep fairly calm. I've always been that way as a coach. It's important because this calmness rubs off on your players, helps them keep their own poise. O. J. Simpson said it better than anyone else: I won't lose the game on Saturday by getting unnerved.

As I mentioned before, game plans are not irrevocable.

Even though we've planned all week, I'm not going to be bound to that plan if it's not working. If we get in a situation where I think a certain pass pattern should be run differently because of the way the other defense is playing, I'll change the pattern, and our players will have to adjust.

We may look so bad we practically fall down coming out of the huddle, but I'll do something to try and get us straightened out—right away and not next week.

When we upset unbeaten Notre Dame in November, 1964, I sent a pass play in to quarterback Craig Fertig that we hadn't used all season. We had practiced it only in the spring. It was midway through the fourth quarter, we were trailing, 17 to 7, and were backed inside our own 20 on third down. But Fertig threw 28 yards to Fred Hill for a first down and we went on and scored. That touchdown got us back in the game, and we won in the last two minutes.

To keep track of what's happening, I walk back and forth on the sideline more than the men carrying the first-down markers, and I see a lot. I'm practically as close to the game as the players, except there's nobody hitting me. I know where we're going to run the ball, so I can watch that area. I can tell if the play worked or not—and why. We also have coaches watching upstairs in the pressbox with binoculars. They talk to us by phones. But I learn more from the players coming off the field than I do from the coaches upstairs.

For example, against Oregon in 1973, our flanker, Lynn Swann, came to the sideline with the rest of the offense and told me that our screen pass to him would work, because of the way the defense was reacting. Swann was a very bright, aware player, and what he said impressed me.

The screen to Swann was the first play I called the next

time our offense was on the field. He caught the short pass and ran 55 yards for a touchdown.

Although I can see a lot, I laugh when some oldtimer tells me he could see all 11 men at once when he was coaching. I can't, and he couldn't, either. You have to look at game films three or four times to see all 11 players.

When the action is over, it's sometimes an emotional strain to cross the field and shake hands with the rival coach, if he's my friend. I've found this uncomfortable with Paul "Bear" Bryant of Alabama, Duffy Daugherty, when he was at Michigan State, and I certainly find it difficult with Washington's Jim Owens, whose team we play every year. But the handshake is one of our profession's rituals, so I do it.

I used to think that it was important as an example of good sportsmanship. It would prove to the fans that everybody should be friends, no matter who won. But now that crowds have this compulsion to run onto the field and knock people down, the handshake has become not only an emotional strain, but a physical one as well. In fact, it can be dangerous. At Notre Dame in 1973, when I was walking across to see Ara Parseghian, I was jarred by a hard blow on my shoulder. Somebody running past had hit me, and I had no idea who it was. So I think now the handshake should be eliminated.

There's no reason for a coach to be subject to all this mindless jostling by people swirling around on the field. The poor guy has already been on pins and needles for three hours on the sideline and he doesn't need any more aggravation. And when people yell obscenities at me—and they do frequently—that bothers me more than anything. I'm amazed sometimes at the way adults act at football games.

But sometimes when I walk over to see a friend we

relax each other with a quip or two. In 1970 we opened at Alabama, the first time I'd ever played my best buddy, Bear Bryant. Everything went right for us. We jumped ahead 32–7 and coasted to victory, 42–21. When I met Bear at midfield, he looked me in the eye and said, "Damn, John, we just ran out of time."

I admit that victory hurt me a little, however, because I knew Bear was unhappy. Coaches have always said they'd rather not play their best friends. This isn't a practical solution, so we just don't talk about the game after it's over. I've hardly ever said anything about our victory over Bryant that year, and he's seldom mentioned beating me in Los Angeles the next year. Usually, we'll go play golf, have a couple of drinks and forget football.

Corky, meanwhile, has become very close to Mary Harmon Bryant, Paul's wife, and Martha Owens, Jim's wife. Corky and Martha meet for lunch every year, whether we go to Seattle for the Washington game, or they come to Los Angeles. A few years ago, the University of Washington team was staying in a Los Angeles hotel, and Corky drove over to meet Martha.

She marched into this big suite and surprised the coaches who had their offensive and defensive plays spread all over the tables. The younger ones panicked and tried to cover them up, but Corky walked over quickly, picked up a card and said, "Jim, this old Statue of Liberty play will *never* work against us."

"Corky," said Jim, "you're holding up SC's defense."

Football is much further advanced than it was 15 years ago, and it's completely different than it was 20 or 25 years ago. Motion pictures have changed it. Today, we spend thousands of hours looking at film, and there are no more secrets.

By studying film of our opponents and stuffing the information in a computer, we can figure out his tendencies —when and how often he'll run a certain play. Conversely, we have to change our own offenses and defenses continually, so he can't pick us apart. We scout ourselves as thoroughly as we scout our opponents. We study our films and put all our plays in the computer, too.

As the season goes on, our work load increases along with the games. By the time we play UCLA we'll have nine or ten game movies to study.

And each week is a new experience. Teams used to rely on one or two basic offensive formations and one or two basic defensive formations. Offenses have gotten more complex, of course, but the greatest complications in the last few years have come on defense. At USC, for example, we have 15 or 16 pass defenses alone—although we wouldn't use them all in the same game. But some teams might use 25 different defensive alignments in a game.

Because of these rapid changes, it takes more intelligence to play today than it did 20 or 30 years ago. But, because coaching staffs have more than doubled in size, there's more teaching of players now.

Many head coaches, some of them fairly successful, pay more attention to the public relations side of their jobs than to this technical side. They have head offensive and defensive coaches—or coordinators—doing much of their planning. I don't believe in this. I don't have offensive or defensive coordinators.

In 1960, my first year as a head coach, I ran the offense and one of my assistants ran the defense. We had a losing season. Now I split my time. To me, it's important that the head coach doesn't divorce himself from one part of his team. Besides, I enjoy coaching both offense and defense. Just planning one phase wouldn't be enough challenge for me.

I believe defense teaches you about offense, and offense teaches you about defense. I've never designed an offense without figuring out how to stop it. When I was an assistant coach at Oregon for nine years, I spent almost three hours a night doing nothing but thinking about football. Corky almost went out of her mind. Plays were scattered all over the house. Even today, I spend at least an hour a day drawing them.

I draw plays on tablets, I draw them on cocktail napkins, and I draw them on tablecloths. I'll draw anywhere. If I'm watching a movie on television, I'll be scribbling plays at the same time. I like to think of myself as an innovator, rather than an imitator.

The first pass we completed against Arkansas in 1972 came from a design on a bar booth tablecloth. The same season, I added a new pass play the day before our Rose Bowl–deciding game with UCLA. I concluded that if UCLA lined up the way I thought they would, they couldn't stop this pass the first time they saw it. I was right. We tried it only once, and the pass went from Mike Rae to Lynn Swann for 25 yards.

Some coaches improvise like this, some don't. Some feel the idea might be good, but because you can't practice it, you probably can't do it well. I figure you can succeed if you put the pressure on your best players. I knew Swann could run the pattern, and I knew Rae could hit him with the pass. Putting in plays this late is almost like street football, a little bit of that old drawing the play in the dirt.

Whenever I draw new formations or plays I always fill in the formation with an actual lineup of my players. After studying it, I'll redraw the formation and move a player to another position. Then I'll draw it again, move someone else there and switch the first guy to another spot. Under each lineup, I'll jot down the advantages and disadvantages. And, all of a sudden, I may realize, hey, we should be playing some kid in another position.

We probably change players' positions more than most teams do. Sometimes, coaches will decide for all time, "This young man is a *right* tackle." Well, he might help you win better somewhere else.

Since my assistants know how much I'm thinking about football, they don't barge into my office with stacks of trick plays. They had better think them through first. If they can convince me of a play's worth, I'll accept it. But I don't want to hear that it's a great play because the Miami Dolphins use it. It must be discussed in terms of our players, not Miami's. If the play demands that the strong-side guard be the best blocker in the world, and our strong-side guard weighs 207 instead of 250, then it may be great theory, but it won't work.

To stay abreast of the game in the off-season, I accept several invitations to speak at clinics for coaches. After I've lectured, I'll sit down and hear what the others have to say. By traveling around the country and listening to as many coaches as possible, I'll learn as much or more than they'll learn listening to me.

When you get older you tend to become less receptive to ideas, but you can't stop listening to them. I feel coaches should be like doctors who go to seminars to find new methods of operating. Any coach who thinks he knows it all has got a defeat waiting right around the corner.

Too many people waste their time at clinics and don't get out of them what they should. A good speaker, like Frank Broyles of Arkansas or Bob Devaney, the ex-Nebraska coach, will explain what he does and why he does it, and then some clown in the rear of the classroom will say, "Heck, if I had his players, I could do what he does, too."

This is like hearing a great surgeon describe how he operates and responding, "If I had his scalpel, I could do it, too." Why don't they just listen?

Besides, the coach with the best players does not always win. He has a better chance of winning. Too many people—fans, sportswriters and some coaches—want to give material all the credit for a man's success. I know coaches who can lose with good players. Getting them to perform well after you recruit them is not as easy as everyone thinks.

Consider what Ara Parseghian did in 1964, his first year at Notre Dame. He went 9-1 with the same personnel that had a 2-7 record the previous season. He took John Huarte, a quarterback who had sat on the bench for two years, and made him the Heisman Trophy winner. Ara had the same players, no bigger, no faster than the year before. Unless you're dense, you have to say, hey, this man is a pretty good coach.

How about old Bear Bryant? People say, "Alabama always wins. So he should always win." They didn't always win. The four years before Bear arrived, Alabama won eight out of 41 games. One season the record was 0-10. His first season Alabama went from 2-7-1 to 5-4-1, and he's been winning ever since.

I've heard others say it's easy to win at Nebraska. Well, from 1956 to 1961, Nebraska never had a winning season. They won only 19 of 60 games. In 1962, Devaney's first year, they were miraculously 9-2.

So when these people talk at clinics it's worth listening. It always amuses me to see a top coach talking while some young hotshot is diagramming a play for somebody else. Instead of learning, he's telling what little he knows.

I may have very strong ideas about what I want to do offensively and defensively, but I'm not stubborn enough to resist change if I think there's a better way. And I'm not too shy to ask for help, either.

Let me give you a striking example of how much Frank Broyles helped me in 1962, and how I returned the favor in 1964. I had been USC's head coach for two years, when I went to a clinic in the middle of summer and heard Frank talk about his Arkansas "50 Defense."

At the time I wasn't happy with my own defense, even though we had used it all spring. We had a potentially explosive offensive team returning in 1962, but I knew we couldn't play defense like we did in 1961 and be successful. In 1961 our opponents outscored us.

I copied down every word Frank said. After he spoke, I chatted with him for a while, then came home and spent three weeks deciphering his comments. I called him and asked him to send me a couple of Arkansas game films, and I studied those, too.

Then I took his defense and wrote in the names of my own players, and I could see that the Arkansas defense, with a few alterations for our personnel, would be effective for USC.

It was. We won 11 straight games and my first national championship and allowed only 55 points during the regular season. But the public gave my new offensive formation, the I, most of the credit.

The same year Broyles had a 9-2 record. But in 1963 he slipped to 5-5, and came to me for advice. He wanted to learn all about the I-formation. We helped him install it. The result? In 1964 Arkansas went 11-0, won the national championship, and went on to win 22 straight games.

As long as I've been coaching and as successful as I've been, I'd make a radical change like I did in 1962 all over again if I thought we weren't playing well. I revamped my defense in the middle of the 1971 season and turned a losing season into a winning one, and I'd change it tomorrow if I thought it was wrong.

You may wonder why Broyles and I could be so honest with each other, since we were opposing head coaches. That's because we weren't scheduled to play for many years. It would be wrong to discuss technical aspects of the game with somebody you played every year. That's why Jim Owens and I confine our football discussions to team discipline or morale, and not how you run off tackle.

I've probably talked more technical football with Charley McLendon at LSU than anyone—we'll talk about it all season—but we've never played.

Simply changing formations or plays, however, doesn't make coaches successful. And if you do it too much it may hurt you. Since we all like to doodle, it's hard not to keep making changes. You get fancy and think, well, we'll run this way and that way, and pretty soon you've got so many ways to run that the players that have to do the running make mistakes. And the players who have to block make mistakes. And you're the idiot who put in more plays than the kids could remember.

There are nights during the season when I sleep only four or five hours. Sunday, Monday and Tuesday I'm up by 5:30 in the morning. The rest of the week I'm awake by 6:30 or seven. If I'm tired, I just have to apply will power and force my body to accept that schedule. But I don't mind. I figure once you die you're not going to get up anymore, so I appreciate every chance I get.

Most of the time I like getting up early, anyway, although I realize there are people who hate it. Corky does. She's terrible in the morning.

When I get up at dawn, however, I don't run around

and jump up and down, inhaling, exhaling and opening windows. I simply put on my robe, come downstairs if I'm home, start the coffee perking, get some orange juice and read or watch a little TV. I enjoy that part of the day.

The first part of the week I don't have the luxury of sleeping at home, however. We work so late—to around 11 or 12 at night—that I stay at a downtown hotel, which is just a few miles from USC.

If I'm home, I often have help getting up. Our scrappy little dog, Alfie, is also an early riser. He awakens out on the patio, runs up an outside stairway, goes down our long balcony and barks at our bedroom door. If he's seen me downstairs—we have sliding glass doors—he won't go to the bedroom. But if he hasn't, he'll go up there and bark until I let him in. He's my backup alarm clock.

After I get up, I often start reading newspapers, which I've found to be an invaluable source of information. I read 16 or 17 a day from other schools and other cities, trying to pick up some bit of information that will give USC an edge. Just by reading, I'll often tell an assistant more about an upcoming opponent than he'll tell me.

For instance, I might discover an article that says a team's starting right cornerback was injured in an automobile accident and won't play, a fact nobody knew in Southern California. Or, if the newspaper lists how our opponent is going to line up on defense, I can tell by size what formation they're planning to play. This is important for the first game, when you haven't had a chance to study any recent films. My whole talk to the squad on Monday before the 1972 opener with Arkansas was based on what I'd read in Arkansas papers about their spring practice.

Newspapers aren't the only additional source of information. Perhaps a visiting scout may have indicated how he feels we can be stopped, tipping the defense his team might use. Scouts are idiotic. They have a compulsion to talk. I always ask our radio announcer if he interviewed another team's scout at halftime. The scout might have said something that will help me decide what to do against his team.

To be a head coach you must be on top of everything. You have to drive yourself and drive your assistants to make sure everything is covered. You can't say, "I won't worry about this problem, because my assistants will handle it." What if they don't? No matter what I assign my staff to do, I'll always check and make sure they did it.

Working this hard takes tremendous discipline, and I think it carries over to my personal life. I can discipline myself in other ways. I usually lose weight during the season, for example, which makes up for all the pounds I gain the rest of the year on the recruiting and banquet circuit. But in 1972 I didn't lose. I kept going up until I tipped the scales at 202, which was some distance from my old playing weight of 172.

Those pounds snuck up on me. I wear stretch pants and they kept stretching, so I felt fine.

I went for a health checkup and my doctor glared at me. "John," he said, "you get out of here and lose that weight. You're much heavier than you should be, unless you're going to play guard for your own team."

So I trimmed off 21 pounds in six weeks. But dieting didn't bother me—except for one phase of it. I began to have an insane craving for sweets. I could be anywhere and all of a sudden I'd be daydreaming of a piece of pie.

That's why you shouldn't drink too much when you're on a diet. I've had friends tell me I can drink all the liquor I want on a particular diet. But alcohol knocks down your inhibitions, and you fall off the diet.

This is what happens to Ray George, one of our assistant athletic directors. Ray, God bless him, gets up in the morning after a big night, grabs his head and says, "Son of a bitch, I drank too much. But the worst thing I did was eat those two pieces of pie."

So discipline is important in the life of a football coach. I laugh at coaches who are fat and go out and preach about discipline. But we all don't talk about it as much as George Allen, coach of the Washington Redskins. You can't meet George without him telling you within five seconds how hard he's working:

"You know, John, I worked 27 hours yesterday. Rest of the coaches were all out enjoying themselves. Not me. I was slaving away. That's how to win, John."

George seems incapable of having a good time—even in the off-season. He doesn't do anything for fun but eat ice cream. He's always saying that he's going down for a dish of ice cream.

In my off-season, for example, I enjoy playing golf. My handicap is 14 and I'm probably the worst 14 in the world, but I play.

But George—and I've known him since the 1950's when he coached at Whittier College—is an evangelist for work. After the 1972 season we met at the Washington, D.C., Touchdown Club, where I received an award as College Coach of the Year and George one for being Pro Coach of the Year. He rushed me like a long-lost brother, and in four seconds told me how hard he'd been working since the Super Bowl. I mean, he didn't say congratulations to me or anything. Boyd Dowler, one of his assistants, was over in the corner, winking at me.

A few years ago, when he was still the Los Angeles Rams coach, George visited USC one afternoon to see a professor about methods of saving time. He spotted me having lunch with Dave Levy, one of my assistants. He reached our table in half a second. Then he introduced the professor and gave us this:

"You know where all our friends are, don't you, John?"

"No, George."

"They're out playing golf. But I'm over here, trying to learn something. And you're on campus working, too. Nobody has to play golf. Sleep is all the recreation you need. You gonna be a great football coach, you got to learn something all the time. Right, John?"

If you can believe George, he's successful because he outworks everybody. He doesn't win because he has good players or is smart or innovative or knows how to handle people skillfully. He wins because he's working all year. Everybody else is supposedly out playing golf.

Sometimes my enthusiasm for football gets me in arguments. I like basketball—I played it for several years—but I got into a lively discussion about it with UCLA coach Johnny Wooden one day and made him mad at me. John is a friend of mine, but I triggered an argument when I said, "John, you've got an easy sport to practice."

He countered that basketball was a physically demanding sport, and I snapped again that it wasn't, and we took off from there. Well, compared to football, I don't see basketball as a very trying sport at all. You don't have to be as physically tough. It's just a matter of getting into condition. They tell me how difficult it is because the players have to run so much, but running is just running. I've watched players float along on the outside of the action, run up and down the court and not touch anybody for ten minutes, then come to the bench and get their breath.

If you don't want to join the contact under the basket, you don't have to. You might not stay in the game long if you don't, but as I said to Wooden, you're not forced to mix it up.

The fact that you can't avoid the contact is one of the

factors that makes football so demanding. Many of the players also have to overcome immense personal frustration. In basketball, as in so many other sports, every player can score. Every player touches the ball. An offensive lineman may not touch the ball all season, knocks the hell out of the man in front of him all afternoon, has the hell knocked out of him, and no one even knows his name. Half the time you can't even see him. But he has to keep hammering away.

That's why I admire the people who play my game.

MY EARLY LIFE

"There weren't many cookies floating around"

MY FRIEND, Bear Bryant, has always said he worked so hard and became such a successful coach because he had great motivation. He didn't want to go back to the miserable life he knew growing up in a small town in Arkansas. I know what Bear means.

I became such a success because I didn't want to spend my life working in the coal mines of West Virginia.

Our family enjoyed a very comfortable existence when my father was alive, but he died suddenly the year I was 13 and just as suddenly we became poor. So I matured early. I worked as a paper boy, swept out restaurants and schools, washed bathrooms, delivered wet concrete in a wheelbarrow and was an electrician's assistant in a mine —I either worked or we didn't survive. But I think the struggling boyhood was good for my character.

The more money a family has, the less pressure there is on the children to mature. You just don't have the same responsibility. Consequently, I think kids from families that are wealthy or near-wealthy may have a more difficult time in life. People that don't have responsibility don't take responsibility. It may come as a shock when they're forced to.

Of course, my boyhood wasn't unique in the 1930's. Most people were poor and most people, young and old, worked hard, particularly in the hilly coal-mining country where I grew up.

In the town of Shinnston, where I played high school football and basketball, all the athletes were heroes. There were only two kinds of young men in Shinnston, those headed for the mines and those who excelled in sports so they could go to college and escape digging coal. My ambition was to get a college education and return to replace my coach, Mickey McClung. Or come back and be his assistant.

McClung was Shinnston High's only coach, and he really liked his job. He worked very hard—and I couldn't help but be impressed by his enthusiasm.

But Mickey wasn't the first person to inspire me toward coaching. When I was younger and living in Fairmont, West Virginia, I admired Pat Tork, my junior high coach. For a while I was very intrigued by his job.

McClung died many years ago, but Tork, the father of former world pole vault record-holder Dave Tork, worked until 1973, when he retired from the physical education department at the University of West Virginia. I leaned a lot on Pat when my father died. He was very, very good to me when I needed him.

I was born July 5, 1923, in the McKay house in Everettsville, West Virginia. Everettsville was a tiny coal-mining town that doesn't exist anymore. When the coal dried up, the people left. The first person I remember, besides members of my family, was the policeman who rode his brown horse through the streets. He rode to stay out of the mud.

My mother and dad were Scotch-Irish from Pennsylvania, and moved to West Virginia after they got married. All my other relatives lived in the Pittsburgh area.

Dad, whose name was John, was a mine superintendent who made a very good living for that time and that area. My mother, Gertrude, now lives in Spokane with my older sister, June. She had five children to raise.

Jimmy, who is a retired Air Force colonel, was the oldest. Then came June, myself, Richard and my younger sister, Punky. Richie, my youngest son, is named after my younger brother, who was killed during World War II.

The McKay family was always on the move in northern West Virginia, and I lived in seven different places before I was 16. But wherever we settled I was very active in sports. In fact, I became a professional when I was very young. Every Sunday June and I wrestled for a nickel. The paymaster was our young Catholic priest.

Like other Catholic families in those little towns, we often invited the priest over. Ours was Father O'Brien, who was taking care of his first parish. Father O'Brien usually had breakfast with us on Sundays after celebrating Mass and that's when we wrestled. June is three years older than me, and at first she won most of the time. She was stronger and could pin me. But I was maturing fast and once I beat her, I never lost again.

Like my dad, I hated to lose at anything. When I was older and one of my teams lost, I'd storm home and go to my room without saying a word. I had a quick temper as a boy, and, again like my dad, I was impatient, independent and always ready to accept a challenge.

One day, when I was about six or seven, we kids were all at home with a girl who sometimes took care of us. She was burning trash in the field next to our house.

I looked at that fire like I look at football teams today.

"I can jump over the fire," I said.

"No you can't," said my older brother.

Now I was really charged up, and I ran and leaped over the flames. But my pants caught on fire.

I hit the dirt and rolled around on the ground to put the fire out, but it left a scar inside my left leg—from my ankle to my knee. It's still there and will be until I die. That day I learned an important lesson: If you're gonna jump over fire, jump high.

My father was athletic, too. He played baseball every Sunday before I was born, and later the two of us threw a baseball back and forth on the front lawn every night. Baseball was my favorite sport when I was young. Dad was about 5-10, 175 or 180 pounds and could run like hell. Which is just like me.

I was very close to my father, and he was very good to me. But he was like most fathers in that era. They'd get up at five in the morning, head for work and wouldn't get home until five at night. Then we all had dinner, and if there wasn't anything else to do, dad was in bed by eight or nine. The family never saw him at breakfast.

You hear today that fathers don't spend as much time with their children as they used to. But I don't really believe that. It seems like they were gone much more when I was growing up. Sunday was an important day for us, however, because dad would be home and we'd have a picnic.

My father treated me a lot like I've treated my oldest son, Johnny. Dad was very interested in me, but he didn't sit around at night and spend much time talking to me. I believe my children know what I feel about them, but I never have spent hours lecturing them, and never will.

I was pretty much of a normal kid, I guess. I do remember being fascinated by uniforms. One day, when I was about four, I was visiting an aunt whose husband had been a World War I Army officer. His picture, in uniform, was on the wall. I crawled up on the piano and took the picture off the wall. Then I pulled it out of the frame, looked at it and realized I didn't know how to get it back in. Today I laugh about my ingenuity—I stuck the picture back up on the nail and poked a hole through my uncle.

My father always made us pay for anything wrong that we did. I broke a window once and he marched me over there immediately to apologize. Whoever got in trouble had to face the consequences right away. Sometimes dad would simply make me apologize, and sometimes he'd take his leather belt off and swat me about five times across the backside. That would usually straighten me out—or up. Yes, it stung a lot.

Even so, I almost never cried. I knew as a boy I wasn't going to get much sympathy by doing it. I don't think crying is necessarily a sign of weakness—I got tears in my eyes talking to my team before one of our games with Notre Dame. But for the most part I'm a little embarrassed by crying. Maybe there's too much pride in me. But I know one damn thing: I'm not unemotional. I just hide it sometimes.

Although as a boy I spent more time with my father, I had a wonderful mother, too. She was very good to me. She raised children like they're supposed to be raised—gave us independence and let us grow up. She's always said I was easy to take care of, anyway, because I could entertain myself.

I guess mom has been excited by my success, but she never says much to me about it. Every once in a while she flies down to visit us, and last year we sent her back to West Virginia to visit her old friends.

But, as I said, I was almost exactly like my father in personality. He had a tremendous influence on me. When there was a problem, he made a decision. And he feared nobody.

Like me, he wasn't a glad-hander, and the way he treated other people has always stuck with me. I guess I picked up that part of his personality, too.

Next to USC is a restaurant named Julie's, where my coaches and I go several times a week to sit down and talk. But I'm still not at ease going in there and running around to all the tables shaking hands. Like my father, that bothers me. I figure people will say, "Well, here's the big phony shaking hands with us."

Sometimes I'd like to be more outgoing, and then suddenly I'll just think, "Oh, hell, let me get in my booth and have a drink with my coaches."

I'm by nature a loner, and I've always been that way, although as I said earlier, I become even more aloof just before games. But even in the month of, say, April, I may want to be left alone, and people who don't understand will think, "Ah, the son of a bitch has won some national championships, and now he doesn't speak to anybody."

They don't realize that before I ever won a game I didn't talk to many people. In college, I think I once went ten days without talking to my roommate in the fraternity house. He kids me now that the first thing I said after that protracted silence was:

"Uh, as long as you're taking your laundry downstairs, would you take mine, too?"

When I was a boy I didn't have many friends, although I was very close to the ones I had. Today, my best friends are mostly quiet people.

I still hate to go through receiving lines, and I'd rather not eat than go through cafeteria lines where you're right out in the open. I don't like to go to large cocktail parties, either. I hate to feel that people are looking at me. I suppose I'm basically shy.

When I was a boy and my parents had company over, they had to drag me out to meet them. Once I felt comfortable, though, I could be a bit of a ham. Sometimes we older kids would put on skits for our grandparents, and I would play the clown.

It's funny, but I don't worry about people looking at me at games. I always assume that anyone with any intelligence is watching the players and not me. Corky watches me, though. She wants to make sure I take good care of our wide-receiver son.

As a coach, I've been forced to become a public speaker, which wasn't easy. Though my father wasn't a coach, he was a good extemporaneous speaker. He had a sharp sense of humor, and he could be sarcastic, too.

My Aunt Ethel told me a story about their school days, when he got caught short and had to come up with a quick answer. He and my aunt, so the story goes, were assigned an essay to write. Dad did, but his sister put it off and finally didn't. She stole my father's and skipped off to school first.

In class, she was ordered to read her paper; so she read dad's. It was a small class, and my father was called on next.

"Ethel took my homework and read it," he said. "So now I'll sing it."

When I was old enough, my father would take me to work with him during the summer. We'd have breakfast together at a cafe at 5:30 in the morning, and then I'd go to the mines and watch him work. I'll always remember one statement of his. He would introduce me to the men, and when we were walking away, he'd say, "Now, that's a good man, Jack." Or at other times he'd say, "That's not much of a man." Invariably, he was right. At least at my age he seemed right.

I've never forgotten that. Over the years I've never picked an assistant coach and kept him very long unless I thought he was a good man. That doesn't mean he has to think like I do. But there are assistants who have been with me for 10, 12 or 14 years, and I feel that if I suddenly died, I could depend on them to help take care of my family.

Since my father was a mining superintendent, and non-union, our family was always being threatened in the early days. It was a tremendously violent era in the Southern mining country. Miners were paid very poorly—they never seemed to have any money at the end of the month —and conditions were bad, too. Unions were just getting started, and the National Guard was often called out to quell riots.

I remember dad had a permit to carry a gun, but nothing scared him. Two or three times he got calls that warned him dynamite had been planted under the house, and, although I barely remember it because I was so little, our front porch was blown off one night. On another occasion we were all evacuated at one in the morning after a dynamite threat, but nothing happened that time.

Finally, when I was about five, my father moved us from Everettsville to Arnettsville and later to Morgantown. There was a mine disaster that killed 96 men and he decided he was fed up with the company he worked for. He decided to go into business for himself and leased his own mines after that. He also leased a company store, which was robbed twice. Those were tough days.

Besides violence, the era was also marked by strong prejudice—and not just against black people. There was prejudice against Catholics, too, and we knew we were different. We heard about it every place we went. But it never bothered me too much, although June told me later that the phone company made sure she knew that she was the first Catholic they had ever hired.

The only time we were scared was when the Ku Klux Klan, which didn't like Catholics, paid us a visit. Our parents were away at a party one night when we lived out in the country, and we kids were home with a baby-sitter. A flash of light attracted us to the front window. Peeping out, we saw six members of the Klan walking in a circle a few yards from the house. They were wearing white sheets and carrying a burning cross. A few minutes later they rode away into the night.

My father tried to raise us without prejudice. He never lectured us much, but the one thing he preached all the time was to be fair. He said people should be treated according to what they were, instead of who they were.

Dad's right-hand man, whose name also was John, was black. He was always with my father, planning, organizing and solving problems.

I remember John seemed old to me, but everybody seemed old to me when I was a kid. John was a super guy, just great to me and my brothers and sisters. I remember him now because he used to wear an old black felt hat, the kind some of my players wear to be "with it" in the 70's. That old hat was droopy, all beat up and sweat-ridden. I always thought John probably wore it to bed.

When I was ten, I heard my first Rose Bowl game on the radio. It was the 1934 game and Columbia beat Stanford, 7 to 0. The rest of the family went to another home for dinner, but I didn't want to go and begged my dad to let me stay and listen. So I stayed there alone and heard the game on a radio that was bigger than I was.

Columbia and Stanford played in a heavy rain, which I thought was very funny. We had an uncle who lived in Pomona, California, a few miles from Pasadena, and he was always bragging about the great weather out there.

When I was a little older, dad bought three Shetland ponies, and from then on we always had some to ride. Jimmy, June and I rode bareback and played cowboys and Indians, chased each other everywhere, up and down hills, across pastures and through water.

To be economical, my father bought a cow, too, but he didn't know anything about farming, so he hired a man to milk it. The cow was considered very valuable. One Sunday we were walking to Mass when the cow escaped and started running away through an open field. Dad was wearing his best suit, but he chased the cow, caught her, grabbed her by the tail and wouldn't let go.

Mother was screaming, "Let go, you're tearing off her tail!" Dad's suit got ruined, and the rest of us stood there amazed at the sight. But my father wouldn't let that cow get away. He captured her—and he really didn't hurt her tail, either.

At the age of 12 I enrolled at Barnes Junior High in Fairmont, West Virginia. But in the middle of the school year we moved to a little town out in the country, several miles away. That meant I would have to switch schools, but I didn't want to, because I was playing basketball and softball for Pat Tork.

"Jack," said my father, "you can stay at Barnes if you walk home every night."

"Sure," I said.

And I stayed at Barnes—and walked home often. It was a distance of seven miles, clear across the city and out through the country. But I didn't think it was any big deal. Sometimes my father would drive me home, but I didn't want to phone him, because it was inconvenient for him to come and get me. My children, of course, have had a much easier life in many ways than I did, and today they often kid me, "Here he comes, he's gonna tell us again that he walked seven miles to school."

Well, it was a hassle, because I had trouble getting from school to the house on time for dinner. Dad's standard rule was if you didn't get there on time, you didn't eat. So I had a choice. When I was hungry, even if I had just finished practice after school, I raced home. If I dawdled along the way and the family was eating when I arrived, dad would just point upstairs and I went up and missed dinner.

When my father died in 1936 at the age of 45, it was a stunning shock. We didn't know there was anything wrong with him. Dad caught what he thought was a bad cold, and a doctor came by the house, checked him and agreed. Within a week he was dead. When the autopsy was performed, they discovered he had suffered from pneumonia.

His death really hurt me because I was so close to him. As I said, we were very similar, and he loved me very much. My father had always been a strong man and taken care of everything, and suddenly my mother was left alone with five children. Fortunately, many men, like Tork, picked up the slack for me. But I missed my dad a lot. The sense of loss was tremendous.

But as I have told my own children, this can happen to a family at any time, and you can't fall back and give up.

When my father died, however, we went from living well to near-poverty overnight. We never had to go without food, but there sure weren't many cookies floating around the house. Everybody had to work hard. When I was 15, I got up at five in the morning, went down to a restaurant at 5:30 and cleaned it out before going to school. They usually gave me a meal every day, and sometimes two, but I didn't get paid in cash.

Later, when I was in Shinnston High School, I made $15 a month as the janitor's assistant. The job was part of a federal anti-Depression program, the NYA (National Youth Administration). I scrubbed out bathrooms and swept the classrooms with a broom, sawdust and oil.

Handling that broom was probably one of the best things I ever did, talent-wise. I'm sure you've seen that old janitor's trick. You spread that sawdust and oil down, and then sweep it right out. Picks up all the dirt. I don't know how many rooms I had to clean. I never counted them.

Meanwhile, I was playing sports every chance I got. We had moved back to Fairmont, and shortly after my father died, Tork fixed it so I could go across town and play on the Fairmont High team, even though I was a ninth grader in the junior high. The junior high didn't have football. So every afternoon I'd pedal six miles on my bicycle to the high school for practice and I made the team. They told me I was the first ninth grader to ever make it, and there couldn't have been many more after me, because they soon wrote a rule against it.

This was the first time I played with pads on, although we had played tackle football for years on sandlots.

The next year, 1938, mother decided to move from Fairmont to Shinnston. While she was working out the details of the move, my aunt suggested June and I move in with her in Elizabeth, Pennsylvania, and go to high school there for a semester. Mother sent us up and I played football in Elizabeth, but I never stayed the whole semester.

Right after Christmas, I hitchhiked to Shinnston, where my mother had found a home, and where she lived until just a few years ago. I enrolled in the high school there and arrived in time to play basketball in 1939.

There were about 700 boys and girls in our school, but it was the smallest in the northern West Virginia league we competed in, called the Big Ten. A lot of kids didn't live in the town, which had a population of about 3,000, but were bused in from houses around the coal mines.

I was an All-State back in football, and they say today I was All-State in basketball, too, but I don't think I really was. We did win the Big Ten title both years in football, and I led the team in scoring. By that time I had ballooned up to 160 pounds. We ran the old single wing, and McKay was the wingback in formations to the right and tailback in formations to the left. I switched with Babe Loretta, a friend of mine who died several years ago.

The blocking back always called the signals after we lined up, but I called the plays in the huddle my senior year. Since I was often the tailback, I had to pass as well as run, but I wouldn't say I was a proficient passer. If the play called for me to throw, I threw, but not always with the greatest enthusiasm. I usually got it to the guy I was throwing to, or at least I always got it to somebody on one of the teams.

I loved running. Recently, I found an old Shinnston newspaper, printed after our first USC national championship in 1962. The paper gave me high praise, as it reminisced about my high school career.

"McKay," said the article, "was a breakaway runner in football and was quite adept at eluding his opponents."

In my era—and that includes my college career, too—we didn't have face masks, all that extra padding they have now or tape all over our hands, arms and shoes. We had shoulder pads, hip pads and a leather helmet you could put in your back pocket.

When I was at Shinnston, Coach McClung often had me over at his house for dinner, but it had nothing to do with the fact that we were poor. He invited all his signal callers over for strategy sessions. It's possible Mickey also took a stronger interest in me because I didn't have a father, but he never talked about it. But he did impress me quite a bit. He was a sharp dresser, very handsome, had infectious enthusiasm and really enjoyed coaching football.

I played guard for Mickey in basketball, and one year we won the Big Ten title in that sport, too. In fact, the Shinnston yearbook predicted I would go on to play basketball for the old New York Celtics.

As I said, being a high school football or basketball star made you a big man in Shinnston. A person would have to live in a small town to understand that. There just wasn't much to do, except go root for the local team. At that time, there wasn't even much to listen to on the radio.

The town's biggest hero was Joe Stydahar, who later became a pro football coach. He was playing with the Chicago Bears then, and when Joe came home, everyone turned out to greet him. He was very respected. Whenever there was a little violence, like a fight in the pool hall, he would always help settle it. It was easy. Joe would march in, grab the man who was causing the trouble, lift him up and take him over to jail.

When I graduated in 1941, the yearbook printed a will for the departing seniors. Our book said, "McKay wills the junior class his wonderful sense of humor." I imagine people who have since found me difficult to get along with think, "Maybe the son of a bitch did leave it."

After graduating from high school, I proceeded with my plan of going to college. I was offered a football scholarship to Wake Forest, so I went down to North Carolina in August to enroll. But before I took any classes, my mother suddenly became ill. At first, doctors thought there was something wrong with her heart, so I rushed home. It turned out her condition wasn't serious, but I decided to stay home and go to work.

A fellow by the name of Ted Brennan gave me a job in the Bethlehem Mine just outside Shinnston. I was only

18 and didn't have any experience at coal mining, so I went to work with Joe Stydahar's dad, Pete, helping to build a substation for electrical power.

You see, there were two types of coal mines—shafts, which went straight down, and tunnels, which cut through hills. Bethlehem was a tunnel mine, and they had cut a new tunnel through a different hill. Every time they did that they had to build a new substation to provide power for the mine cars which carried the coal. The cars ran on tracks.

I worked on that substation in fall and winter, and the temperature often dropped to five or six degrees below zero. So when I walked to work every day I used to take a shortcut through the mine tunnels, because the temperature was warm inside.

But I had to work in the cold. My job was wheeling concrete, which was one of the hardest things I've ever done. I'd pick it up in a wheelbarrow, as it came wet from the mixer, and then wheel it to the substation across a plank about as wide as a swimming pool's diving board. It was heavier than hell to try and pick up, let alone push around. If it ever started to tip, you couldn't stop it. The whole load dumped.

After my first two days on that job, I didn't think I'd be able to lift my arms for the rest of my life. But, after two or three weeks, I got used to it.

As soon as the substation was built, I was out of a job. But the Japanese had bombed Pearl Harbor and I wanted to get in the service. I couldn't enlist immediately, however, because the country was just getting mobilized and there was a shortage of uniforms, weapons and almost everything else. So I took tests for the Navy and the Army Air Corps and passed both. Whichever one called first would win me.

By the time I took those tests in January, I had also

been hired for a new job at Owens Mine Number 32. If I hadn't tried to enlist, I doubt seriously that I would have been drafted, because there was a shortage of coal miners. Jobs like that were considered very important during the war.

The number 32 on that mine became a happy echo later in my life. O. J. Simpson, who led us to a national title and two Rose Bowls in 1967 and 1968, wore 32.

My best friend at the time was a young man named Bill Martz, who is still very close to me, and his dad, Roy, helped me get the job. I became an assistant to the head electrician, Cy McCoy, and also worked in the car barn where we made the cars that the miners loaded with coal. It's surprising how big those cars were and how much coal they carried. One of the other guys working in the barn with me was Pete Stydahar, Joe's brother. Since Joe's father was also named Pete, this sometimes got confusing.

I had to go in and out of the mine almost every day, because McCoy went inside every time there was an electrical failure, which was about every day. I carried his tools, and Cy would say, "Give me the wrench," and I'd slap the wrench in his hand like some sort of electrical nurse.

Truthfully, I didn't mind the coal mines, although I never dug coal, and they didn't scare me when I was inside. My dad had taken me in since I was four years old. But it sure wasn't creative work. All I cared about was the money. I made $6.75 a day.

Finally, in the summer of 1942, the Air Corps called me up. I was shipped to Columbus, Ohio, with about 200 other young men. The 200 gathered together looked like about ten million to a small-town boy. From Columbus, we were sent in civilian clothes to San Antonio, Texas.

I've always been amazed that the United States survived the first couple of years of the war. When I arrived in San Antonio I saw soldiers train with sticks, instead of guns.

I took another battery of tests in San Antonio, including a more complete physical. They hadn't given us much of one to get us in there, but I understand they had a reason for that. One of the tests was to determine my fitness for flying. I was very interested in being a pilot, because my brother Jimmy already was one.

But the doctors ruled that my depth perception would have made it difficult for me to learn to fly. Ultimately I could have learned, but they wanted people they could teach in a hurry, so I was eliminated. They gave me a choice of two other jobs, navigator or bombardier, and I had to appear before a board to state my preference.

Well, I was disappointed I couldn't be a pilot, and I didn't hide it when I appeared in front of the board. I said, "The only thing in an airplane I really cared about was flying it."

"If that's all you think of the Air Corps," snapped a young officer, "then you're out." So they stamped on my form "GDO," which meant ground duty only. I should have kept my mouth shut, but I told the truth. Sometimes in a spot like that it can be a mistake.

Sentenced to ground duty, I was assigned to a school to become a physical training instructor. The Air Corps picked me for that because I had been a high school athlete. From San Antonio, I was reassigned to San Marcos, Texas, where the biggest navigational school in the world was being built. I was there a year and a half.

In a way, it was my first coaching job. I stood on a platform all day and led 300 to 400 men at a time in calisthenics, including cadets, officers and mechanics, who all exercised at different times. I gave several classes. I had to shout like hell, and getting up in front of all those people helped me overcome some of my shyness.

Our staff ran the recreational and physical-fitness programs for the entire base, which had a tremendous number of personnel. We conducted indoor classes and gave physical-fitness tests—and I kept in shape by playing on the post basketball team.

As the months slipped by, many of my friends were shipped out, and I wanted to go, too. I was interested in gunnery, but I could never get released to go to gunnery school. People talk about the bravery of certain soldiers, "because they volunteered for such dangerous duty." Well, you didn't volunteer. If they didn't want you to do something, you couldn't do it.

I did discover that the Air Corps couldn't refuse a transfer to a course in foreign languages, which was supposed to help train men for the Army of Occupation after the war. It was almost 1944, and the country's confidence was building fast. So I took an intelligence test for that course, passed it and was transferred to another base—prior to going on to the University of Michigan for language school.

Those of us assigned to the language school were discussing it one day, and suddenly I realized what going there meant.

"You know what's going to happen to us?" I asked.

"What?" said one of my friends.

"We're going to study until the war is over, and then we'll still be in the service, because we'll be in the Army of Occupation. We're going to be in the Army forever."

I couldn't see that. So I phoned Duane Purvis, who was the commander of the physical-training program at San Marcos, and he got me shipped back. I applied for gunnery school again, and this time I was transferred.

I was sent to Kingman, Arizona, passed a test in B-17 gunnery and was then assigned to take the B-29 gunnery course in Las Vegas. From there, I was attached to a crew, sent to another base in Salina, Kansas, and then shipped overseas to the island of Tinia in the South Pacific as a B-29 tail gunner.

Sitting in the back of a B-29 taught me two things: how to meditate and how to smoke cigars. You had to do something to pass the time. Was I a good tail gunner? Outstanding. I never shot myself once. But I never shot down any planes. The Army Air Force had what seemed like a million surplus tail gunners, and the war was winding down by that time.

After a while, many of us were shipped back to the U.S. and sent to Maxwell Field, Alabama, to play football and basketball for the Third Air Force. They figured we were just as valuable entertaining the troops in the States as sitting on an island in the South Pacific doing nothing. It was already 1945.

Jimmy, who flew B-17s, and I were the lucky brothers. Earlier in the war, Richard, who was serving on a Navy minesweeper in the Pacific, asked for a transfer to submarine training. The Navy refused the transfer and sent him into the Atlantic on another minesweeper. His new ship either struck a mine or was hit by a submarine, but it was blown up and nobody was ever found.

First my younger brother was reported missing, and then finally he was presumed dead. Because it dragged on like that, it was traumatic for all of us, particularly my mother. Richard was only 18.

After more than three and a half years, I was discharged from the service in January, 1946, and enrolled at Purdue University. The man who pointed me toward Purdue was Duane Purvis, my old commander in San Marcos. Duane had been an All-American football player at Purdue.

I had also considered LSU and Kentucky, but Purvis

contacted Purdue, told them I was a pretty good basketball player—he had never seen me play football—and the school recruited me to come up and play basketball.

But I didn't get out of the service in time. I arrived and signed up for the second semester. Basketball season was half over, and spring football, which went on for months in those days, was starting. So I went out for spring football, did well and played for the varsity as a 23-year-old freshman.

I always thought I was a good basketball player; in fact, some people said it was my best sport. I had a good one-handed set shot and was a very tenacious defensive player. Make that tenacious, but clean. But I never played basketball in college. In fact, I never played another game in my life. About all I did was shoot baskets with my son, Johnny, when he was old enough to lift the ball.

I was a starting defensive halfback for Purdue in 1946, and occasionally played right half on offense. I had trouble playing offense, however, because I had never run from the T-formation before. Taking handoffs from the quarterback right on the line threw me. I was used to getting the ball deep in the backfield in the single wing.

I did catch ten passes for 196 yards, which made me the team's second leading receiver, but my rushing total of 76 yards wasn't impressive. That tied me for 38th place in the Big Ten.

Cecil Isbell was our coach, and I listened to everything he said. I was always trying to absorb football. There was still no question in my mind about my future. If I could, I was going back to Shinnston to coach.

I was very happy at Purdue, played with some tremendous people, many of whom went into coaching themselves, like Henry Stram of the Kansas City Chiefs, Abe Gibron of the Chicago Bears and Bob DeMoss, who later coached Purdue. DeMoss was our quarterback and finished second in the league in total offense.

But even with all those fine minds on the team, our record was only 2-6-1.

At the end of the season, Isbell left to coach the Baltimore Colts in the old All-America Conference, and Purdue wasn't sure who the new coach would be. Meanwhile, the trainer, Tom Hughes, went to Oregon to become trainer there, and he told Oregon's new coach, Jim Aiken, that I was a pretty good player. Aiken contacted my old high school coach, McClung, who was a good friend of his, and had Mickey call me.

Mickey helped convince me to transfer to Oregon. I figured that if I played there Aiken would give me a good recommendation in West Virginia when I started coaching. This was more sensible than depending on Purdue's new coach, when I didn't even know who he would be. So I saw no reason to stay at Purdue.

Going to Oregon turned out to be the turning point of my life.

PLAYING AND COACHING IN OREGON

*"The right place at
the right time"*

IN 1951, I was spending my first season as an assistant
to Oregon's new coach, Len Casanova, when he had a
back operation. The doctors put him in a cast from his
neck to his waist. One day Cas called me into the bathroom and explained that he needed help in dressing and
undressing. So I had to pull down his pants.

"Damn it," I said. "I knew I should have read the fine
print in that contract."

However, I did more in Oregon than work as a valet.
From 1947 to 1959 I played football for two years and
coached it for nine, earned my degree, met and married
Corky and had four children.

My first impression of the town of Eugene when I
arrived in the fall of 1947 was that it rained a hell of a

lot. I went to the University of Oregon, as I had to Purdue, on the GI Bill, which paid for my tuition, housing and books and saved all the schools a tremendous amount of money. That's why the cost of sports at universities in the late 1940's was so small.

Today, you hear old athletic directors talking about costs being much higher and they forget that after the war most of the scholarships for athletes—I'd say about three-fourths—were paid for by the government. It cost me nothing to go to school, and I was able to earn an extra $75 a month by working on campus.

Since I had transferred, I had to sit out the 1947 season and lose a year of eligibility. But I was able to practice with the team, and I got to know all the players. They included Norm Van Brocklin, still a friend of mine, who quarterbacked us to the Cotton Bowl in 1948, and tackle Don Stanton, who set up my first date with Corky.

I enrolled in the school of physical education so I could fulfill my goal of going into coaching. But I learned most of my technical knowledge from the football coach himself, a gruff-voiced, ornery bugger named Jim Aiken. Jim took over the year I arrived and had a major influence on my coaching career.

Before Aiken arrived, Oregon had not had a winning season since 1935. Jim, meanwhile, had won 88 percent of his games in 14 years of high school coaching in Pennsylvania and Ohio, and then gone on to post a 64 percent winning record in 11 years at Akron University and the University of Nevada.

Van Brocklin had been on the team in 1946, but he hadn't even lettered, because he was the fifth-string tailback for coach Tex Oliver, who played the single wing. If you remember Van Brocklin's playing days, you can imagine how funny he looked. How could he play tailback? When he tried to run, it was just like a man running in place. His legs moved, but he never went anywhere.

Aiken changed our offense. He switched to the T-formation and made Van Brocklin a quarterback. Everybody knew Van had a great arm, but, nonetheless, somebody had to put him in the right situation and teach him. Van Brocklin was fifth-string for another coach, which at Oregon was really bad, but Aiken taught him the T for the first time in his life, put him behind a great blocking line, added good receivers and spent hours talking football to him. Van would be the first to admit today that Jim helped him tremendously.

While I practiced and watched in 1947, Van Brocklin passed for 939 yards and nine touchdowns, and the Ducks won their last six games to finish 7-3 and tied for second in the Pacific Coast Conference. Jim Aiken had Oregon football on the move.

Jim's greatest asset, which you must have to be a success in my business, was his ability to teach. Some coaches are strategists, but they're not worth a damn as teachers. They're like professors who have great minds but can't get anything across to their students. But at Oregon, under Jim, when we went into a game, we were completely prepared offensively, no matter what the other team tried to do.

I've seen many teams with good players that didn't function very well at all. Some coach wasn't teaching them.

In Aiken's era, the head man really did a lot of actual coaching. His entire staff was only four, including himself, and he got right in the middle of his players. This fancy stuff, where the head coach at many schools doesn't do anything but stand around, is a recent phenomenon. When Jim handled the offense, nobody else said a word.

He was a strong presence as a man and never talked

to the players much off the field, but he was a very sound person and we respected him very much. Van Brocklin and I still refer to him as "The Old Man," and his picture is up in my house. Football and his family— that's all Jim cared about. When he got older he ignored his doctor's orders to slow down. He died of a heart attack in 1960, right after making a speech. His death really upset me.

Jim taught me something that makes me a little hard to live with now. He said a coach should always do what he believes in, no matter what anyone says. He emphasized that if you listen to your critics you'll start to hunt around, rather than coach. You can only practice so long and only do so many things, so you must stick with what you believe in. And if you have to practice something two million times to learn it, you practice it two million times.

In 1948, my junior year, Aiken coached us to a 9-1 record. Van Brocklin passed for 1,010 yards, George Bell led the team in rushing with 648 yards, and Johnny McKay led in scoring with eight touchdowns. Bell, Woodley Lewis, who became a pro star, and I alternated at the halfbacks, and Bob Sanders was our fullback. It was a pretty good team for those days, different than the teams now, because we were all older, 23, 24, 25. Most of us were service veterans.

It was a two-platoon era, but we didn't have very many players, so 17 of us did 98 percent of the playing. We were called "The Sacred 17." I played defensive halfback. Van Brocklin, of course, played only offense. When the defense took the field, Aiken got him the hell off.

We'd work Monday, Tuesday and Wednesday on offense, and then on Thursday we'd just line up in the defense we were going to play, and figure out who was to take which man. Not all schools did that in the late 1940's, but Oregon only practiced defense for a day.

I was a cocky guy on the field. In fact, I probably thought I was better than I was, because I never got as much acclaim as I thought I should have. But I still hold the Oregon career record for best rushing average per carry, 6.4 yards a try.

And, truthfully, if I hadn't injured my knee both seasons, I would have done better. I wasn't very big—only 5-9 and 172 pounds—but I ran for 114 yards and scored three touchdowns in my first game, against the University of California at Santa Barbara. I had 385 yards by the time I got hurt in our fourth game against Idaho, including 154 in that game alone. But I missed the next game and most of another and only carried 16 times after that. I ended up with 483 yards and a 6.7 average. Van Brocklin also threw me ten passes, and I returned punts and kickoffs, too.

When the season dragged on and I wouldn't get the ball, I'd think, my God, don't they even think I can run? It would make me mad. I really enjoyed playing and practicing.

I could outrun a lot of people at 30 or 40 yards, and I had a big line to follow. But I admit I was getting older, 25 in 1948, and I don't think I could run as well as I could when I was younger. If I played at USC today, that is if I were still a kid and not 51, I wouldn't be a running back. I'd be a flanker. I could always catch.

Of course, you always improve in your own memory, as the years march by. I remember Len Casanova used to brag that he got off an 87-yard punt as a kid. So I found a football like the ones they used in the old days and waited until a party we had at Oregon. Then I asked Cas to come out in the street. I kicked that ball, and it went 20 yards in the air and then rolled about six blocks. The damn thing was practically round.

Despite our great season in 1948, we had a big disappointment. California was voted into the Rose Bowl over us. We lost only to Michigan on the road and finished up 7-0 in league play. California went 6-0 in the conference and 10-0 for the season. We weren't scheduled against each other. Even though we were the only team in the history of the Rose Bowl pact with the Big Ten to be allowed to visit another bowl, the vote still depressed us. We wanted to go—and felt we should have gone—to Pasadena. We had won seven games and Cal six, so we had taken one more chance.

Instead, we went to Dallas for the Cotton Bowl, where we lost to SMU, 21 to 13. I felt we should have won, although SMU was awfully good. They had Doak Walker and Kyle Rote.

It was just before that season started that I met Corky. Her real name was Nancy, but she'd had the nickname Corky all her life. Her father tagged it on her because she was born the same time as Corky in the Gasoline Alley comic strip.

"My dad," says Corky, "thought I looked exactly like the other Corky, who was a baby boy. I never thought that was a very flattering comparison. A fine thing for a father to name his first-born child. Except for little boys, dogs are the only things called Corky. Somebody is always yelling for his dog, and I'm always looking up."

Corky's parents, Ken and Louise Hunter, are big USC fans today, however, so I can forgive them, even if she can't. Besides, I like the name.

It was during two-a-day drills in August of 1948 that Corky came up from Southern California to visit her cousin, Polly Stanton, Don's wife. Corky had just enrolled at USC and paid her dorm money, but she was only 17. Once she got to Oregon she stayed, which, she says, proves to her the value of recruiting trips to a campus.

Corky had never spent much time on a college campus before, and I guess she was enchanted by all the ball players and the fun we were having in the summer before school started. The weather was great, too. Oregon people never tell you about the winter.

One day, after a morning workout, Don and I and Van Brocklin went to Don's campus Quonset hut, where he and Polly lived, like all married students. Corky was over there talking to Polly. We all sat around, drank some soda pop and talked for a while. I've always accused my wife of seeing me and deciding to stay in Eugene, because soon after she canceled at USC and enrolled at Oregon.

When we met, the first thing that attracted me was her personality—she laughed a lot—and her sparkling eyes. I thought she looked exactly like the actress June Allyson. She still does a little bit, although she's even better looking than June now. She had a husky voice like June Allyson, too, and we got along fine.

But I didn't ask her out.

Corky isn't shy. She convinced Polly to convince Don, who was one of my best friends, to push me into taking her out. Don asked, I agreed, and I still can't recall the exact day we first went on a date. It wasn't that momentous to me at the time.

I do remember that the weekend before was the Idaho game, when I got hurt for the first time. I was playing defense and came up to support our end when Idaho ran a sweep. Somebody hit the end and he fell into my left knee. It felt like a hot poker went through it. The knee swelled up immediately. We beat USC by a point the next week and all I could do was watch.

The old method of treating bad knees was to wrap them so tight that you were automatically a cripple for a while, because you couldn't bend your leg. So the injury always looked worse than it was, and I was on crutches for about a week. I was leaning on them when I went to pick up Corky for the first time. We had a triple dinner date, with Don and Polly and another couple.

Corky's always said she's the nonathlete in the family —and she's right. I met her at the door and she offered to help me down the stairs. She did. She tripped, tugged on me and the two of us fell all the way down.

"Uh, I'm sorry," she said. "But you had so much Ben-Gay on that the smell knocked me over."

I don't know why—I guess I wasn't real forward in chasing girls—but I didn't ask her out again. She called me a month later and asked me to a sorority dance. She claimed she had been trying to call me all that time and I was avoiding her. At the dance we had a couple of boilermakers, I turned on the old McKay charm, and six months later we were on our way to marriage.

"I think you just gave up," she says. "I wore you down."

I was a lot older than she was, seven years older, and she did chase me all over the campus. She dropped to nine units once and spent most of her time in the men's P.E. department. It got to be a standing joke. "Here she comes again," all the guys would say.

I've always loved movies—when I was growing up they were the cheapest entertainment I could find—and Corky and I must have seen a million together. I saw even more alone. In college, I spent most of my free weekends in movie theaters. I would take Corky on a Saturday night, go to a matinee by myself Sunday afternoon and then return to the Theta house Sunday night, pick her up again, and we'd go to a double bill. I have the utmost respect for the ability of actors.

Cowboy movies have always been my favorites. On Sunday nights in the off-season, I still take out the TV guide and scout for all the westerns coming up. I get my game plan ready for the week. I've seen many, many good movies on television. For that, I'm indebted to the used-car dealers of America.

I read once that Corky and I also courted on hay rides. This isn't true. I think we went on one Oregon hay ride. We couldn't have taken very many, because she has hay fever.

Finally, we got pinned, then engaged and got married in June of 1950. Corky brought up marriage more often than I did, but there was a slight problem for me—money. I definitely didn't want to get married while I was still in school, because there was no way I could support a wife. Truthfully, there was no way I could support one after I got out, either.

Oregon was on the three-semester system, and I finished classes at the end of the second term, early in the year. Since graduation was held only in June, I took some extra units of practice teaching, while Corky quit school and went home to San Bernardino to prepare for the wedding.

After graduation, I drove down and we were married in a San Bernardino church. I was two weeks short of 27, and she was 19. There's a picture taken as we left the church, and it makes it look as though I'm running out. But I wasn't. I just moved so fast in those days that even when I walked it looked like I was running.

Thanks to Aiken, I was ready to begin coaching by the time I got married. But I started in college, instead of in high school. My chance came when I hurt my knee again late in 1949, my senior season. We started fast, like we had in 1948, by winning four of our first five games, to run our conference winning streak to 13 straight. And then injuries began to pile up, and we lost our last five games. Besides losing several key players during the season, we lost Van Brocklin before it even started. Van didn't want to play his senior year, because he was eligible for the pro draft. He had been in school four years. The Rams drafted him, and he signed.

But even though we finished 4 and 6, Aiken could have had another excellent team. Despite everything, we were still pretty explosive for that era. We averaged 25 points a game. I lasted until the ninth one, before my career came to an end.

Before I got hurt for good, I rushed for 378 yards, averaged 5.9 a carry, caught 17 passes, intercepted three and scored five touchdowns.

The knee I had injured in 1948 bothered me all season. It was okay in the spring of 1949, except for swelling every once in a while, but it began to hurt when we started playing games. Before each one the doctor jammed a big needle into my knee and shot it full of the same medicine women took to relax their muscles during labor. Each time it seemed like he injected about a quart of that stuff.

In the seventh week I gained 98 yards against Iowa, including a 37-yard touchdown run, but that was my last big game. Against Washington the next week I ran a sweep, started to cut back, and somebody hit me from behind. The knee hurt like hell. But I kept playing and caught a four-yard touchdown pass, as we lost by a point.

Next week we went to California. Early in the game I ran a sideline pass pattern right in front of their bench.

I went up for the ball, came down on the knee wrong, and it gave out. That was it.

I fell right at the feet of the California doctor, who was Brick Muller, an All-American end with the Bears in the early 1920's.

"Son," said Brick, looking down at me, "I'm sorry, but you're not going to play any more football today." I never played any more, period.

However, my knee was never operated on. I assume the injury was torn cartilage, but I don't know. In those days they didn't operate as often as they do now. Today, a guy barely hits the ground and somebody's out there cutting on him.

As we rode the train back to Eugene after the Cal game, Aiken told me I'd be his backfield coach in 1950. I spent the last week of the 1949 season working with the offensive backs.

It was the first time I had ever thought of college coaching. Undoubtedly, I would have gone into high school football after graduating, although Shinnston had lost its great appeal. I probably would have tried to get a job in Oregon.

The 1950 season was Aiken's last. Perhaps the game had caught up with him, and certainly having a small staff hurt his recruiting. In 1950 and 1951 there were very few top-quality football players at Oregon. The 1950 team lost nine of ten games.

Several months after the season the league recommended that Jim be fired for breaking conference regulations, chiefly for holding extra practices in the summer. Orlando Hollis, the faculty athletic representative, reported the results of the conference investigation to Oregon's president, and they held a meeting with Jim. He resigned in the middle of the summer of 1951 and never coached again.

I think this was the real beginning of the breakup of the old Pacific Coast Conference, because the Aiken case spawned bitterness in the Northwest. Later, in the middle 1950's, when other league schools, including USC and UCLA, broke recruiting regulations, their presidents did nothing to their coaches. Yet, the league had said earlier they wanted offending coaches fired. This may have led to the harsh penalties which stripped USC and UCLA seniors of eligibility for three straight seasons. People in the north still remembered Aiken.

The only season I coached under Jim I made $2,800. But before I took the job I was drafted by the New York Yankees of the old All-America Conference and offered $8,200 a year. The pro offer didn't tempt me that much, however. I figured if I really wanted to go into coaching it would be senseless to postpone it. Otherwise, I might be 30 or 31 my first year, and that's a little late to begin. Besides, my knee had already been hurt two straight years, and at 27 I was much older than most players going into pro ball.

For me even to make $2,800 as an assistant took some bargaining by Aiken. Oregon's original offer was $2,400, but Jim went in to see the athletic director and emerged with $400 more. Those weren't my most affluent days. In nine years as an Oregon assistant I never made more than $7,500 a year.

In 1951 I almost left and went into the FBI. With Aiken gone, I thought about my salary and my wife, who was expecting our first baby, and figured I better start making some money. I also felt the new coach should have the right to pick his own staff. Gordon Wilson, an ex-fraternity brother of mine, knew the chief of the FBI bureau in Portland, so I talked to him and we agreed it might be a good idea for me to go to work there.

My career as an investigator never got started. Oregon

hired its new coach, Len Casanova, before I could leave. Cas had been head coach at Santa Clara for four years and Pittsburgh for one when he was hired. He had taken Santa Clara to the 1950 Orange Bowl and beat Kentucky.

He brought his top assistant, Jack Roche, with him to Eugene, but he needed to hire more coaches. Oregon's athletic director, Leo Harris, was not only a good friend of mine, but I think he felt I was a pretty good recruiter, too. He explained to Casanova that Gene Harlow, another assistant, and I had signed contracts before he came and it was pretty late in the summer for us to find other jobs. So he ordered Cas to keep Gene and me at least a year. I decided to stay—and there went my FBI career. But if Casanova had argued with Leo that he didn't want me, and I had found out, I sure as hell would have left.

As Cas puts it, he "inherited" me—and I stayed for eight years. Len is still one of my best friends. He was the godfather for my daughters, Michele and Terri.

He coached Oregon for 16 years, was later athletic director, and probably taught me more about dealing with people than anyone I've ever known. My problem as an assistant coach was my temper. I used to get furious with the players too often, and he'd jump me. One time I threw a player off the field, and Cas made me bring him back. I didn't like it, but I had to do it.

I've never seen a young coach who doesn't overcoach. He assumes he knows so much that he wants to impart it all right away—and he talks too much. We all did it. You find out eventually, however, that most of the kids aren't as interested in the game as you are. This infuriates you until you learn to accept it. Finally, you learn how much your players can take. Bear Bryant says it best: "Don't get so involved that you forget to let them play."

Cas also taught me to handle people as individuals,

rather than as a group. The assistant must know who to push hard, who to pat on the back and just what the capabilities of each player are. If you demand that everyone perform exactly the same way, no matter what, you'll go crazy every time a kid moves his hand or foot the wrong way.

I began to understand this after four or five years. Being older helped. Cas also gave me quite a bit of responsibility, and I had to grow up in it quickly. We had only a four-man staff at first, and later no more than five. I coached both the offensive and defensive backfields. All the coaches worked both ways.

From about 1954 on, I designed the offense and Roche designed the defense. When Roche would draw his defense I'd suggest how it could be attacked and then how it could be improved to counter that attack. I was always looking at movies, reading football books and drawing plays. I went to every clinic I could. If I was going to be successful, I felt I had to know as much or more than the people I would be coaching against.

Although Casanova is my close friend, I have to admit he once made a statement about some of my offensive ideas that I've always disliked. He said:

"I've never known a man with more ideas on football attack than McKay. Some of the stuff he suggested was too far out for us at Oregon. We had to reject some of his plays because we would have needed motorcycles to make them work."

Now, I wasn't a flaming radical. I think he just believed that I was trying to change more quickly than he wanted to. Some of my ideas were that shifting and sending players in motion should be used more on offense. I felt this had to be an advantage.

In the early 1950's nobody wanted to try that. But football coaches are like everyone else, you know. If something's going good for them, they figure they may as well keep using it and not change.

One of my ideas, which Cas said he had never seen done before, was to have George Shaw, our quarterback from 1952 to 1954, roll out. Cas liked the rollout and we used it and got a lot out of it. We figured we didn't have a great line, and since George was a very good runner and passer, he could really operate by rolling out.

I didn't remember seeing the rollout in the T-formation before that, but I couldn't say I invented it. Sometimes you have a new idea and then discover somebody else thought of it 20 years earlier. What is a rollout pass anyway but a running pass in the old single wing? The man rolling out is just taking the ball from a different spot.

In 1957, the year our Ducks went to the Rose Bowl and almost upset Ohio State, I made another suggestion which Cas utilized immediately. We were on the bus to the Stanford game when I suggested that we start the game without an offensive huddle.

Stanford was unique in that era, because they used multiple defenses, and they used to get in their defensive huddle and stay in it for a long time. We figured if we didn't huddle, they couldn't, and they'd have to stick with the same defense. Thus, the advantage would be ours.

We took the opening kickoff and used our two-minute, late-in-the-game-emergency-offense to march right down the field and score. Every time Stanford got in their huddle we were already at the line of scrimmage. I think that upset them. We won, 27 to 26, although Stanford was probably better than we were.

I've never used the no-huddle offense again, however, and don't think I'd consider using it now. It's a gamble with some merit, but not very much. You might try it if you feel you're tremendously outmanned.

Our leading rusher in 1957 was a quick little halfback named Jimmy Shanley, who still reminds me more of myself than any other player I've ever coached. With people like Shanley, Jack Morris and Jack Crabtree, we had a racehorse team that year.

I remember how shocked I was when I left Oregon and came to USC in 1959. All the players ran the 100 in about 20 minutes.

During my years as an assistant at Oregon, I met the man who suggested I come to USC, badgered me until I agreed to, and then was instrumental in my becoming head coach. His name is Nick Pappas, now USC's director of athletic support groups. Nick led the Trojans in rushing back in 1935 when he had more hair.

Pappas was a USC assistant under Jess Hill from 1950 to 1956, and he and I often bumped into each other while scouting. I guess my scouting methods impressed him. When Nick was scouting, he spread paper everywhere and worked furiously, taking down everything that happened on the field. Meanwhile, I scarcely took a note, puffed cigars and went out at halftime for hot dogs. Nick spent his halftimes shuffling through all that paper. It looked like a paper drive.

Occasionally, he missed a player or two and he'd have to ask me how an end was slanting or where a tackle lined up or something like that, and I'd tell him. Or I might peek over his shoulder and correct a defense he had copied down. So Nick would leave me and tell people, "That son of a bitch McKay is a genius." Well, McKay wasn't a genius. He just had a more simple method.

I was convinced—and Cas didn't care how I scouted, because he didn't believe in it that much—that most scouts were wasting their time. I believed that teams at that time had a defense they wanted to play, and they would use it perhaps 85 percent of the time. Some of them would get so involved that they'd stay in it 95 percent of the time. They'd change only a small percentage of the game.

For example, Red Sanders' UCLA teams in the mid-50's played what we call a 4-4, or wide-six, defense. I'd watch all the other scouts draw a diagram every time UCLA lined up, putting down the whole Bruin defense. Their sheets would already have an offense penciled in, and across from it they'd put down 11 defensive players, tackle here, guard there, tackle over there.

I thought this was ridiculous. I knew where UCLA was lining up 85 percent of the time. So, unless they lined up differently, all I had to say to myself or write down was "60." I watched UCLA and it was 60, 60, 60.

I could then see the game while the other scouts were laboriously writing. There's no way you can draw 11 diagrams, write 11 names and watch the whole play. But this was one of the things that coaches wanted. It was stupid.

So the other scouts would miss a man or two and ask me what defense they were in, and I'd say brightly, "They were in 60. This guy was here and that guy was there." And they'd think I was a genius.

But all I looked for was the change. Now, if UCLA did switch defenses, I was watching instead of writing, and I wouldn't miss the change. But the others were so immersed in paper work that they didn't realize that 85 percent of the time this team was in the same damn defense.

When they watched the offense, scouts would want to know who pulled on every play, things like that. I didn't care. Where'd they run the ball? That's all I wanted to know. If it was UCLA, they were always in the single wing. So I'd write, "Cameron off tackle, strong side. One.

Cameron off tackle, strong side. Two. Reverse, Decker. Three. Davenport up the middle. Four."

When it was over, I would total everything up. Cameron ran the ball off tackle this afternoon 24 times, 15 of them to the strong side. They ran three reverses with Decker and Davenport went up the middle nine times. They threw the ball to the split end four times.

The other scouts would ask, "How'd they block the defense?" I'm thinking, what do I care how they blocked the other team's defense? I don't care how they blocked it. Their strategy isn't based on the other team's defense, it's based on their own offense. They do exactly what they want without worrying about the defense. You see, I was gauging the mind of the coach. I figured Sanders would always do certain things, someone else would do another.

I've always thought coaches worry too much about scouting, anyway, because of movies. Over the years, when I sent out scout Joe Margucci or Dick Beam, our current scout, I have told them I don't want any diagrams. Look for quickness and speed of all the players, because the films we get can be misleading.

If you only scout Notre Dame by film, for example, you'll be in trouble, because they're sneaky, like we are. They slow their films down so the players don't seem as quick as they really are. Some of them look like they're running in glue. I've fallen for that routine before. You think somebody you're going to play isn't too fast and then you get down on the sideline and they're running every which way and knocking the hell out of you. Other teams con you by speeding their films up. They look like the Keystone Kops.

Besides impressing Pappas when we scouted together, I guess I startled him a couple more times when Oregon beat USC. One time we stung them with a surprise quarterback sneak off tackle that went 66 yards for a touchdown. Another time they were favored to beat us, but we shut them out, 25–0. They never could figure out our defense.

After both games, the USC coach, first Jess Hill and then later Don Clark, went into our dressing room to ask Casanova about the quarterback sneak and then about the defense. Pappas went with Hill and Clark. On both occasions Cas gave them his big charming smile, pointed at me and said, "Ask John. He put it in." Pappas filed away all those memories.

Like the Depression years in West Virginia, those years at Oregon helped me, because we were always scrambling. I scrambled on and off the field. Corky started having babies, my salary stayed low, and I had to take jobs on the side.

One spring practice I was a night watchman from seven at night to five in the morning. Another spring I worked in a warehouse. In summers I got jobs in the lumber mills, which was tough physical work paying about $2 an hour.

I picked up extra money by sweeping out the basketball pavilion and took advantage of other fringe benefits, like free T-shirts, sweatshirts and football socks. I shaved in the training room and had my hair cut for a while by a player who was a barber. Corky became very adept at finding new ways to cook hamburger, I drove an old car, and we scrimped on clothes.

Working so long for so little money makes you buckle down and fight as hard as you can to get ahead. Maybe my tendency wouldn't have been to buckle down so much if I had been making a living wage.

I also prepared for my future in another way. I learned

to give talks. Casanova used to force me to go to high school banquets, and I always had the same stock answer: "Oh God, Cas, don't send me again."

For many years I hated to speak. I still don't enjoy it very much. But if you have to do it, you learn how. I remember nights, however, when I'd look at my watch and start sweating. I'd count the minutes and seconds until I had to get up and talk.

When I first began speaking I wasn't convinced that anyone was really interested in what I had to say. That's the big change in me over the past 20 years. When you first try speaking, you think, "Gee, here I am talking, and who am I to be talking?" Later on, if you've had some success, you realize, "Hey, I can do this more easily, because they are interested in what I have to say."

Today I believe very strongly that a coach must inject humor into his talks. No listener wants to hear a speaker drone on in a serious tone like the world is going to end tomorrow.

Some coaches give the same talk every time. I try to be different. I've listened to colleagues of mine say, "Now, we're gonna have a real fine team this year, and at left end we have Joe Doakes, who's 6-4 and 237 pounds. At left tackle we have Pete Fish, 6-5, 284 pounds, nice young fellow," go on down the line. I think, damn, if I was going to do that, I'd just pass out the roster. Coaches who speak that way are mentally lazy.

Over the years I've been criticized by some fans who claim I never tell them about the team. But I assume they're all educated and can read the papers. If they can't read, they can come to me personally and I'll read the lineup for them. Seriously, what am I going to reveal in a short talk? I may say, "I believe we're going to have a good team this year. Some of the stars are. . . ." That's about as far as I'll go.

Even worse than a dull talk is the one that's loaded with fiery clichés. I hate to talk that way. So many coaches, for example, keep repeating how hard their teams are going to hit you. Hell, everybody hits in football. I just shook my head when Oregon State's Dee Andros got up to make a talk a few years ago. Dee's a friend of mine, but, boy, he started off, "Our motto this year at Oregon State is G-A-T-A. That's for Get After Their Ass."

After he finished firing up the crowd, Dick Enright, the Oregon coach at that time, came to the microphone. Enright said he didn't know why Oregon had declined before he came, but things were going to be different now. People were going to have to fasten their chin straps to play Oregon.

And I'm thinking, I hope so. There's an NCAA rule that says you have to fasten your chin straps.

I have an assistant who jumps up to speak, and his line is something like, "Oh, it's great to be a Trojan, and the Trojans are going to beat their ass on Saturday and stomp all over them."

"Change your style," I'm always saying to him. "The crowd isn't going to play the game. Relax."

So many coaches talk that way as if it's a routine and then plop down, that I feel they must be more scared than I was. I'm still not always comfortable. But at least I look relaxed. They look like they're pressed into their suits.

I think most fans just want a few football stories with a little humor. Much of the humor is in exaggeration of simple incidents.

I don't memorize my speeches or write down any lines, but somehow they just come out of me flippantly. Later on, when I analyze some of the lines people laughed at,

I don't think many of them are funny. That's why delivery is so important.

Once in a while I'll use a story to illustrate a point. It doesn't take great intelligence to do that. For example, I might be talking about the importance of confidence— in football or in any endeavor. Then I'll use my story on Bear Bryant. It goes like this:

"One time I was staying down at Bear's house in Alabama, and early one morning he shook my bed and insisted I go duck hunting with him. Bear is a very persuasive man. So at 4:30, Bear and I and Jack Daniels got behind a duck blind. We waited and waited. No ducks.

"Finally, after about three hours, here comes one lonely duck. The Bear fires. And that duck is still flying today. But Bear watched the duck flap away, looked at me and said, 'John, you are witnessing a genuine miracle. There flies a dead duck.'

"Now that is what I call confidence."

Relating the story to myself, I have been given confidence in my own life not by shooting ducks, but by making several big decisions and having them turn out well. I decided to go into the Air Corps, decided to go to Purdue, decided to transfer to Oregon, decided to marry Corky, and, finally, decided to go to work at USC.

I had coached at Oregon for nine seasons when I drove down to Southern California in early 1959 to recruit and also attend a clinic in Santa Monica. At the time USC had lost an assistant coach and was looking for a replacement. The day I walked into the clinic Nick Pappas and USC's head coach, Don Clark, were there. They had been kicking names around for the assistant's job. Nick pointed at me, turned to Clark and said, "How about Johnny?"

Clark said he didn't think I would leave Oregon. But Don called me aside and asked me anyway. I said I'd have to think it over.

USC haunted me all the way back up the Coast to Oregon, and I spent two or three weeks making up my mind. It was a very difficult decision. One faction was saying I'd be the next head coach at Oregon, while Nick and other people were arguing that I could more easily spring to a good job from USC. But I was a little in awe of USC, I guess. And there were drawbacks. At the time, the Trojans were in a slump—they won only one game in 1957 and four in 1958—and they were finishing an NCAA probation, which kept them ineligible for the Rose Bowl in 1959. There was no talk of any more money, either.

You always change your mind a lot when you have to make a major decision like that, and I did. There were points for staying and points for leaving. One day I'd walk into Casanova's office and say, "I'm going," and the next day I'd come back and say, "No, I'm not." At the end I think I was changing every half hour.

I went to see Cas at his house one afternoon, but he had gone to Portland, so I discussed the offer with his late wife, Dixie. She said I'd be foolish not to go.

At home, I was getting a lot of pressure, too. Corky really pushed hard for coming to USC. She had always wanted to go home, and now she had a medical reason for wanting to leave Oregon. Every spring she had terrible hay fever attacks. It got to the point where she was going to the hospital for treatment and taking shots all the time. Occasionally, we had to get up in the middle of the night and drive to the coast so her sinuses could drain. The hay fever got worse every year, and at the end she was taking codeine.

Corky's other argument—and she claims this was the last time she won an argument with me—was that we had been at Oregon so long we were in danger of becoming fixtures. It was time we did something else. Casanova, she argued, was always going to retire, but he hadn't, and John McKay better take a chance and go somewhere else. I was 35 years old.

Pappas, meanwhile, was relentless. He spent half his time on the phone trying to talk me into coming down. He used everything against me. He discovered that Corky had always loved the beach in Southern California and said, "Wouldn't it be nice if your wife could go to the beach again? You know how much she loves it."

One day I made my decision. The McKays were going to Southern California.

I waited for our last child, Richie, to be born, and then came right down in March. I never regretted the decision. Don Clark was tremendous to work for, and he'll always be one of my best friends. I worked like hell for him, and I think I got some people to play well who had failed before, like fullbacks Clark Holden and Jim Conroy. They had ability, but they needed someone to help them realize it. I coached the offensive backs and ran the offense, and, even though we had a bigger staff, helped out with the defensive secondary.

Our team started with a good spring practice and kept the momentum. The Trojans were a little amazing. They had several good linemen but no speed at all. And Willie Wood, although he was a great athlete—he became an All-Pro safety for Green Bay—was a limited quarterback who had a bad shoulder besides.

We didn't run very well and we didn't pass very well, but we won our first eight games, three by shutouts, including a 17–0 smashing of Ohio State. Although ineligible for the Rose Bowl because of the recruiting violations in the middle 1950's, we beat the Rose Bowl team, Washington, 22–15, handing them their only loss in 11 games.

But we lost the last two games of the season—to

UCLA and Notre Dame—and poor Don Clark was attacked by everyone. All the criticism made me mad. I remember storming into my house one day in December.

"Corky," I said, "this is a horseshit town. The man won eight games and lost two. SC had been at the bottom of the barrel, and for a while we had a chance at the national championship. Now everybody's complaining. Let's get the hell out of here."

Although I was furious for days, the criticism from alumni and sportswriters alone wouldn't have driven me away. But I was thinking of leaving. I was worried about my own future. Despite the furor, we had turned in a good season, and since Clark was coming off an 8-2 year it would be easier for him to recruit. The program had begun to straighten itself out, USC was getting off probation, and Clark was only 36 years old. Where did that leave me? I was 36, too, and figured I'd better look for another job that would pay more money. In December, 1959, I had a wife and four kids and was making $9,000 a year.

I decided to go into pro football. I talked to Van Brocklin, who was then quarterbacking the Philadelphia Eagles. Van told me that he had been promised the Eagle coaching job, if Buck Shaw quit in 1960. He offered me an assistant's job, and I decided to take it.

Van Brocklin and I are still good friends, but I've occasionally wondered what would have happened if we had coached together. He's stubborn and hot-tempered, and I'm stubborn and hot-tempered. I suppose a personality clash would have been inevitable.

But our initial plan fell through. Eventually, the Eagles talked Van Brocklin into playing one more year, and Shaw went on to coach one more year. In fact, they won the world title in 1960. But, after Shaw retired, the

Eagles hired Nick Skorich as coach instead, and Van went on to Minnesota to become the first coach of the Vikings in 1961.

Before all that, however, an astonishing thing happened. USC made me head coach.

Everybody at Oregon thinks to this day that I came to USC with some sort of deal promising me the job. There's no truth in that. It was a miracle I became USC's head coach. If this school hadn't hired me, I might never have become one. I was stunned when I was offered the job.

Clark resigned and recommended me, and I'll never forget him. Don gave me an opportunity most coaches only dream about.

I had no inkling he was thinking of quitting, but apparently he had been considering it for some time. He had a year left on his contract, but he wasn't making much money, either, and was under severe pressure from his brother, John, to help run John's big industrial laundry company. His brother had suffered three heart attacks, and told Don he had to join him as a partner immediately. Today, John Clark is happily retired, and Don is a successful businessman.

Although his decision was an economic one, Clark admitted he had been hurt by all the criticism.

"What are they going to do in this town if USC comes up with a bad team?" he said. "It amazed me to run into all the dissatisfaction with our past season. I know many of our fans were hoping for an undefeated season. Well, so were we when we had gone that far. Coaching in Los Angeles is certainly complicated. There was no reason for me to think it would grow less complicated.

"And I got to thinking where I'd be in four years when I was 40. I would still just be making house payments.

The financial advancement just wasn't there in coaching, and that's something I had to think about with seven children."

Before the announcement of Clark's resignation, USC vice president Francis Tappan, who supervised the athletic department, asked Clark who should get the job. Don recommended me. Then Tappan asked Pappas, and he recommended me. So Tappan went to the president, Dr. Norman Topping, and said it had to be McKay. I was hired the next day.

I must be one of the luckiest guys in the world. There's nothing you can do to try and become a head coach. Nothing. Just work hard and be in the right place at the right time. It's unfortunate that our profession is not one in which you can take an examination and move up. You just can't.

Since I had been the only new addition to the USC staff, and we had gone from a losing team to one contending for the national title, I probably got more credit than I deserved.

The night before Topping offered me the job I went to a restaurant with Jerry Frei, who had been an assistant coach with me at Oregon. Pappas was so excited that he tracked me down at the restaurant and found Frei and me sitting at the bar.

He pulled me aside. "John," he said. "How would you like to be head coach?"

"What are you talking about?" I said. "Are you putting me on?"

"No," he said. "You're going to be called in tomorrow and offered the job."

I still couldn't believe it. The next day, December 14, I was sipping coffee in the student union when Topping called me into his office. He told me Clark was quitting and asked if I would like to have the job. It took me half a second to say yes.

Topping has since retired as USC president, but he and I have remained close friends, and I'll always remember the support he gave me from the beginning. I know I wouldn't have stayed without him. I can't think of anything worse than being at a university where the president isn't behind you 100 percent. Topping was always accessible, too. If you have to go through 27 channels to reach the president when you have a problem, you'll never get anything done.

Dr. Topping said USC wouldn't make the announcement until the next morning, but since there had been rumors about Clark leaving, he was afraid a reporter might call our house and learn by accident. You never know what kids will blurt out when they answer the phone. So Topping said no one should spend the night in our house.

I rushed from his office and called Corky. I couldn't even believe the news as I told her. How could they pick me? I'd been at USC for only nine months.

"Corky," I said, "brace yourself. Don Clark has resigned and I'm SC's new head coach."

"Don't be funny," she said.

"I'm not kidding," I answered. "I really am the new coach."

She yelled and went a little crazy on the phone.

"Calm down, Cork," I said. "Listen to me now. Take the kids and go over to your parents' house for the night. And don't tell anyone."

Corky, bouncing like a rubber ball, hung up the phone —and then realized she couldn't tell anybody.

First she called her parents and told them she was packing and leaving home with all the kids and asked her mom and dad to come and pick them up. Her mother got mad, because she assumed her daughter was leaving me, and said she wasn't going to come.

"I can't tell you anything over the phone," Corky said, "but it's good news." That didn't soothe them.

"My mother and dad marched into our house with fire in their eyes," she told me later. "They had no idea what I was up to. A neighbor who helped me pack really thought I had flipped out."

So Corky whispered the news to her parents and left with the kids. It was a good thing, because a sportswriter did come by late that night and wound up camping on our front lawn until morning.

But I wasn't there, either. I spent the night with Don Richman, the USC publicist.

At ten the next morning, USC had a press conference to introduce John McKay as the new head coach. But Braven Dyer, the most influential sportswriter on the *Los Angeles Times,* screamed because it was held so early the day after Santa Anita Racetrack's big cocktail party. He wasn't just mad, he was indignant.

Many of the other writers were confused. Several wanted to know how to spell my name. One of them wrote, "SC names Mr. Who," and another referred to me as "a talented but relatively obscure assistant."

A television sportscaster said: "Don Clark has resigned and Jim McKay is the new coach at USC."

By this time, my brother Jimmy was a B-52 pilot, stationed near Seattle. He was an Air Force colonel, and was startled to get calls from people who wanted to know if he was leaving the Air Force.

He phoned the next day. "Listen, John," he said. "I have enough trouble flying these planes. Don't get me any coaching jobs."

The confused reaction by the media didn't bother me.

That's the way I would have reacted, too. Who was I? I was nobody.

Topping was positive, however, as he made the announcement. "We are hopeful," he said simply, "that John McKay will be with the university for many years to come."

Then I made those statements all young coaches make. We're going to work hard at recruiting and coaching and we're going to have a fine team and carry on the tradition, and all that. And that was it.

It was incredible. The right place at the right time. I'm sure if Clark hadn't resigned I would be in pro football today.

RECRUITING

"I'm very close to his mother"

FOOTBALL COACHES OFTEN WORRY about the field they're going to play on or the weather conditions they're going to face. But if we had the best players, I wouldn't mind playing you in Nome, Alaska.

And, of course, you get the best players by recruiting. There isn't a coach in America who can win with poor material, but it's his responsibility not to be in that position.

Recruiting is a very difficult job. Except for losing, it's the worst thing about college coaching. For several months it's almost a full-time task, and it gets even tougher at USC when we go to the Rose Bowl regularly. While we're getting ready to play Michigan or Ohio State, the other schools get the jump on us by spending December talking to prospects.

Recruiting is complex, because of all the NCAA rules governing it, and it's frustrating because so many kids today are arrogant and so many of their parents are skeptical. When I'm talking, some of them even imply that I'm a liar. It's vicious, because coaches claim that other coaches cheat, and it's a dogfight, because there's more competition than ever for the best players. But recruiting can also be humorous and very rewarding.

Morally, it's improved tremendously since about 1960 —and the NCAA should take most of the credit. There still is illegal payment of athletes, but nowhere near as much as there used to be. It was the greatest vice in the old days, and it was as rampant at USC and UCLA as it was everywhere else.

In the 1940's and 1950's, there were a lot of players coming out of the service—after both World War II and Korea—and many of them were older, married and had children. They couldn't live on regular scholarships. So support groups donated to the athletes to enable them to stay in school.

Because of the GI Bill, schools spent less money on scholarships. So if X university would give each player $50 extra to come and play, then Z university could afford to do the same.

Under present NCAA rules, you can offer an athlete room, board, books, tuition and $15 a month for incidental fees, a figure that hasn't gone up for several years. What can a student-athlete do with $15? He is also barred from having a campus or off-campus job while school is in session.

In our conference, the Pacific-8, we can only offer room, board and tuition. No books, no $15. Until five years ago, it was only tuition, and the athlete had to work on campus to help pay for his room and board.

But there's so damn much hearsay about recruiting today. For example, someone will say to me, "Don't tell us that O. J. Simpson didn't get a big car, an apartment and an education for his wife."

"He didn't," I'll respond.

And they'll wink and say, "You wouldn't tell us if he did."

You can't win. Now I'm a cheater and a liar, too.

I believe that if it's necessary to cheat in intercollegiate athletics to be successful, they aren't worth having. And I've never believed in the innocence of an 18-year-old boy who takes something extra. He's heard of the rules, and he knows he's breaking them. I have no patience with that stale rationale people use: it's like cheating on your income tax. Why not do it? Everybody else does.

Recruiting rules are so intricate now that it's possible to break one and not realize it. This is why 90 percent of USC's recruiting is done by my assistants, our current players and me. Maybe 10 percent is done by ex-players. We don't want alumni involved anymore, because the more people involved, the more chance for infractions.

We used to be able to entertain a player lavishly at dinner and take him to another city to do it. But now, in order to cut down the cost of athletics, a new NCAA rule says that a recruit can only be taken out in an area contiguous with the campus.

In our case, this means we can only go to dinner in the city of Los Angeles. Unfortunately, Los Angeles is the most undefined city in the world. We have to give all our recruiters maps. There are areas in the San Fernando Valley which are in Los Angeles, and some of them are three times as far away from USC as Santa Monica is. But we can't take a recruit to Santa Monica.

That's absurd, isn't it? Even so, it's hard to write rules encompassing so many schools and so many circumstances. To stop people from taking unfair advantage of others, the NCAA occasionally winds up with a rule that's a little crazy. This one can be difficult for parents to understand. If I go to Santa Barbara to see a boy, I can't take him out to dinner. His parents have to entertain me.

There are rules covering everything you could possibly think of. As harmless as it sounds, a coach can't take a prospect out to play golf.

So, every time a rule is passed, we send out a flood of memos to make sure everyone understands. The alumni have to be watched carefully, because they're the ones who could easily slip an athlete illegal side benefits.

Grade tampering got heavy publicity in 1973, when Oklahoma was suspended after it was discovered that the grades of two Sooner recruits had been changed at the high school level.

Grade tampering goes on, but I don't think it's widespread. And it can happen to a university without its knowledge, because the official high school transcript is sent to the admissions office, not the athletic department. It's often very tempting for the high school to raise grades to help the athlete, before forwarding the transcript.

I didn't like the old 1.6 rule for qualifying, because it left this avenue open for cheating. First of all, it was the worst-named rule in the history of sports, because it gave all the critics of athletics a perfect target to fire at. People assumed it meant a student with a 1.6 high school average, which is between C− and D+, could get into college. "Boy," the critics said, "they're letting in players that don't even have a C average."

But it didn't mean that at all. It was simply a formula that took your high school rank and your score on the College Board exams and predicted whether or not you would get at least a 1.6 average your first year *in college*. The higher your class rank, the less you had to score on your College Board test; the lower your class rank, the higher you had to score.

Assume I was recruiting a player and went to a high school principal and asked for his class rank. The principal would ask why I wanted to know. I would tell him I'm a coach from USC and I want to find out if this young man qualifies 1.6. Okay, says the principal. We'll send it to you. So it's sent to our registrar's office, and they report the player qualifies.

Now maybe that principal wants the player to go to college. Maybe his coach is worried about him and wants to help him go. Do you realize how many grades have been changed over the years by school superintendents so their students could go to college?

Most people always assume athletes are the ones given special favors. But it can be done just as easily for girls. Some dad knows the principal, goes out and plays golf with him, and says:

"You know, if my daughter Susan had just a little higher average, she could get into Stanford." So the records are fixed, and who's guilty?

The new rule for admission stipulates that the athlete must have a 2.0, or C, average in high school. But the same temptation is there. A coach goes to the principal, says he's interested in a certain player.

"What's Joe's average?" he asks. "1.98? That's too damn bad. If he had a 2.00, he could have gotten a four-year scholarship."

The principal might seek out a teacher who liked Joe and say, "You know, if Joe just re-took that test you gave him last year, do you think he could get a B instead of a C?"

"Well, certainly," says the teacher. "Joe's a nice young-ster, been good to us here. And his folks can't afford to send him to college." Now it's done, the altered grades are sent to some other college, and that school can be hung out to dry. It could be us that comes along second.

Then it comes out in the paper that USC cheated. "No," we say, "we didn't have anything to do with it."

"Don't kid us," everyone says. "That's how you got all your guys in." And the first school which recruited this boy points out that his grade point average didn't qualify when they checked. We have no defense, and the public scoffs, "Ah, they're all doing it."

Whenever I hear that generalization from someone, I tell him to go to hell and get away from me. If I say I don't cheat, and someone says all schools do, then he's calling me a liar.

I could never convince the public that USC is completely honest, and many other college coaches have the same problem. But I'll be happy to take a lie detector test.

A couple of years ago we recruited and signed a player, and then his father gave him a new car to drive to college. A sportscaster announced that it was clear why this star had chosen us.

"He's going to USC," said the broadcaster, "because they gave him a flashy new car."

In this case, the boy's father got madder at the sportscaster than we did. He didn't want people to think he couldn't afford to give his own son a car.

Unfortunately, our own fraternity causes a lot of this public skepticism. A coach gets beat, and he responds, "No wonder I lost. The other guy's got all the players, and he cheated to get them." So he satisfies his alumni.

Sure we're competitors, but some of our own worst publicity comes from saying silly things like that. We're working against each other. And I think all of us, myself included, have been guilty.

People have queer ideas about ethics, too. After the NCAA suspended UCLA running back James McAlister for the 1971 season, because of alleged tampering with a College Board test, a fiery story appeared in a newspaper before our game with UCLA in 1972. In the story

McAlister said he'd been waiting a year and a half to get even with us, because we turned him in for cheating.

We didn't turn him in; hell, I wouldn't do that. But if we had, what's so wrong about that? We had an honor system in certain classes at Oregon, like they do at West Point. I wasn't about to cheat, but I'll be damned if I want a guy to sit there and cheat for an A, while I work my brains out for a C.

I have come to believe that we shouldn't have NCAA rules restricting admission of athletes. Every school should admit who they want to admit. Let the grades arrive, and let the admissions office decide. That's the way it is with other students.

Basically, a lot of faculty people in the NCAA passed the qualification rule to impress the educators. But the way to determine whether the youngster should compete is bring him into college and see what he does. Does he pass his work? Then he's eligible to play.

The NCAA doesn't even have a rule for the most important factor: progress in school. Some leagues have the rule, some don't. The NCAA simply says you must carry 12 units to be eligible. They don't care what you do with those 12 units. You can flunk them, drop them after the season or never even show up for class.

Our league says you must not only carry 12 units a semester, but pass 24 every year. Therefore, you are progressing toward a degree. And that's what the NCAA says they want.

As I've said, many things about recruiting irritate me. For example, we've had coaches use racism against us. To white players they'll say, "Don't go to USC. It's in the middle of Watts."

To blacks they'll say, "Don't go to USC, because until recently they never had any black athletes."

One day, a year ago, a black father brought his son, whom we were recruiting, into my office. The young man was very nice, but his father kept repeating he had heard USC was prejudiced. I tried to say this wasn't true. I pointed out that our first All-American back in 1925 was Brice Taylor, who is black. I admitted USC had a lapse for many years before I got there, but I said I could prove that throughout the country there were few or no blacks playing for major universities. Of course, it was much the same in professional sports, including baseball, football and basketball.

I told him that in my tenure at USC no school anywhere could have had better rapport with black athletes, and it lasts, because many of them recruit for us after they're through playing. Without them, I would have been a complete failure.

This father was still arguing. I pointed out that on our national championship team of 1972, 11 starters were white and 11 were black. Of my All-Americans, 11 were black and 13 white. (The total is now 14 white, 14 black.) And if he wanted to take quarterbacks, USC was the only school on the Coast that had started a black quarterback full time, Willie Wood in 1959, and Jimmy Jones for three years, 1969 to 1971. We had also had two Heisman Trophy winners, and they were both black.

But this man still wouldn't accept what I was saying. Finally, I got mad.

"For you to tell me I'm wrong because of something that happened at USC 20 or 25 years ago," I said, "is totally absurd." I asked him to leave.

Well, this is the way it is with many parents, black and white. Most of them are very nice, but a small percentage have some fixed ideas that are ridiculous. While this father was claiming USC is prejudiced against blacks, I got letters from other people who said I had too many blacks on my team. But I ignore all those people. I play the best players I have. But there's no way to convince the cynics.

Obviously, parents discuss more than race. They're often skeptical about other parts of the program. I'll describe it to them, and they'll say, "We were told this player got unfair treatment here," or "You don't live up to your promises." I deny the charges, but they'll respond, "That isn't what we know."

That infuriates me. I'm not interested in talking to those people anymore, and I'm not interested in talking to their sons either. If they're going to question my honesty, I don't know why they would even consider having their son play for me.

But I don't find most parents aggressive. Some come in very much in awe, and about half of them are nervous. They want their sons to do well, and they're very concerned.

By the time I meet parents my assistants have already been recruiting their boy for a long time. The assistants all have different recruiting areas, and ultimately they will set up an appointment for the player to visit the school and talk to me. As a rule his mother and father will come, too.

If the assistant coach feels it's important for me to eat dinner with the family, I'll do that, but I prefer to meet them in my office. In a year, if we recruit, say, 25 players, I might go out to dinner with three or four of them.

Occasionally, I find myself in embarrassing situations. Several years ago an assistant and I were out with a family. The mother sang in a church choir. She was very polite as I talked about the benefits of USC. But as time wore on, I could tell she was getting impatient. Suddenly she said:

"I don't understand this bullshit the other coaches have been giving me. But, wherever he goes, I hope my son has a better opportunity than my husband here. All he was good for was making love."

Her son tried to interrupt.

"Shut your mouth, boy," she said. "If it wasn't for that, you wouldn't be here."

I guess mom liked me, because her son went to USC.

When we do hold our meeting in the office, I'll talk about an hour, find out if the boy has a specific major in mind and try to get the USC literature to him. I'll discuss our program and tell him where I think he can best play on the team. Then I'll offer the scholarship and spell out what kind of aid is available.

Many parents, particularly the mothers, will at first profess great interest in their son's education. It seems to be their major concern. Then, when you get right down to the crunch and don't get the kid, mom will often say, "I don't blame him. He just didn't think he could play at your school."

So I have kind of discounted that malarkey about the education from most parents. Like everyone else, they want their boys to make the team.

Parents say the damndest things. One mother told me, "When you own an athlete like we do, you have to make sure he goes to the right school." And I thought, I didn't know parents owned children.

A proud daddy said, "I've known my son ever since he was a little boy." Which is not unusual.

Many parents feel they must convince you how good their son is, although you've already shown your interest by offering a scholarship.

"He made all-league in San Bernardino, you know," says the mother. "He scored 20 touchdowns."

And I say, "Yes, ma'm," and listen for about 35 or 40

minutes and think, boy, did they figure I would invite him down here if I didn't know all that?

Meanwhile, the son is trying to impress me by flexing his muscles every four seconds so I can see how big his arms are.

The parents should realize I already know their son is good enough to play for us, and should be more concerned about whether or not they like the university. What I'd like them to ask is if their boy can get into dental school or business school or engineering school. What are the requirements for those?

The line of reasoning used in picking colleges sometimes borders on the hilarious. When I was an assistant at Oregon, I lost a boy once because I smoked a cigar while I was talking to him. He went to Oregon State. Damned if it didn't happen again a couple of years ago. I lost another player, this time to Washington, because he didn't like my cigar either.

In 1973 we lost a player to UCLA because his dad liked Coach Pepper Rodgers' television show better than mine. That's what they told me.

If I were an ordinary parent trying to help my son choose a college, I would first assess his skills, find out what he wanted to do, and if I knew anything about football, look at the offense the team is using. If my son is a split receiver, for example, he shouldn't play for a wishbone team, because they never pass.

Then I would tell him to study the various schools and see if they can offer him the degree he's interested in.

And, as we studied each one, I'd ask, what is the coach's record? What has he accomplished? What kind of man is he? I don't think very many parents study records. There's a difference in coaches, just as there's a difference in doctors or lawyers. And that difference matters.

Many young players claim they always want to win and they pick schools that are always losing. It amuses me when I hear how easy it is to recruit at USC. It's not. A lot of players won't come because they assume they're going to sit on the bench. The typical American youth loves competition, but not at his position.

When Tommy Prothro was coach at UCLA, he mimeographed our roster and sent it around to all the recruits to try and scare them—to try and prove there was no way they could play at USC (some coaches told O. J. Simpson he wouldn't play for us). But if the kids we're after would use simple mathematics, they would understand this isn't true. Almost everybody we've had plays, because our squad is smaller than most of our opponents'. We've never used the limit of scholarships since I've been at USC. Obviously, if you recruit fewer people, the percentage who play goes up.

It may sound preposterous when you study USC's record—almost 60 national championships in all sports—but we've never had many athletic facilities. We have no athletic dorms, no fieldhouse, little practice space, and, until recently, barely enough office space to turn around in.

So we have to keep the number of players down. Not only is there limited room to practice in, but the school's tuition cost is very high. I'd guess the average number of football scholarships at most big schools, counting freshmen through seniors, has been about 130. An NCAA rule now limits everyone to 105. The highest we've ever had is 91, and one year it was in the high seventies. But we can't come up with a million excuses for losing, so we better select the right people.

People sometimes accuse us of taking athletes so they won't play anywhere else. That isn't true. I don't believe in giving anybody a scholarship if I don't think he'll play.

I would get awfully angry at one of my assistants if he had a two-year record of recruiting six kids, five of whom couldn't play. Then he's doing a damn poor job.

My feeling—and sometimes I'm not sure if my coaches do exactly what I think they should—is that sometimes you're just wasting your time trying to recruit a youngster. Right away, you should ask him if he has a choice of schools. Most boys grow up thinking, I'm a Texas fan or a Nebraska fan or a Notre Dame fan. So you should ask him if there's a school where he has always thought he'd like to go. If he says yes, he's probably better off going there. What he's going to find out in one 48-hour visiting period is not going to counteract what he already knows about his favorite school. He's been thinking about it for 17 years.

Then we ask what major he's interested in.

"Well, coach," he might say, "I want to be a dentist."

"Son, we have an outstanding dental school. Here is the proof."

"But I'm thinking of going to. . . ."

"They don't have a dental school."

"Yes, I know, but they said they would help me when I got out."

"Look, now you're just falling for an argument. If you really want dentistry, go to USC."

I also try to sell players nearness to home. You will play in an area in which your name can later open doors for you. The farther away from home you go, the bigger name you must make. Otherwise, you're not going to be known when you return to your own community. We're lucky at USC, because we're located in a large metropolitan area with great potential. About 98 percent of the athletes who play for us end up living in the Los Angeles area. People still remember, for example, that Ben Wilson was the fullback for our national champions in 1962. Today he's a vice president of Wells Fargo Bank.

If a player goes to South Bend, Indiana, or Lincoln, Nebraska, or any other small town, he'll probably leave that environment when he graduates.

We tell our recruits that they'll play for a winner and face the best teams and players in the rest of the country.

We sell USC as a private university with smaller classes, but one still large enough to be tremendously diversified.

And we promise that we'll get a summer job for everyone who wants one.

We have never set out to recruit anybody from out of state. Of our 1972 national champions, 37 of the top 40 players were from California. Out-of-state players generally have no feeling for Trojan tradition and might not be susceptible to the benefits of playing in Los Angeles.

Mainly, however, if we search outside California, we're spending more time and money to see players, and the odds against getting them are greater. There's an old cliché, too, that the farther away a boy is, the better he gets. Distance makes him sound like a superstar.

So we'd be flying everywhere to capture these players, while right in Los Angeles there's a tremendous wealth of talent. More consensus All-Americans have come from the Los Angeles area in the last 25 years than from any other urban area in the country. Over the same period California was second only to Texas in All-Americans produced by states.

Even so, if a very special player from out of state expresses interest in us, we'll go after him in an instant. A good example was Gary Jeter, a defensive tackle from Cleveland, who was good enough to start for us as a freshman in 1973.

Ironically, there is occasionally one advantage in recruiting players from outside California. No one tells them they're not good enough to play for USC.

Coaches lie a lot about personnel. We might recruit and sign a boy that other coaches have ignored. He turns out to be a star, and they'll say, "No wonder SC won. Look at that player they've got. Nobody else could get him." We've had players like tight end Bob Klein and flanker Bobby Chandler who are pro starters today, but they snuck into USC with no one else after them.

Clarence Davis, one of our All-American tailbacks now in pro football, had a bad junior college game on a muddy field, and several coaches in our conference decided he wasn't so promising. It's surprising how many players we take that nobody else wants.

Even though there was frantic competition for O. J. Simpson, a couple of coaches in our league didn't think he was a superstar. Tommy Prothro of UCLA went to one of O.J.'s JC games, sat next to one of my assistants, and said he didn't think O.J. was a great player. He does now. Of course, the gimmick from UCLA was, "Well, we couldn't have gotten him in school, anyhow." That line has become a cliché.

Mike White, the coach at California, said before the 1972 season that USC wasn't going to be top dog anymore, that the Pacific-8 had leveled out. We beat Cal, 42 to 14. Said White: "It's hard to beat a team with material that super."

A top recruiter is one who does a superb job in evaluating the players when their quality isn't always that evident. We've learned to judge youngsters on their potential for development in two or three years. Many high school seniors are two or three years away from their peaks.

It doesn't matter if the boy is a second-stringer or all-league. Maybe he's awkward because he's younger than the others in his grade. Maybe he's a slow halfback who could be a quick college center. Three of our best linebackers on the 1972 national champions, Dale Mitchell, Ed Powell and Ken Gray, were high school running backs.

I don't want to imply that we don't make any mistakes in recruiting. Of course we do. But we work very hard at cutting down those mistakes.

We're looking for quickness and a certain amount of size. At some positions you can get by on quickness alone. But at others size is important. It's not enough to be quick at tackle. When we played Notre Dame in my early seasons at USC, their defense was bigger than our offense, and we couldn't block them. So we recruited taller players who put on weight.

We prefer tall linemen because they can add pounds and not slow down. If you recruit a shorter lineman, you'll discover the more weight he gains, the slower he gets. Many tall linemen are easier to recruit, too, because they might have been a little awkward in high school, since they grew so fast. So maybe they didn't play very well. We recruit linemen for potential more than we do backs. There's a tremendous maturation in a boy between 17 and 19.

To be realistic in our judgment, we also have to be wary of taking someone else's word about the height, weight, or speed of an athlete. Everybody I've known has a tendency to exaggerate.

When we ask our own players how tall they are, a lot will answer 6-1. I'll bet you many of them are 5-11, 5-11½, 5-11¾. It's normal in football to stretch yourself.

When it came time to list heights a couple of years ago, my own son grew an inch in one day.

If we ask an alumnus how big a young man at his old high school is, he might answer 6-2, 210. That means 6-1, 190.

I've asked some people how fast a player is at running 40 yards and gotten the answer, "He runs 4.3."

And I've always thought, well, if he does, he's the greatest player in the world. Earl McCullouch, a split end for us who tied the world record in the high hurdles, ran 4.4. Simpson ran 4.4. Who are they kidding?

The return to two-platoon football in 1964 has made the biggest difference in the size of college players. If we still had one-platoon ball, we would need smaller athletes, because there's no question that a leaner man will be in better shape over the long haul.

Every year we lose two or three good players because they've been told by someone else that they'll play at their favorite position. But since we're recruiting for potential, we try not to commit ourselves by telling a youngster that he'll play the same position where he starred in high school. There are many kids, for example, who are high school quarterbacks or running backs just because they're the best athletes. They shouldn't stay there.

I'll tell a youngster that if he wants to play a certain position he'll have an opportunity, but I won't promise that I'll never move him. We've had brilliant flankers who were high school quarterbacks, including Bobby Chandler, Rod Sherman and All-Americans Hal Bedsole and Lynn Swann.

Gene Washington of the San Francisco 49ers, one of pro football's best wide receivers, was a quarterback in high school, and Stanford promised Gene he would be a quarterback for them. We told Gene he wouldn't be. We said he'd be a receiver, because there was no way he could be as good at quarterback as he would at flanker.

Washington ignored us and went to Stanford. For a while, he was an inconsistent quarterback. Then Stanford got Jim Plunkett and Washington became the damndest flanker you ever saw.

UCLA has a quarterback named John Sciarra, who went to high school with my son, Johnny, and our quarterback, Pat Haden. I liked Johnny Sciarra and saw him a lot, because he used to visit our house. But I had never met his mother and dad. When I tried to recruit him and met his parents, I knew we had no chance to get him.

Sciarra was a year behind Haden in high school and had played behind him as a junior. That's because Haden was the greatest prep passer in Southern California history. But Sciarra had talent. When he started as a senior, he was Southern California's prep player of the year. But his parents figured Haden would start ahead of him at USC, too, and had already built up an animosity against us.

But we kept trying. Finally, I went to Johnny's home. I don't visit too many houses, but Sciarra is an excellent athlete. He was a very good shortstop in high school, too.

"The most important thing to Johnny is baseball," said his father. "That's where his whole future lies—although he's a better quarterback than Haden."

"Well, I don't think he's a better quarterback than Haden," I said. "I want to be honest on that. I think his future, if it is in football, is as a defensive back. He can be an excellent one.

"But, if he wants to play baseball, you should consider that UCLA has won only one league baseball title since World War II. USC has won 24 of the last 28, ten national titles and produced dozens of major leaguers.

"And did Johnny ever consider how many football players at SC have played baseball versus the number at UCLA? Mike Garrett, Willie Brown and Anthony Davis all skipped spring football to play baseball. O. J. Simpson missed one spring practice and half of another to run on the track team. Johnny would play baseball at USC, and he'd play for the coach who won all those titles, Rod Dedeaux."

"What you say doesn't make any difference to me," said his father. "I'm sure he'll play baseball at UCLA."

Those parents knew my son and knew Haden, had a boy who loved baseball and yet wouldn't accept what I said. You look at USC's baseball record and you'd have to be crazy to go elsewhere if baseball is your sport. Well, Johnny went elsewhere. And in spring of his sophomore year he didn't play baseball, because he was warned that if he did he wouldn't even be the second-string quarterback.

Even though John Sciarra started occasionally at quarterback as a sophomore and took over as a junior, he has no more chance to play professionally at the position than I do. But I thought he had a chance to be a pro defensive back.

Coaches are like Army recruiters. Many of them will say almost anything to get a youngster. That's not my way. You will play where you can best help our team. I think you'll find that where you can best help the team is where you can best help yourself. But in most cases it's the parents who insist their sons can or cannot do something. Many of them have a heck of a lot more to say about where their boy goes to school than they admit they do.

Recruiting was easier when I began doing it more than 20 years ago. First of all, pro football wasn't very important and college was more than just a vehicle to the pros. Today, when a player asks if he can make it in pro football and we honestly answer we don't think so, he considers it an insult.

Second, the kids are pressured by more schools today. Any time you try on two suits it's not hard to make up your mind. But when you see about 25 of them, a decision doesn't come easily.

Often the attention goes to the boy's head. One of the most aggravating things about recruiting is talking to the athlete who's having fun trying to make up his mind— the one who's arrogant. I despise arrogant athletes. I like basketball, but I'd rather be back in the coal mines of West Virginia than be a basketball coach. Why? Because if you're recruiting a hot dog you can never humble him.

One day our very successful basketball coach, Bob Boyd, brought a brilliant 7-foot high school player to USC and I agreed to talk to him. Bob was desperately trying to land him. So were a lot of other people. When I talked to the prospect, he wouldn't even look at me.

I'm thinking, damn, look at me. I'm not that bad to look at. Look at me and I'll look at you. Let's discuss this. But he's up there on Mount Olympus.

"How are you going to pick your school?" I asked.

"I'll put down all the good points each university has. The one that has the most good points I'll go to."

"What are you going to major in?"

"The education part's not that important."

He's going to weigh USC's good and bad points and he doesn't even know what his major is going to be.

"Well, maybe I'll be in cinema," he says.

"Well, do you know what school in the country has turned out the most Academy Award winners?"

"Washington State," he says.

"Washington State? USC is the school that has won all the Academy Awards."

He didn't even know USC had a good cinema school, and he's the guy who was going to put down the pluses and minuses. Washington State? Do they even have a motion picture theater in that little town?

The young man ended up going to another school. And I thought if he wanted to do that, fine. Say that. But don't give us 16 or 17 ideas like you're looking for the best cinema school and Washington State has it. You're talking to adults. What you want to do is play basketball. Admit it.

I think many basketball players become arrogant very young because they're taller than everybody else. Therefore, they're better than everyone else in their sport. And the money for them in pro basketball is phenomenal—much more than in football. But I don't think kids are forced to grow up in basketball, like they are in football.

We recruit cocky football players, too. We'll talk to a player who says he always wanted to go to USC or UCLA. Fine. A few weeks later, we'll check again.

"Well, now," he says. "Notre Dame's got a good chemical engineering school, and Colorado's got skiing, and Arizona State's got warm desert. It's hard to say."

"What are you going to base your decision on?" we have to ask.

"Oh, I don't know. I've still got to go to Idaho, Montana, several other places."

"Idaho? Are you going to play at Idaho?"

"No, I just want to take the trip up there."

And Idaho has to pay for it. You immature punk.

Boy, would I have liked to have that arrogant basketball player for one day in a football scrimmage. But what can his coach do to humble him in basketball? Give him the four worst reserves and play him against the varsity? All they can do is outscore him.

But we can take a cocky halfback, put him behind the third-string line and make him wish he had never been born. That is a comeuppance. When you think you're great, there is a way in football to prove that you're just another human being. In football, no matter how good you are, you can't dominate alone. The other players must help you dominate.

After a while, most players learn they have to depend on their teammates, and if they don't, they're in trouble. That's why football is the greatest team sport there is.

I've been in football a long time, but the biggest thrill in my life was the first time I saw my son Johnny play in high school. When he was growing up I almost never tossed a football around with him. Occasionally, we'd just shoot a few baskets.

As a high school junior he became a star split end playing at Bishop Amat, and Corky kept pestering me to come out and watch him. She said he was pretty good. But I've learned never to believe mothers where their sons are concerned. Assistant coach Craig Fertig saw him and said he was good, too, but I figured Craig might be saying that just to please me.

One night I went to see Bishop Amat play—and I was stunned. I knew immediately Johnny could play in college. The first time I saw him he made one of the greatest catches I've ever seen.

I found myself getting as excited on Friday nights rushing to Bishop Amat games as I did on Saturdays coaching USC. While we watched, Johnny set new Los Angeles area prep records for career, single season and touchdown catches, and then finished with a flourish by being named

Co-Player of the Year in Southern California. The other award-winner was Pat Haden, his quarterback and best friend.

They were both high school All-Americans and formed the greatest pass-and-catch combination in Southern California high school history. Haden passed for 82 touchdowns and completed 62 percent of the passes in his career. In his senior year alone he threw for 42 touchdowns and almost two miles of yardage.

Johnny caught 106 passes as a junior and 97 as a senior. Of those 203 receptions, 47 were for touchdowns. As seniors, the boys led Bishop Amat to the Southern California high school championship, after being runners-up as juniors.

Recruiters came running from all over America, doubly inspired because Johnny and Pat announced they would attend the same university since they were such close friends.

"If one of us had an itch," said Haden, "the other would scratch himself automatically, and both of us would feel better."

When they were a little younger, they often played touch football on our front lawn, and I would referee. I got to know Haden very well.

Before their senior season, a problem developed for Haden. His family planned to move to San Francisco, but he wanted to continue playing at Bishop Amat. So Johnny asked him to move in with us, and Pat accepted. Now I had the quarterback and the split end under my roof.

Every time I came home, said my friends, I was breaking the NCAA rule which limits the number of recruiting visits. People wanted to know about all the free meals these two fine prospects were getting.

Actually my boarders were recruited by dozens of universities, and there was no guarantee at all that they would come to USC. Johnny was afraid if he did that and became a starter, fans would yell he was first string only because I was the coach. Corky was worried that he would be singled out by the other players.

I seldom talked to the two boys about USC, because I wanted them to make up their own minds. I encouraged them to visit more schools than they actually did. But recruiters poured into our house. Many nights some other coach would be downstairs talking to Johnny and Pat and I would be upstairs reading, trying to pretend the recruiter wasn't there.

Fertig was assigned the job of trying to snag Haden and McKay for USC. Since they had known him for years, they had fun with him. What they did was practically drive him crazy. But this was nothing new. When Craig was a USC player, Pat and Johnny used to hang around our hot August practices eating ice cream. They made sure he noticed.

The recruiting lasted for months, with Johnny and Pat flying to Notre Dame, Nebraska and Stanford. But the list of others interested went on and on, including Alabama, Colorado, California, Princeton and a host of Big Ten schools.

Trying to be impartial—which was difficult—I told myself I would have been happy to see Johnny play for Bob Devaney at Nebraska or Ara Parseghian at Notre Dame or Jim Owens at Washington. Or, of course, Bear Bryant.

Everywhere I went people asked me where my son was going to play college football. It reminded me of the time when I had gone to Alabama to play in a golf tournament with Bryant. A nagging sports question then was whether or not Joe Namath was going to remain in pro football. Fans kept interrupting Bear on the golf course to ask him. At the same time there was a controversy about O. J. Simpson's holdout with Buffalo before his first pro year, and people kept bugging me about that.

So Bear and I had some cards printed that said, "Damned if I know," and just passed them out.

During the recruiting-Johnny turmoil, Bryant phoned our home and Corky answered. "Paul," she said, "concerning my son and where he's going to college, would you please send me 200 of those cards?"

I didn't use the cards, but I did develop a standard line to lob back at the questioners. When they asked if Johnny was coming to USC, I said:

"Oh, I think the Trojans have a heck of a chance. I'm very close to his mother."

One night I was out drinking with the then California coach, Ray Willsey, who had actively recruited Johnny and Pat. I invited Ray over to the house for a nightcap. All of a sudden it was 3 A.M. and we discovered we were very tired. I insisted Willsey spend the night with us, rather than drive back to his hotel. He agreed.

Just before he tucked himself in bed, I went down to see him. "Ray," I said, pointing to Johnny's room, "I hope you know you're breaking an NCAA recruiting rule by staying overnight with an athlete."

While the other recruiters visited, Fertig kept tracking the boys for USC. One day I decided to shake him up a little at one of our staff meetings.

"Craig," I said, puffing thoughtfully on my cigar, "I think we should just offer a scholarship to Haden and ignore my son. I don't think Johnny can play for USC."

Fertig was stunned. His face got red. "But, coach," he stammered. "Johnny is damn good. He can play for us."

There was silence in the room.

"How can I coach this kid," I asked, "when I can't even get him to take out the garbage?"

Although I rarely spoke to Johnny and Pat about USC, they wouldn't leave me alone. They needled me about the other schools they visited and pictures painted by other recruiters. They even told me they were very interested in Stanford, which is not one of my favorite schools.

"If it was between Stanford and Red China," I said, "I would tell you, 'Good luck in Peking.' "

On another occasion the two boys really shook me up by signing a letter of intent to go to Nebraska. Since Nebraska isn't in our league, they still could have come to USC, but they admitted they liked Nebraska.

That night I bumped into Johnny alone in the living room. "Son," I winced, "you can't be doing this to me. I need that quarterback."

While Pat and Johnny pondered, I listened to various opinions on the sensibility of having my own son play for me. There have been many father-son combinations in sports, some which worked out, some which didn't. One coach that encouraged me was Jack Curtice, who had recently concluded his career at the University of California at Santa Barbara. At Santa Barbara, Jack had coached his son Jimmy, who was the starting quarterback for two years. I knew Jimmy, knew he had played very well for his dad and was liked by the other players. I assumed if he could do it, Johnny could, too. So I wasn't apprehensive about that.

Besides, I always figured that if Johnny made a mistake at an SC practice it wouldn't be the first time he had caught hell from his father.

Suddenly one day—when they still had seven more recruiting trips planned—Pat and Johnny announced they were tired of traveling, tired of recruiting and tired of thinking. They canceled their trips and signed with USC to a chorus of several sighs of relief.

Now I grinned when everyone threw me a new question. Why did Johnny decide on USC?

"I paid his bills for a long time," I said. "After 18 years he owed me something."

COACHING IS TEACHING

"It's just like a classroom"

ONLY A COACH can have real empathy for another coach, and I understood exactly how Missouri's Dan Devine felt when his team had a horrible breakdown in the middle of the 1961 Orange Bowl. Missouri was playing Navy and had put together a painfully slow march which finally reached the Navy one-yard line. There, the quarterback called for a pitchout, and favored Missouri was about two seconds from a touchdown. So they thought.

Unfortunately, Missouri's right end missed his block on a Navy defender named Greg Mather. Mather lined up in one of the gaps of the offensive line, burst unchallenged into Missouri's backfield, picked that lateral right out of the air and ran 98 astonishing yards to score.

On the sideline I imagine Devine was contemplating suicide. Next to him was the assistant coach in charge of the man who had missed the block on Mather. "You idiot!" the assistant screamed at his player.

Devine glared at his coach. "Who," he said, "was the idiot who taught the idiot how to block?"

I've always thought Devine's remark summed up football coaching very succinctly. There is nothing mysterious about developing a good team, because coaching is nothing more than teaching. Head coaches coach assistants, and then assistants impart the techniques to the players. The better job they do, the better job the player will do.

Over the years I've grown very mad at assistant coaches whenever their segment of the team continued to make mistakes. I always tell them not to blame it on the kids.

"You are a damn poor teacher," I'll snap. "This is not that difficult a game if *you* teach the players properly."

Sometimes young assistant coaches aren't good teachers; they're great strategists. They've got ten million plays that will win the game, with no thought about teaching the people that have to play that game.

I believe strategy will win some games, but not very many. I don't believe I'm going to earn my living by deceiving anybody. I'm going to earn it by recruiting good players and then working hard teaching them to block and tackle, so that whether I deceive my opponent or not, I'll move the ball and stop him from moving it. We don't beat people with surprises, but with execution.

There are occasional exceptions. The best strategic job we ever pulled off was against Oklahoma in 1964. The Sooners were ranked second in the nation, had the home field advantage and were favored by a touchdown. We won, 40 to 14.

We had prepared for that game since spring. We were a good team, but not good enough to win by 26 points. However, we got in a formation nobody had yet used as far as we knew. Today it's one of our standard formations. We took the split end and put him way out to one side, and then put the flanker, Rod Sherman, about half-way out on the same side. We opened the season the previous week and beat Colorado without using this formation.

Many teams in those days used basically an eight-man defensive front, with six linemen and two linebackers or five and three, with only three men deep. We decided that if Oklahoma did that against this formation we would win, because we'd have a big advantage. Most coaches change their offenses in a game quicker than they change their defenses—they don't like to change their defenses—and we can take advantage of that stubbornness.

The way Oklahoma lined up on defense there was no way to cover Sherman, and most of the time Rod was wide open. He caught seven passes. When they moved a player out to cover him, we just audibilized to tailback Mike Garrett and ran him off tackle for good yardage.

We also rolled out our quarterback, Craig Fertig, another ploy we hadn't used the week before. And Craig completed 16 of 28 passes for 212 yards, with no interceptions—despite throwing in a 40-mile-an-hour wind.

"If my mother were passing left-handed," said Craig later, "she could have completed them today."

Oklahoma was so confused that Fertig, who was never a very good runner, scored twice by simply faking to Garrett and keeping the ball. This is still a good play for us, and often we'll fool our own team with it. We'll call the quarterback over when we're down on the goal line and tell him to call "26 cut," which is a handoff to the tailback, but to fake and keep the ball. When he does that, everybody, including the tailback, thinks the tailback is going to get the ball. There have been times we've used that play, and everybody in the stadium has hit the tailback, only to look up and see the quarterback holding the ball in the end zone.

That Oklahoma game, however, was a rare example. We normally will fool a team in every game on at least one play, but we won't fool them all day. If our success depends on deception, and the other team isn't deceived, we can't block them.

Reverses, which we run ten or twenty times a season, are examples of plays built on deception. They're always a gamble that the opponent will react a certain way. If he does, the reverse looks like the world's greatest play. If it doesn't work, we can lose about 15 yards.

The same is true of gambling on defense. If we have a weak defensive team, playing a strong offensive team, we might stunt and shoot linebackers on every down. If we guess right we'll look fairly decent. But over the long haul it will get us killed. When you jump around on defense and get caught, there is a gaping hole.

Coaches who have had the most success at any level —college, pro or high school—believe as I do in teaching fundamentals properly. I think the main reason many others fail is because they're continually looking for offensive gimmicks that will make them winners.

You can't draw a play on a blackboard and pronounce, "If we do this and this and this, the play will work." Yes it will work if the protection doesn't break down, if the quarterback throws accurately, and if the receiver catches the ball. You better make sure your players know how to block, throw and catch.

When coaches are working on the field, it's their job to make the players listen, just like a professor in a classroom. We don't want any whispering. The coach doesn't talk to one student in his class; he talks to everybody. You'd like to be very calm on the practice field all the time, but that nonsense doesn't work. If you talk to players I coached at Oregon, they'll tell you I was a mean son of a gun at practice, and I was. But they heard me.

You can hear me at a USC practice, too, although I think I've quieted down the last few years. Sometimes I regret my blowups, and I remember one which proved embarrassing.

We were having a nervous, frantic week before a Notre Dame game several years ago, when one of our student managers noticed a man standing in the third-story window of the classroom building that overlooked our old practice field. We didn't want anyone to watch us, so the manager was sent up to the room to ask the man to leave. He was a big, burly guy, and he refused. He kept watching practice.

The manager came back and reported to assistant coach Dave Levy. I overheard the discussion and stalked over. "What's the matter?" I demanded.

"Coach," said Levy, "there's a man who appears to be spying up there in the window, and he won't leave."

"I'll get him to leave," I said.

My Irish temper got hotter and hotter as I approached the fence next to the building. Looking up at the window, I shouted:

"You goddamn spy, get out of that window! And I mean right now!"

The man fled.

The next day my staff and I were sitting around a table, discussing Notre Dame, and athletic director Jess Hill entered the room.

"John," he said, a little perturbed, "did any of your assistant coaches swear at the dean of the religion department yesterday?"

"Oh, no, Jessie," I said. "You know how it is out there. The coaches get a little riled up sometimes. Someone must have yelled at one of the players, and that poor man misunderstood."

*　　*　　*

Football is an unusual game because of its violence. Basically, most people do not enjoy knocking other people down. You must have confidence to play the game, and some people never get it—even though they have the ability. To other players, physical confidence comes late, and they don't like contact as much as some do. This doesn't mean they don't have any guts.

I hate that word, anyway. I never allow any of our coaches to use it. Courage is an overused word, too. We're not trying to make Marines, we're trying to make football players. It's the responsibility of the coach to give the player confidence by teaching him the right techniques.

There are so many little techniques which are important that the average fan never sees from the stands. For example, how far apart do your backs stand? What spot should they take off from? Which direction should they go? What is the right stance? What is the timing of the pitchout from the quarterback to the ballcarrier?

A few years ago, we helped a buddy of mine, Henry Stram, coach of the Kansas City Chiefs, put in the I-formation. Two weeks later Henry phoned and complained that he couldn't get the pitch to the tailback to work. The ball kept hitting the fullback, who was the leading blocker. It turned out that Henry didn't have his backs lined up in exactly the right place. That's how refined the game is. A man can be a great athlete, but if he doesn't learn the right techniques, he won't fulfill his potential.

Some of the techniques are very difficult to learn. Blocking is the toughest. It's the most unnatural movement, because it's the only part of the game you play without using your hands. A boy grows up using his hands for everything, and now we tell him he can't use them. Because experience is so important in offensive linemen, you seldom see a sophomore start, let alone a freshman.

Pass blocking is the hardest technique of all to master, because the lineman has to learn to keep his feet moving when he makes contact. The natural tendency when you block someone is to stop your feet.

Can blocking be made more natural? Sure. By holding.

Everything else has to be taught, too. Great runners aren't born; they're made, and I'll discuss that in detail later. Passers are not born, either. Certainly, some players have more ability to start with, but somebody has to refine that talent. I think I can do that.

You hear so many coaches moaning, "Oh, we don't have a passer, so we can't pass."

I don't buy that complaint. How much do they work on passing? Troy Winslow was our first-string quarterback in 1965 and 1966. Some of his passes floated so slowly I could have autographed them in the air. But we worked and worked and worked with him. One year he completed 61 percent of his attempts and the next year 59 percent. Both seasons he threw for over a thousand yards.

If a passer wants to be good, he has to learn to release the ball correctly. Take drop-back passing. Here come the linemen, all standing 6-4 and 6-5, charging in with both hands in the air. You've got to throw the ball over their hands to find the seams in the defense. That's some challenge.

To be able to do that, the passer must be taught to release the ball high, particularly if he's short. Let's say you're 5-11—and we won a national championship with Steve Sogge who was a 5-10 quarterback on his tiptoes—and you drop back to pass. When you release the ball, you must throw it from straight over your head. Now how tall are you? You're 6-2 or 6-3, because the ball is coming off the tips of your fingers from way over your head.

Take another quarterback who actually is 6-2 in height, and let's say he doesn't pass the correct way. Assume he throws it three-quarters or shoulder high. Who's the taller passer? The man who's 5-11 and throws from over his head.

We had a quarterback once who stood 6-4. He started out with a big advantage and yet he threw sidearm. Just wouldn't change. That's like cutting off your head. It made him about 5-7, and he never did play much for us.

Of course, there are other ways of throwing, besides the drop back. When a quarterback rolls out, for example, he doesn't pass the same way. But again there are proper techniques. A right-handed quarterback must face upfield, or get his shoulders square with the line of scrimmage before passing. If he rolls left, we want him to throw somewhat sidearm for maximum accuracy.

We have four ways of passing at USC: the drop back, the rollout, a half rollout and the play action pass, or pass off a run fake. We never use all four in the same season. You must build your offense around what your quarterback does best. We did a lot of things with Mike Rae in 1972 that we never attempted with Sogge in 1967, but in both years we won the national championship. Mike was several inches taller and could throw better, so we threw much more often and threw longer.

Because we adjust our offense to fit our quarterback, I always say his role is highly overrated. I don't believe the team with the best quarterback will necessarily have the best offense, and I know you can have a great team without a great quarterback. He doesn't have to have exceptional physical attributes.

What he must have are intelligence and the ability to lead. You can't be stupid and play quarterback, because you put too much of a burden on the rest of the team. As for leadership, a good quarterback stands out when he walks into the huddle. Everyone know he's there. Others are just number callers. They say, "28 blast on two . . . break," with all the enthusiasm of a guy edging out of bed on a cold winter morning.

Quarterbacks are rare people. They all have big egos. Without this confidence they can't win. But all of them, particularly the top passers, think they can throw the ball into a crowd. Excellent passers often force the ball where it shouldn't go—and the result is usually an interception.

This is one reason we like rollout passing. If the receivers are covered, the quarterback can still run and pick up a few yards, instead of taking a loss or throwing into a mob.

In practice we completely alternate our quarterbacks. We give each one the best players to see what he can do with them. We challenge them. We don't want to say, "Pete, you're a pretty good quarterback," and have Pete thinking, "I'd be a hell of a lot better if I had the first-string line and backfield."

So we give them to him. Many coaches always have the second-string quarterback working with the second-string line and backs. How can they determine how good he is? I've seen the pros stick a rookie quarterback in the fourth quarter of an exhibition game with seven young linemen and decide that he didn't look very good. Well, the poor guy couldn't get out of the way of the avalanche.

As the season progresses and our number-one quarterback is firmly established, we still alternate the top two or three. Running backs come in all shapes, sizes and speeds, and we want our quarterbacks used to working with all of them. You never know which lineup you'll be forced to play in a game. At Washington in 1971 we had so many people injured that we had to use our third-string fullback and tailback in the last four minutes. But they teamed up with our number-one quarterback, Jimmy

Jones, to drive into field-goal range and we won by a point on a kick.

I've often thought the ideal situation—to further prepare your quarterback—would be never to start him. Let him stand on the sideline with the coach without any ball handling or passing responsibilities and calmly assess what the defense is doing, while the second-string quarterback runs the attack.

But, of course, the quarterback would go crazy because he wasn't starting, his mom and dad would get mad, the newspaper people would howl, and if he was successful, everybody would complain that the dumb-ass coach had him on the second team.

What about working with pass receivers? They can't wait to run downfield and catch the ball. So assume you're a split end and the other team puts a linebacker in front of you. What are you going to do now, run around him? No, that's a mistake. If you try and run around him, he figures to push you with his hands anyway, and then you're going sideways. Don't let him get the first shot. He'll drop back and wait to hit you again, and you're still not past him. Meanwhile, the poor quarterback is back there running for his life, wondering where the hell you are.

We tell our ends, you pop the linebacker first and you'll go where you want to go. Use your power on him, instead of the other way around. He won't expect that.

Once they're in the open field, we want our receivers to read the defense on the run and adjust. They're given a lot of leeway on changing their cut, depending on how the defense is playing them. If the receiver breaks into an area where he'll be covered, the ball will be intercepted. We call this adjusting "ad-libbing."

Ends have to learn the proper way to catch the ball, too. My son Johnny learned very early a technique I've always believed in. When you catch the ball, catch it with your hands. Don't cradle it in your arms. Clutch it like you'd pick up a cantaloupe. Johnny has one advantage I didn't have—big hands. But I always caught the ball easily, because I grabbed it that way.

The end must also learn to concentrate on the ball. You have to catch it before you can go anywhere. So look it right into your hands.

Catching is like any other skill. The more a person works at it, the better he'll get. So many players who could be very good don't try. When fall practice starts, I can always spot the ones who have hardly caught a ball all summer. The last day before drills, they're thinking, "Practice starts tomorrow, so I'll start working out tomorrow." Heck, your sister can throw to you if you can't find anyone else. Raymond Berry, one of pro football's greatest ends, caught passes from his wife in the off-season.

It's not easy to teach all these techniques to many trackmen who decide to become receivers. They're so infatuated with their own speed that they think it makes up for everything else. But who isn't fast in football today? We want a player who can catch.

Many games are won or lost by the specialty teams. Let's briefly consider some of the techniques we teach the players on our punting and punt-receiving teams.

If the punter is deep in our own territory, say inside the ten, and he gets any kind of bad pass from center, we instruct him to run out of the end zone and take a safety. We don't want his kick blocked for a possible touchdown, and we don't want him to run and get tackled on the two or three. That's giving up a touchdown, too.

If the punt is made and the other team signals for a fair catch, we order our players to run by the receiver. If he drops the ball, they'll have a better chance of recovering it. If the receiver elects not to catch the ball, our players can touch it down themselves and keep it from rolling into the end zone. Nothing frustrates me more than to talk about this rule and then see a couple of our players stop five yards away and stare at the guy signaling for a fair catch.

When our opponents are punting to us, we teach our safety to let the ball go if it's still in the air at our ten. One of our worst plays on a punt was pulled off in 1967 by All-American Mike Battle. Mike signaled for a fair catch on our one, which was bad enough. But he also dropped the ball. Michigan State recovered it and scored a touchdown.

If two men are deep to catch a punt, we don't want the man in front to catch the ball if he's anywhere near his teammate, because we then lose a blocker.

Often we use the up man to give directions to the deep man. He yells, "Go," if he thinks the deep man should catch and run. Of course, you can make an enemy on the basis of this decision if you're the up man and you see nine or ten people racing down to cover the punt, and still turn around and yell, "Go!"

Speed, quickness and agility can be improved through proper instruction and hard work. Years ago, coaches gave up on slow linemen, but today we feel we can increase foot speed. Most linemen we've had became quicker. We make them jump rope, play handball and play paddle ball. We also have several agility drills.

Quickness is more important than speed for linemen, because they play in a very small area. They spend most of the game in what we call the box, seven or eight yards wide and seven or eight yards deep. The defensive lineman that doesn't have quick feet won't be able to rush the passer. If he runs the 100 in 9.9 and doesn't have quick feet, we'll knock him on his back.

Jumping rope is good for linemen, because it helps develop their coordination. Handball also is good because it doesn't allow them to favor either side of their body. People naturally grow up either left- or right-handed and favor that side. But in football the ability to use both sides of your body is important.

I'm not a great advocate of weight lifting, but I feel that when a youngster gets stronger he gains confidence. So we have a weight-lifting program in the off-season. But all players lift according to their position. We don't want our quarterbacks to have overdeveloped muscles.

Traditionally, my teams have been strong in the fourth quarter, and the amount of running we do is one of the major reasons why. I think we run as much as any team in football and more than many, but we probably do it in a different way. We throw a tremendous number of passes in an average practice session. So the wide receivers and the tight end and the backs and the quarterback are running all the time in a passing drill.

Many times after a drill like that we'll take the offensive linemen and sprint them for five minutes. Then we'll go to another drill, say on pass protection, and then sprint the linemen again.

Our linemen never stand around for an hour and a half and then go shower. At the end of practice, no matter what day it is, we'll end up sprinting again. We don't always sprint our backs and ends, however, because they've already been running pass patterns and other plays all afternoon. When our backs carry the ball on a running play, we order them to run full speed about 20 yards downfield—every time.

If a player gets hurt, it only takes him a week or two to lose his great conditioning. Some people don't understand this, because football players don't run as much in a game as, say, basketball players. But that's not the point.

Imagine running ten yards and lifting 210 pounds. And then running ten yards and lifting 210 again. Or let the 210 pounds hit you every time. You better be in shape. And if you can't run, you won't be. You can lift weights forever and run out and collapse on the first play.

And the game itself has become much more wide open, so that today a player's wind is tested to the utmost. On a normal running play, the flanker sprints 20 or 30 yards.

We don't scrimmage during the season, but confine our hard hitting to spring and early fall practices. To run plays during the regular season when we're not scrimmaging, we'll organize a defense made up of reserves and put all the players except the secondary in foam-rubber aprons that cover their bodies. The aprons look like the protectors baseball catchers wear, but they run all the way down the legs. They keep the defenders from getting seriously injured and keep the offensive line from hitting hard muscle when they block.

Once the defenders are protected by aprons, we can tell our players to go full speed. We want the offensive linemen to get off their blocks as fast as they can and hit as hard as they can. Since the defensive linemen have their hands free, they can force our running backs to adjust when they dart into the line. We announce we're going to run the off-tackle play, and the defense can do what it wants. If they want to slant out, so the backs have to cut back inside, that's fine, because now our ballcarriers are running just like they'll have to on Saturday.

I've watched other teams practice with their defense lined up holding dummies, which are big heavy bags, and I've wondered what dummies they'll play in a game. We want our backs to learn to run to daylight, and if the defensive linemen are holding dummies, all you do is hit them and they can't react. Their advantage is gone, because they can't use their hands.

At the other end of the field, we don't put our regular defense in aprons. We want them to practice recognizing plays and reacting to the ball at full speed. They practice against reserves, too, and they bump the runners and receivers, but they usually don't tackle.

We never want our top running backs tackled in these practices, either. The reserve defensive players, including the secondary, just bump them with a shoulder. I don't want to have a back tackled and injured on some Tuesday, trying to find out if he can run. I know he can run —that's why he's on the team.

Our quarterbacks are also protected in practice, and sometimes we extend this protection to full-scale scrimmages. In the spring of 1973, when we had only one top quarterback, Pat Haden, we rarely let him get tackled.

The reason was simple. We alternate the offensive lines as we scrimmage. Let's say we've inserted a sophomore lineman, Joe Doakes, at right guard to see how good he is. Haden drops back to pass, Doakes blocks the wrong man, and here comes a first-string linebacker, like All-American Richard Wood, who blind-sides Haden and breaks his leg.

No one even blocked Wood. And our season is ruined because we have just taught a third-string guard not to block the wrong man. So we make it quite clear to the defense: you will not tackle our quarterback. We're trying to teach the linemen how to block and who to block, and there's no sense in the quarterback taking the brunt of all this learning.

I've never lost a quarterback in practice, except Troy Winslow in 1966 in a freak accident. He was just running around end and turned his knee. Nobody even touched him.

Any coach who doesn't protect a quarterback is not only shortsighted, he's crazy. At UCLA, in the spring of

1973, Mark Harmon, who was a very good wishbone quarterback, broke his collarbone on one of the last plays of a scrimmage. Here they had been scrimmaging for an hour, and their first-string quarterback was running the ball again. How was he going to get any better at running? He had nothing to prove.

Go ahead and show the world how tough your quarterback is, and you may blow your season. If the injury had occurred in the fall, Harmon probably would have missed the season. He did come back to play, but his injury was still inexcusable.

There's nothing revolutionary in our system of coaching. We just spend a tremendous amount of time on teamwork. Some people have the quarterbacks over here, halfbacks over there, guards in the middle, tackles in another spot, and they come together as a team about 20 minutes a day. In the fall we'll spend almost an hour, maybe even the whole practice, trying to get our players to understand that football is a team game.

When we add a new play we explain to every man the reason for it, the theory behind it, and what we expect of each player. We want all 11 players to know as much about the offense as the quarterback; so we explain it to all of them. Then, when we play a game, they'll understand what we're trying to do.

Theory is important to us. Some coaches believe you tell your tackle to block the opposing tackle and forget about everything else. But if something goes wrong, he'll just figure the play is no good because he doesn't understand the theory behind it. But, for example, we'll gather our offense and say something like this:

"Gentlemen, we're trying to fake a sprint-out pass. We expect the defensive end to react and come after the quarterback. But instead, quarterback, you hand the ball off to the tailback. We'll call this play '26 cut.' If you guards do this and you tackles do that, and you, center, do this, the play will work.

"If it doesn't work, if the end doesn't react that way, then they can't stop our sprint-out pass. But we must have this play to make sure they're not bringing that end across to stop our sprint-out pass. You understand, guard? You understand, tackle?"

This is why we like an experienced offensive line. They know all the plays. If a play doesn't work, they know what to do about it. They figure, "We're going to be able to block this play for good yardage somehow. They can't stop us all afternoon."

An inexperienced line says, "Oh, shit, they stopped the play, and we didn't make a yard. What are we going to do?" What they're going to do is go in a state of panic for about 20 minutes. By that time the game's over.

We want our defensive players to know as much about our defense as possible, too. USC's defense has a basic weakness, and all the players know what it is. We're willing to give up something to stop teams somewhere else. If a team exploits our weakness, we know how to conpensate for it. When it happens, our kids don't panic, because we've told them what to do, and they understand why.

You just can't beat experience, because mental mistakes beat you more than physical mistakes—in any sport.

I get furious at people who make mental mistakes. I don't like anybody out on that practice field who isn't concentrating. If I'm good enough to say we'll practice only an hour and a half, while other schools are practicing two or three hours, I don't see why the players can't concentrate.

Sound teaching needs a motivating force, and I think

it's accomplished, at least somewhat, by instilling fear in the players—fear of being a failure, fear of letting their teammates down, fear of abuse if they don't do the job well. We work so hard to be successful, all of us, that some player who blows an assignment is letting us down. He's trying to get us beat, because he doesn't have enough pride to remember his assignment.

We explain to the players that physically we may ask them to do something they can't. If you're a 220-pound guard and we ask you to block a 280-pound tackle, maybe you can't. But you can try. But if you don't attempt it; if you block the wrong person, or run the wrong pass pattern, or run to the wrong hole as a back, then what you're telling me is that you're not interested in what we're doing. Therefore, you're not my kind of player. I don't know why you would play the game. There are easier ways to go through college.

Before our Notre Dame game in 1964, I exploded at Craig Fertig, our quarterback. I yelled I'd throw him off the team if he didn't stop throwing so badly. Now, he was the only quarterback I had, and he knew it.

"But, Craig," I snapped, "you're not going to come out here and be casual throwing the ball because you're the only guy I've got playing the position. If you are, you won't play for us. If you don't want to do the job, I'll center the ball to the goddamn tailback and run around end 55 times. Or maybe I'll kick on first down and play defense. But the only thing you're entitled to is doing your job right."

And he did his job: He threw the touchdown pass that upset the Irish and knocked them out of a national championship.

Sometimes I'm not really mad, but I'll act like I am. I might yell and throw a clipboard around to shake up the team. I believe there's a little bit of actor in the makeup of all coaches, and occasionally we have to be theatrical. We have to study not only the individual players, but the mood of the entire team. Are they coming off a big victory, and do they think they're the hottest cats in town? They haven't beaten everyone yet, and they better learn they're not the best team in the world. So I make a conscious effort to prod them.

I love players who enjoy practicing, the ones you don't have to beg to do anything. That's why I liked tailback Anthony Davis right away. From the first time he carried the ball in practice, he ran all out. And I figured a player with his kind of ability and desire just had to be good.

I can't stand players who think practice is a great big chore. The one you don't want is the one who's thinking, "Hope we can get done soon so I can go see my girl, or go to a beer bust."

But we can't get a young man to put out mentally and physically unless he wants to. We could force him to run wind sprints forever as punishment, but that wouldn't get him ready to play football. So we look for older players with great talent who lead by being the hardest workers on the team, and we single them out as examples.

We hope that if the younger players see a guy like Davis or 1973 All-American flanker Lynn Swann or tackle Ron Yary, an All-American in 1967, people who never stop trying, just never make a mental error, they'll realize how important it is. You can't practice relaxed. We preach all the time that football is a game of mistakes. And if a player doesn't concentrate in practice, his mind will wander in games.

The UCLA game we lost in 1965, the one that knocked us out of the Rose Bowl, was lost on one man's mental error. Although the score didn't indicate it, we were beating them badly, because they couldn't move the ball. But we kept fumbling and couldn't pull away. Still, we were going to win. Suddenly, our 16–6 lead dwindled to 16–14 as Gary Beban hit us with a 34-yard touchdown pass and two-point conversion.

Next, UCLA recovered an onside kick and had the ball on their 48 with just under three minutes left. I called the secondary over before sending them on the field.

"Listen," I said, "I don't give a damn what Beban does, you three guys play deep. If he rolls out, let him run. He's gotta throw the ball deep to beat us. You do not rotate the way he rolls. If he rolls out, ignore him and stay deep."

If UCLA had been near our goal line, the defensive backs obviously would have been told to rotate to the side where Beban was rolling, but not at midfield.

On the very first play, Beban rolls to the right, and our safetyman ignores me, leaves the middle of the field and swings to the side where Beban is. Our halfback on that side, meanwhile, has stayed outside where he's supposed to be. Their split end, Kurt Altenberg, cuts to the middle—and there's no Trojan there.

At the last instant, our safetyman realizes what he's done, runs back, dives and just misses Beban's pass to Altenberg. Bam. Fifty-two yards. Touchdown. And we're out of the Rose Bowl. That kid of ours is going to see that ball forever.

Mentally, he knocked us out of the Rose Bowl, let everybody down, because he couldn't remember one thing. Physically, he was good enough to play. But he wouldn't think. We called time out to tell him to stay in the middle, but he wouldn't believe us. He wouldn't stay there. That's a mental mistake. You get many of them, and you're about 7 and 3 or 6 and 4, no matter how much talent you have.

Often, after a winning game, I will go into the dressing room far from elated. I know there are certain things that happened that might have caused us to lose to a better opponent. Winning may be the important thing, but as I'm walking off the field, I know I've got only three or four days of next week to get us straightened out. The players don't pay any attention to that. They're bobbing along to the dressing room, congratulating each other, and then they're going out to celebrate.

The player I'm going to get the maddest at is the one who I believe isn't doing what he's capable of. I hate to yell at young players or reserves who aren't going to play much anyway, but I'm really going to get on some ace who's loafing. All players can't perform equally, but they can all give the same effort.

I try to get my assistants to check their personnel after every practice. If they've been hard on a kid, I don't want them to leave without talking to him. My rule is: If you've given a player hell, tell him you still love him. Tell him you're just trying to improve him. Sometimes an assistant coach may not want to do this—and I remember how hard it was for me—but then I have to force him.

Of course, if we coaches get mad every time we see a mistake, we're going to be mad all the time. Mistakes are going to happen in a game, despite all our planning and hard work. Another advantage of having experienced players is that they know they've made mistakes before and survived. They can shrug them off. A young player is worried about being benched, and he's so busy thinking of his last mistake, he makes another. He should be concentrating on what he's going to do next.

As you get more experience in life—and I've tried to explain this to my children—you're able to accept the fact that you will make mistakes. But we're going to rebound from them. We're not going to play a perfect game—either in the stadium or in the world. Nobody ever has.

I've heard the theory that USC is not sharp on offensive fundamentals because occasionally we have several penalties or several fumbles. But we do so many things, change the plays so often, shift, go in motion, that we're putting more of a mental and physical burden on the players. Therefore, we have a higher margin of error. The way not to fumble or make any mistakes is to get in a tight T and run three straight quarterback sneaks.

We have several different ways to block. For example, we can block our blast play with the tailback off tackle 14 different ways. As the game proceeds, we determine how we'll block it for the most success.

If the quarterback changes the play at the line, the blocking assignments are also changed, and our players have to be bright enough to understand the changes immediately.

A multitude of blocking assignments and techniques can confuse a lineman, and he may pull the wrong way, leaving a hole for a defender to shoot through and smack the runner just as he gets the ball. The result may be a fumble. Of course, I'm going to try to minimize those mistakes, but in the final analysis, I'm not interested in the number of fumbles or penalties we have. I'm interested in who won the game.

And we win. No one puts an asterisk next to our score which says, yes, USC won, but they fumbled four times.

Of course, if you fumble and lose, then you're fumbling too much. Fumbling was probably the greatest contributor to our disappointing 1971 season when we lost four games. We fumbled the ball so many times inside our opponents' 20-yard lines it seemed like we were jinxed. Certain backs will consistently fumble, and if you've made a mistake and recruited them, you're stuck.

We had no choice that year but to play the fumblers. There wasn't anyone else.

Fumbling will not only cost you games, it will contribute to poor morale, because the other players, particularly the line, will say, "Hey, no matter how hard we hit, those other guys are always screwing up."

Just as I demand that my players concentrate, I place the same demands on myself at practice. I'm in my twenty-fifth year of coaching and I've never missed a day of practice. I don't care what happens. If I'm dead, I'm going to practice.

Sometimes I may get a little flippant out there, chat with a sportswriter, hum a tune, comment on the weather, or even break up the players with a joke, but I'm concentrating just the same. No player at USC can say I don't know what he's doing.

I learned the importance of concentration early. That's the way my high school coach, Mickey McClung, acted at practice. Jim Aiken was the same way at Oregon. Sometimes now I'll ignore friends on the field and they'll think I'm mad at them. But I'm not mad. Just involved.

All head coaches who really enjoy coaching miss working closely with the players, like they did as assistants. But if I do too much of it now, I'll step on the toes of the coach in charge and reduce his effectiveness and morale. Pretty soon the players will lose faith in him.

But if the assistant can't get something across, that's when the head coach has to cut in and explain what has to be done. Some head coaches like to climb up in a big tower and from on high comes this divine-sounding voice out of a megaphone, "No-o-o-w, defense, you will . . . ," and everybody on the field stops to hear this announcement.

I think I've still got some assistant coach in me, because I would rather go right to the assistant I want to correct and tell him, "You know, Wayne, if we're gonna continue to play defense against the wishbone like this, well, hell, let's give up the game."

But if I yell across the field, I'm just embarrassing him. So I use an electric golf cart and ride from one spot to the other.

I want the players to know I'm looking. If a player comes into my office to complain he's not getting a fair chance, I don't want to send him to his assistant coach. He'd have a perfect right to leave my office thinking, "Coach doesn't pay any attention to me at all. He didn't even know I was out there."

One of the reasons Dave Levy has been such a valuable assistant to me since I became head coach is that he can see a lot of people at once, too. When I can't be at one area, I tell Dave to watch it and tell me after practice who did well and who did poorly.

If we go across the street from USC to the Coliseum to scrimmage, I'll have a camera looking at the players, and then I'm usually pretty relaxed. But I know there's another John McKay watching the players—the camera.

The camera is a marvelous invention. Let's say I've got an offensive guard who comes into my office after a scrimmage to discuss why he's not playing more. Like everyone else, he thinks he's better than he is.

"Well, Charlie," I'll say, "let's go in and turn that movie on and make sure we know what you're doing. You may be a lot better than we think."

A lot of players will suddenly realize that they're trapped and say, "I'd prefer not to see that," but some will go right ahead and watch the film.

Now about halfway through, Charlie mumbles, "Coach, I guess I didn't do very well, did I? I guess I wasn't feeling too good that day."

"Well, Charlie," I'll answer, "you want another day? You want to tell us when you have a day that you feel good? In 20 minutes you blocked nobody. You are watching yourself block nobody for 20 minutes."

So now this player is stuck, and he'll always agree with me, and insist that he'll work harder. He's happy just to get out of the room.

But human nature being what it is, you can bet that he'll probably go and tell his buddies or his parents, "I went in to see the old coach and I showed him."

This is why when we review the films of our games, we bring in the whole team. The backs look at their movie, the defensive players look at theirs, and so forth. Now the player can't get away with lying to his friends on the team. He'll have to go somewhere else for sympathy.

Usually, mom and dad will back him up. Somehow they'll find Charlie's old high school coach who will say that he watched him against Notre Dame and Charlie knocked everybody down. That's ridiculous, but it's what people are like. They don't want to admit their failings.

Sometimes I get a lot of flak from parents. They call me and write angry letters because their boy isn't playing. But I don't think criticism from parents is one of the worst aspects of coaching, because I pay absolutely no attention to them. They should be interested in their son, but they should also understand that there's no way I won't play the best player.

I've never talked to a coach, drunk, sober, in a tree or on a stepladder, who didn't say he was playing the best players he had. Now, if the coach has bad judgment on who they are, then his record will show it, and he'll get fired. But we know who the best players are, because we watch them practice for a long time.

I'm not interested in who's black and who's white; I'm

interested in people who can play football. A sociologist discussed this with me a year or two ago, and he said I was crazy. He claimed I had to be black-oriented or white-oriented, that I couldn't be totally color-blind as a coach. I guess he figured nobody could be. But I don't believe him.

I look for talent and enthusiasm in a football player—and that's all. I don't believe that a good athlete wants to be played because he's black or white or Jewish or Catholic or any criterion you might use. If he does, he's a damn poor risk, and I won't play him.

I believe that people who can't make it are looking for an excuse. The old business cliché, "I'm not getting ahead because the boss doesn't like me," applies to sports, too. There have been players I thought the world of as people. But that didn't make any difference when I decided if they could play or not.

My only other consideration is year in school. If it's close between two kids, I'll always play the senior, if for no other reason than he's performing his last time. I don't con the team. I tell them, "If you want to beat out a senior, don't make it close."

When my son Johnny was a sophomore, some of my coaches argued that he should start at split end over our senior, Edesel Garrison. I disagreed, but not just because Edesel was a senior. Johnny was better at catching medium-range balls, and I knew he could go deep better than people thought, but Garrison was one of the fastest receivers in football. He'd run 9.5 in the 100 and 45.4 in the 440 and made some fantastic plays for us as a junior. He deserved to be first string.

If he started for us, opposing defenses would be at a disadvantage. When he lined up at split end, they had to think, "We better play back, because he has such speed." Once the defense thinks that way they can't come up as fast on all runs we make to that side, because they're dropping back. So I overruled my coaches and Garrison started every game.

One thing I'm very concerned about on my coaching staff is jealousy between the offensive and defensive coaches. This can filter down to the players, so you have to train the assistants. This is a good reason not to have offensive or defensive coordinators, or a strong head assistant on either offense or defense. This divides the team into two parts. I want the team to think it's USC playing UCLA and not our offense against their defense, or our defense against their offense.

Assistant coaches can be like old misers. They want to hoard the best people. They'll argue a player should be a defensive halfback, when maybe he should be a split end. I make all those decisions. I think we have great morale on our staff, and one of the reasons is because we don't have any separation based on petty feelings.

I put a lot of pressure on my assistant coaches, but I think they're challenging to me. They feed me ideas. If I accept them, fine. But if I don't, I'm not going to spend three hours explaining why not.

For better communication sometimes—particularly after practice—we'll go across the street to our watering hole, Julie's, have a drink and discuss the team. Drinking relaxes everyone. It would be tough to meet in my office after practice, because one coach might be mad, or another might be embarrassed because his kids didn't play well and I bawled him out.

Instead, we'll hop over to Julie's, sip a couple of drinks, and soon the whole staff's laughing and we get a lot done.

Of course, if we sat there and drank for three or four

hours, we'd forget what we were trying to accomplish. So, during the season I'll have two or three drinks and then I'm on my way home, usually with backfield coach John Robinson, and we can talk some more.

Some of the biggest business deals in the world have been closed over a martini or two, and I don't think that's a bad idea at all.

RELATING TO
THE PLAYERS

*"I don't want any
robots"*

EVER SINCE the campus unrest in the late 1960's, which
also touched athletic departments, there's been a lot said
about coaches "relating to their players" or "communi-
cating" with them. Most of this verbiage comes from
young head coaches who sound off about how many
hours they're going to spend talking to their team.

They also maintain that they're going to "give the
game back to the boys" by allowing them more freedom.

In this liberal age I'm a pretty flexible man, too. I tell
my players: "You can be a free thinker—but be at practice by 3 o'clock."

It's really amusing that so many coaches are just now
coming up with ideas on how to treat people. Some of
their theories are a lot of nonsense. When a young head
coach talks about handling players, I always want to ask
him if he's raised any children yet, because I strongly
believe there's a correlation between raising a family and
coaching a football team.

You have to know how much freedom to give your kids and how much to give a football team. You must know how much to talk to a family and how much to talk to a team. I think it's more difficult to understand college football players if you've never been a father. Players still have a lot of the child in them.

People say that kids are smarter today, and I realize they use more intelligent-sounding words like "relevant," but that doesn't make them any brighter. Certainly, they're more aware because they've watched television all their lives, and, as players, I feel they're a little more serious about staying in shape in the off-season. But basically they haven't changed since I got into coaching in 1950.

You have good kids and bad kids and hard-working ones and lazy ones, and that will never change.

Adults are always comparing one generation to the last one, but as Darrell Royal, the Texas coach, said last year:

"The trouble with making comparisons in the way people act from one generation to the next is that humans are the most forgetful species on earth. I see only one big difference in football players today. More of them write books."

There are too many coaches—and some of them have been quite successful—who suddenly have a bad year and figure they should immediately change the way they handle their players. It's easy to lose a couple of games and say "I'm wrong" and get every player in America on your side. I won't do that.

How does a coach get the respect of his players? By treating them fairly. He doesn't do it by talking to them all day, and he doesn't do it by doling out milk and cookies. I guess George Allen disagrees. Once a week he passes out ice cream and cake to his Redskins at practice.

But I don't think you're ever going to treat all your players well, because some of them won't let you. They'll defy you to be real good to them. Some might get angry and leave school because you've given them hell, and then they'll say to everybody, "That guy didn't treat me well." There's nothing a coach can do about that.

Most of the time I don't say much to my players, and I never have. I don't see the reason for it. I didn't get to talk to my dad a lot, but I understood him. I think my children understand me, and I hope my team does.

I don't believe you can sit down with my son John, who's now a grown man, or with any group of players and talk them into becoming either better people or better players. Your actions speak louder than words. Some young coaches, like California's Mike White, have tried—and I think found it wanting—to get players to perform by incessantly talking to them. But isn't it a universal complaint of young people that adults nag them too much?

I've heard that players are scared of me, and this bothers me. I guess I have a look sometimes that frightens people away, but I can't help that. It does amuse me when people complain I'm not very friendly with the players. I admit I don't run up and down patting them on the back, or putting my arm around them, but I don't put my arm around my wife all the time either. That doesn't mean I don't care.

I'm completely loyal to every player we've ever had. I'll stick with them and do anything for them. I don't respect any coach who isn't concerned about his kids. They're the ones he recruited, the ones who play, the ones who will win him any fame.

But on every team there will be players who have problems, and the coach will be accused of not understanding. I don't think my team has a legitimate beef with me. I'm not inflexible. That's why I got upset during the campus disruptions when the critics said all coaches had to change. No, not all.

I never thought my change would be that great, and it wasn't. Heck, I've changed over the years in certain areas. I never believed that when you get to be 21 or 26 or 30 years old you've grown up. Mentally and emotionally you can keep growing forever.

When all the trouble started I still had four children living with me, and I felt I was still in touch. When I was home, my kids argued politics and anything else they could think of as loud and long as any youngsters ever did. Sometimes I used to drive them crazy by taking first one side and then the other of an argument.

As a coach I've never had that hard-hat approach where the staff was unreachable by the players. Our offices have always been open, but I just think the assistants should do most of the talking. They should be as close as brothers to the players under them—and I think I was at Oregon. My staff must know what the players' problems are, and I insist that they get involved.

A player will bring in two kinds of problems—personal and team-oriented. He's encouraged to go to his coach, no matter what's on his mind. If his girl friend is pregnant, or his parents are getting divorced, or his car has been wrecked, or he's flunking biology, the assistants will try and help.

But if the head coach is going to attempt to do the same thing for 80 or 90 people, including freshmen, he's going to have to put in a 36- or 38-hour day. As remarkable as modern science is, we don't have that many hours yet.

Of course, sometimes the assistants just can't solve the problem, or the player may insist he just has to see me. Then the assistant will call and say he's sending the young man in, because he doesn't think he's getting a fair chance on the team, or he's upset with the trainer, or thinks he's being abused on the practice field. Yes, they tell me about girls, too.

So, despite what I said, I still may get as many as 15 or 20 players a week in my office, which is more than my college coach talked to in a year.

But are we going to make the first move and invite the players in? No. I believe strongly that it must be their decision. Let the players get to know the coaches. Let the child know the parent. Don't force the parent to understand the child all the time. Players are old enough to come to us. If they don't want to, that's their business.

In talking to either my players or my children, I've never tried to relate to them by acting young. Adults who do that are phony. For example, I don't go around slapping or shaking hands all the time. I didn't grow up that way. I probably couldn't play football today, because I could never shake hands that often. My hands would get tired—or sore. Sometimes there's more contact on the handshake than there was on the play.

When I hear a man who is 40 or 50 years old associating with young people and spouting, "Right on!" or "Let's do our thing," I feel he should knock it off. That's not him. That's what I tell my assistant coaches when they talk like that to the players. When you coach, you must be yourself. You can't change your image.

The way the kids themselves act today doesn't bother me at all. Long hair, mustaches, different jargon, slapping hands, wild clothes are as much a part of their way as a crew cut and corduroy pants were mine. Our entire offensive line grew mustaches in 1972—we called them

"The Mustache Bunch"—and Johnny sprouted enough hair for three of my heads and a Fu Manchu mustache besides. That was their fad, and I couldn't care less.

I allow my players and my family a lot of freedom, because I want them to grow up. I want them exposed to the total picture of life. You don't have to dress alike, you don't have to look alike, and you don't have to think alike. I always allow for individual difference—whether it's coaching a team or raising a family.

I've never been dogmatic about the way our players act off the field. I have very few rules for either my players or my children. In fact, I have just one big one: Respect your fellow man. You should never do anything that would hurt our family, our team or our university. And if you bring discredit to them, you're not much of a person. Respect your parents and brothers and sisters and teammates.

But there's no sense in me standing nearby ordering, "Don't do this, don't do that." I talk only in positive terms, because negativeness begets negativeness. I believe in freedom of choice.

I was very proud when Johnny told a newspaperman shortly after he had enrolled at USC that the best thing his dad ever did was leave him alone so he could grow up and discover the world for himself. Young people have to learn to make up their own minds. Otherwise, all you've got is a robot—and I don't want a robot for a child or a player.

I don't like curfews during the football season. If a guy isn't interested enough in his team to get enough sleep, you've got a bad player. So bench him. I want my players to know it's logical they should get to bed fairly early when they can. But it's also logical that if they've got a big test the next day they may have to stay up late. But they must make the decision, not me.

We only have curfews at two times. The first is during two-a-day practices in the early fall when we keep the players in a school dorm. We practice morning and afternoon, and our doctors believe we should force them to get their rest. So, during that difficult period of about 14 days, we have fairly strict regimentation. And, of course, the night before a game, whether we're in Los Angeles or on the road, we bed the team down in a hotel.

But the rest of the season the players scatter to fraternity houses, apartments, private homes and dorms, and I have no idea what time they go to bed. Johnny has an apartment, and I don't know when he goes to bed either. But I know one thing. He and the others have to report to practice every afternoon, and if they're tired, their legs will show it.

Every time Woody Hayes brings Ohio State out for the Rose Bowl he throws a security wrap around his players that would impress the FBI. He doesn't permit them to talk to reporters—unless he's there as a watchdog—hardly lets them go anywhere, and, until his last trip out, hid them in a monastery just before the game. That was the biggest joke in football.

What the hell are those kids going to say or see that will hurt their team? Coming to the Rose Bowl and California may be a once-in-a-lifetime experience for them. They should have more freedom to enjoy it. You don't have to concentrate on football all the time. You should be able to relax when you're away from it.

Woody changed somewhat before the 1974 Rose Bowl game. He had lost two straight bowls, one to Stanford and one to us, and so he loosened his grip on his players. Damned if they didn't beat us. Maybe he learned a lesson.

However, he still didn't allow his kids to go to the annual prime-rib dinner held at Lawry's Restaurant in

Los Angeles. It's called the Beef Bowl, and Rose Bowl teams traditionally attend to see which one can eat the most. The rest of the Big Ten goes, but Ohio State never has gone. That would really disable your team, going to Lawry's to eat prime rib. You might never play again.

And he continued to restrict his players' freedom of speech. I violently disagree with coaches who don't allow their players to talk to reporters. Being interviewed can be highly educational. It helps the players develop poise, and they learn—what's that overused word?—how to communicate with people.

So we allow our players a lot of freedom. I've even let some leave the team and come back. Linebacker Ed Powell quit angrily in the middle of the 1973 season. After missing a couple of games, he returned, apologized and came back to play. Our plans for 1974 are to start him.

I do draw the line on freedom. When it gets down to actually coaching the team, I'll call the shots. There's a new trend among coaches to have player committees. That doesn't work. When we're talking about football, somewhere, sometime, somebody has to say, "Gentlemen, for the good of all of us, this is what we must do." That's what I get paid for, and I'll never rationalize my position on the football field.

As soon as any coach decides he's going to have a meeting every five minutes to find out what his players want to do, he'll find out they don't want to do anything. And he's a loser. Democracy is a great idea, but in football it takes too long to work.

If you're a player and you don't want to do it my way on the field, fine. That's your business, and there's nothing wrong with it. Except do it somewhere else. We have decided what it takes for us to win, and we don't decide those things by throwing darts at a chart.

Though I encourage communication, it does not mean I'm going to listen to some player explain away his mistakes. I've often thought, what kind of profession am I in where a player doesn't perform, and now he wants to communicate? All he wants to do is con me. And I don't need to be conned.

You can't let your players make crucial decisions for you in a game, either. And there are innumerable ones during a football season. The classic situation, of course, is when the offense stalls near the goal line, and on fourth down the coach sends in his field-goal kicker. All the players wave him off, and the ones on the sideline jump up and down yelling, "We can get it in there, coach."

When it happens to me, I think, "If you can't get it in there on three downs, you aren't going to now." I'll decide what we're going to do. And I do.

As far as I know, we have escaped black-white problems on our team over the years, because I think the great majority of players—and that's all you can go by —believed we were trying with all our power to do what was right. I don't know if all my players felt that way, but I never heard of any trouble. If we had ever been accused by black players of being unfair, and it turned out there was a problem, I would have rectified it immediately. If the problem was with one of our coaches or trainers, he would have changed or left.

When I got into coaching, I think I was perceptive enough to realize that some black players have certain disadvantages, because of school or family background. In lower-income families—and this applies to both blacks and whites—the parents may not have gone to high school and there might not be any books or newspapers in the home. So how can the young man have a fair chance to learn to read? This is a particular ghetto problem.

Reading seems like such a simple skill, but it holds back many people in college. Once you can read competently you have a chance to be educated, but not until. Some of our blacks and some of our whites are low in reading skills, so we enroll them in a course to improve that ability.

I think coaches should help with the social and educational adjustment of their players, and sometimes this is more severe for a black student than a white one. But I think every student has a fairly large adjustment to make when he comes to college. If he's an athlete who comes on an athletic scholarship and doesn't get any money from home, then he may really have a social problem. He won't have the money to dress well or spend on dates. There's just no way to get the money, and there's nothing I can do about it.

Although we've never had any racial problems, there was tension on our team in 1970 and 1971 when we had disappointing seasons. Jimmy Jones, who is black, was our quarterback. In 1969, when Jimmy was a sophomore, he led the team to an unbeaten season and a Rose Bowl victory, but when we lost four games each of the next two years, I was hit by heavy pressure to bench him. Unfortunately, I think many of the letters I received were implying the team was bad because Jimmy was black.

That bothered me. I fought the critics and said I'm going to stick with Jimmy because we won with him, and I'm convinced he's still the best quarterback. I told everyone I didn't give a damn what they said.

Losing breeds poor morale and weakens team unity, so there was pressure not only from the outside but also from some of the players to bench Jimmy, too. In 1970 and 1971 we also had Mike Rae, who is white, and the quarterback who would lead us to a national title in 1972. A football team is just a bunch of people, and a bunch of people always divides on whom each likes best. And we became divided. Each quarterback had close friends who felt he should be playing.

For a long time Jimmy continued to be our starting quarterback—and not because he was black and I felt there might be protests if I benched him. I stuck with him because he was the best quarterback. He proved it every day in practice. He proved it in the games.

Finally, in the middle of 1971, Jimmy's senior year, I decided to alternate him with Rae on every series. I have never done this before or since, but we had lost four of six games, including two in the conference which knocked us out of the Rose Bowl race. I decided we had better get Rae ready for 1972, and he had to play a lot to get ready. I felt, too, that we shouldn't embarrass Jimmy by benching him as if to say this was his fault, because fumbles and poor defensive play had the most to do with the failure of that team.

So, for the next four games, we alternated Jones and Rae and won all four games. I decided not to do that in the UCLA game which ended the season, because I felt Jimmy had done a great job for USC and deserved to play all the way in his final game. We played poorly and tied UCLA, 7–7. But I'd do the same thing again.

Now, if there had been a chance for us to go to the Rose Bowl by beating UCLA, I might not have junked the alternating system, since we had been winning with it. But we weren't going anywhere after that game but home.

I know Jones didn't like alternating with Rae, and I think he became embittered at the end of his career. He heard the boos from the crowd and assumed people were booing him because he was black. Then, when we started alternating quarterbacks and winning again, I'm sure he figured fans were saying, "See, we were right. He couldn't win."

But now he's become one of our most important aides in recruiting. He's helped us tremendously. And the critics will never take away the year when he led us to a 10-0-1 record and threw the touchdown pass that won the Rose Bowl game.

Football coaches are often called callous, because they seem to have a disregard for player injuries. I remember once when everyone was shocked at how I acted when a player was hurt.

In 1972 we were playing California, and Johnny, my son, raced downfield for a pass. It was a floater—the kind we teach our quarterbacks never to throw because the receiver is defenseless. And Johnny was. He turned and waited for the ball next to the sideline, and just as he caught it, a defensive back with a running start smashed him from the front. Somehow, Johnny held the ball. But he sailed out of bounds and lay on his stomach without moving.

As I discovered later, everybody in the Coliseum who knew me watched for a reaction. They were startled when I never looked at my son, just kept directing the team on the field as play continued. People called me unemotional, which I resent, because I'm as emotional as anyone.

But they didn't realize that every time we get someone hurt, the doctors and trainers hurry to him right away, along with an assistant coach. The coach then comes immediately to me and explains what's wrong. Craig Fertig checked and told me Johnny had been hit in the face and was bleeding from the mouth, but was okay.

He had a cut lip and later lost a tooth, but I knew he wasn't badly hurt.

Every time the players come off the field somebody is hurting a little. If I went over to every one, I'd never see the game. After it was over, the writers would ask me what I thought, and I'd say, "Well, I didn't see this game. I had five or six guys hurt and I was watching them all afternoon." And they'd say, "That's a hell of a coach." Going to the injured players is not my job.

Johnny got popped in the face. What good would it do for me to run down and see him? I have never worried about any player, including my son, getting hurt, because football is a game of injuries. We try and minimize them, but we have to live with them when they occur.

I'm not callous, but I've gotten adjusted to player injuries, like a parent gets adjusted to raising children. You have your first baby and you're scared to death when you get up at six in the morning to check it. Michele was our first, and we looked at her constantly. We'd worry sometimes if she was breathing or not.

By the time we had our fourth child, Richie, Corky and I could be lying in bed and we'd hear a thump in his room when he fell out of bed. No one panicked. We casually decided whose turn it was to get up and get him.

In the same way, when you become a football coach and have your first injury, you feel, boy, that's the first time this ever happened to anybody. Then, after a while, you realize there's nothing you can do about it. Injuries are going to happen. You just can't get so involved that every time somebody gets hurt all activity stops for about three weeks.

I hate to see a player get hurt. Besides the pain, it's also unfair because he's worked so hard to be able to play. But I can't put a tear in my eye and go over and say I feel bad. That's not going to cure him.

There are, of course, certain exceptions when I'd feel obligated to get involved. If the coach who checks during a game comes to me and says we have a guy with a broken neck, then I'd sure as hell run down there. But we can't crowd around when somebody twists a knee.

Corky has been very good about her children playing football. She's never worried about them, maybe because she was involved with me when I played. But the day Johnny got hit she said she wanted to wait for him after the game. I wouldn't let her, because I didn't want him embarrassed.

As I said earlier in the book, I've always believed that without a sense of humor football can be almost unbearable—for both coach and players.

Mike Garrett alluded to this once when he said of me: "When we lost or he didn't like the way we practiced, he was tougher than hell on us. But just when we thought he was getting unbearable, he'd crack a joke and that would draw us closer to him."

Well, before and after Garrett, I realized that we're going to lose and we're going to make mistakes, and if I can't laugh about it sometimes I'll just drive myself out of my mind. As for the players, there are times when everything is going wrong, so I'll say something funny to break the tension. I have to show them it's not the end of the world. On other occasions, nothing is wrong, but I think the team is just too grim and I'll kid them to keep them loose. Humor also helps me get some of my points across.

I believe, too, that we should build up to a game gradually. When I talk to the team on Monday, for example, I don't want them to start the week thinking World War III is about to begin. The week is going to include a lot more days. Without being dramatic, I'll discuss quickly what we've just done the past Saturday, how I evaluated our performance, what I consider is the ability of the next opponent, what I think our chances of winning are, what we have to do to win, and that's it. I talk 15 minutes and get off stage.

"Now team," growl some coaches, "we are going to play the most important game of our lives. There will never be another game like this."

I don't know how many times you can play the most important game of your life, and I don't think you're ever going to play it on Monday, unless you're in another business.

I don't give pep talks, anyway. I think it's ridiculous when we as adults end up on our knees begging kids. Just play, I tell them. There is somebody who can take your place if you don't want to play. Don't think there isn't, because no one is indispensable.

As soon as a coach begs, "Please, please play for me," he becomes a whore. Don't play hard for me. Play hard for yourself. It you don't want to, fine. But if we lose don't come sobbing to me.

Boy, do I hate to see that scene in the dressing room where a player gets up with tears in his eyes and says, "We'll get 'em next year." "Damn it," I think, "why didn't we get them this year? Don't worry about the next one. Next year may come and we may all be dead."

I don't believe in slogans for inspiration, either. I don't think they accomplish anything. At USC we have only one, which we usually put in the front of our playbook. It comes from General Douglas MacArthur who said:

> "Defeat awaits for those who stray,
> Dreaming of victories won yesterday."

We can't even use this all the time. It's not appropriate unless we've had a super season the year before.

The Trojans don't run around screaming to get ready for games, either. We used to have a pregame huddle where all the players sprinted out and jumped up and down on top of each other, but I cut it out. All they did was step on the coaches' feet.

We also gave up our Friday pep rallies before the games. They would just end up as a cussing contest, and I don't think you have to swear a lot to win. We had a super rally before we got beat 51–0 by Notre Dame, so what did it prove?

Does a team have to be emotional to win? Well, I've always said nobody is more emotional than Corky and she can't play football worth a damn.

Of course a team must be emotional. But emotion mainly must come from the players themselves. The game itself dictates the situation, and players seem to get up when it's big. The student body helps get them up, sportswriters help get them up, everybody they meet helps get them up:

"Playing UCLA, huh? Wow, is that a big game!"

Against some opponents, however, it's difficult for me to get the attention of the team. All they hear is how they're going to win by five touchdowns. A coach warns them over and over about not having a letdown, and they snicker, "Oh, he says that every week." Sometimes they listen more to other people than to me. Often, there's not a lot I can do about attitude.

I know I didn't give Mike Garrett his pride, for example. He already had it. He hated defeat so badly he'd carry half the other team on his back as he scrambled along the ground for extra yards.

No football team goes at its peak through a schedule of 11 or 12 games anyway. But good teams win when they're down. They don't lose and complain afterward that it wasn't a big game. For USC, every game is a big game. At least, all our opponents think so.

Mainly we hope our players are keyed up so that they're mentally alert, and then their physical action will reflect it. If they overlook an opponent, they're just not mentally alert enough to play the game the way it should be played.

But when a coach is building his team up to a game, he must remember that it's divided into two parts—defense, which is more emotional, and offense, which is more controlled.

A defensive player reacts to plays, but an offensive player has to remember and carry out assignments. The offense is supposed to remain calm to remember whom to block if this play is called and whom to block if we audibilize to that play. If they're jumping and yelling, they may get so keyed up that they don't hear the quarterback, or jump offside or run the wrong way.

Over the years I've found that as people offensive players are by nature a little more calm and controlled. An offensive lineman is more disciplined and organized. He probably keeps his car neater. A defensive lineman is more of a rambunctious, ornery guy who doesn't want to be tied down by too many rules. He just wants to get in there and bang people: grab other players and throw them.

Another important emotional factor in the makeup of a team is togetherness, and that's hard to infuse into the squad, too. I think it mainly has to come from within the players. Every team is composed of different personalities, and you can tell before the season if unity is there or not.

There are some things that we can do to bring team and coaches together, however, and one of my ideas that I think has helped is a steak and beer party at the end of spring practice. We did it for the first time in 1972, after two disappointing seasons in a row. I decided to get all the kids together with the coaches and have a beer bust, so we could tell them how much we appreciated their good spring practice. We've done it since then, and we'll continue it.

We also have skits at the end of two-a-day drills in the fall. First the players mimic the coaches, and then the coaches mimic some of the top players. When the players poke fun at us, they don't pull any punches. To say they get very irreverent is an understatement. In the fall of 1973 I took a water pill before practice one day, and it really affected my kidneys. Two or three times during practice I had to stop my golf cart over in the corner of the practice field and get off to relieve myself next to the fence. I didn't think anyone saw me.

Later that week the players had their skit. The highlight was a song entitled, "Tinkle, tinkle, Coach McKay."

In 1972 we had tremendous unity—I've never had a closer team—and not only did we win the national championship, but we did it with our first full-time mascot. I think he was the symbol of our togetherness. The kids all adopted him as their guy.

He was a dog named Turd.

Turd was discovered by our All-American tackle, Pete Adams, just before the season. He was wandering in the street around the campus fraternity houses. Pete rescued him, and, in a rather casual fashion, became his owner.

One day Turd wandered into practice after Adams, and right then he became a part of the Trojan football team. He slept in the dorm during two-a-day drills—on his back with his legs up in the air—and ate steak at training table.

He was a very unusual dog, and I had the utmost respect for him. He was awfully intelligent. When he got tired, he would run over to my golf cart, hop in and ride around with me.

Turd went everywhere. He followed Pete down to the locker room and he followed him into the huddle. You'd see our offense huddling at practice, and from between the players' legs would emerge Turd's tail. Every once in a while Pete would reach down and pat him on the head.

After the huddle broke, Turd would retreat off to the side and watch the play. If he got bored, he simply went to sleep.

But he'd always pep up at the end of practice. He ran wind sprints with the team every night. He was in good shape and kept the players on their toes, but we didn't let him lag either. Marv Goux, our loudest and most fiery assistant, yelled at him when he'd dog it in wind sprints.

Adams was often erratic about taking care of Turd's appearance, and as the season progressed, Turd got dirtier and dirtier. One afternoon I bawled Pete out in front of the squad.

"Damn it, Adams!" I shouted. "Give that dog a bath!" So the players took Turd down to the training room and put him in the whirlpool. One of them blew him dry with a hair dryer, and another sprayed him with deodorant. He disappeared for two days, and we figured he'd gone off chasing girl dogs.

I think he really helped the team. Every player liked him, and he gave them another rallying point. USC has always had a big white horse that charges around the Coliseum during games, but we never had a mascot that actually worked out with us. The kids respected Turd for that.

Unfortunately, when Adams went to the NFL in 1973, he took Turd with him. So now he's a pro dog.

I wonder how the mayor of Shinnston got in his front door. My high school friends liked cigars, but the tough guy in the hat is me.

Some people said basketball was my best sport. This was in the Army Air Corps in San Marcos, Texas.

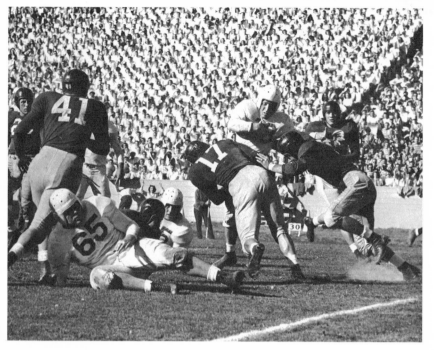

One of those good and bad days. As an Oregon back, I ran for 154 yards against Idaho in 1948, but I also hurt my left knee for the first time.

Corky got her man—and I couldn't be happier. It was June, 1950.

Oregon, 1950. I was a brash, young assistant coach with holes in my right shoe.

I may not look excited, but this was the day I worked half a life for. Don Clark (far right) quit as USC coach, and they picked me (far left) to replace him. Athletic director Jess Hill watches the transfer of power.

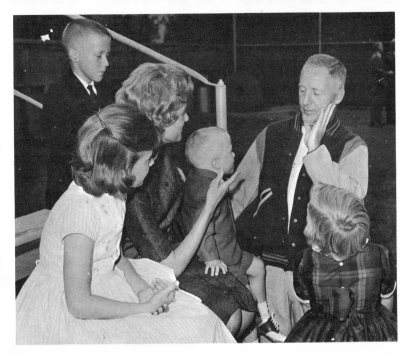

The McKay family joins Dad at practice in 1961. Johnny and Michele are sitting on the steps, Richie is perched on Corky's lap, and Terri is studying my elbow.

I couldn't have been happier. It was 1967, and we beat Notre Dame at South Bend for the first time since 1939. Later we won the national championship.

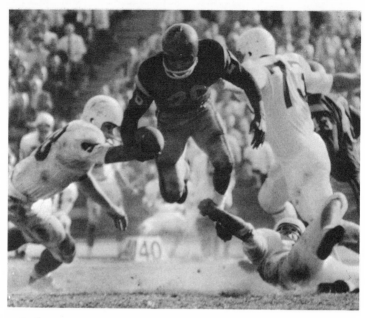

Mike Garrett could do everything—even hurdle for yardage.

Garrett had already won the Heisman Trophy when he left the Coliseum for the last time as a Trojan. November, 1965.

Two of my greatest tail-backs. 1974 senior Anthony Davis talks with 1968 Heisman Trophy–winner O. J. Simpson, the best runner in pro football.

Running always looked easy for O. J.

The first time Clarence Davis carried the ball in a USC scrimmage he ran for a touchdown. In 1969 he turns it on in the Coliseum.

Look out Notre Dame, here comes Anthony Davis. A. D. took this kickoff back to the Irish end zone for one of his six touchdowns in 1972.

A devastating play for our 1972 national champions: Sam Cunningham blocking and Anthony Davis running.

Smiles all around in the McKay home. Quarterback Pat Haden (left) and my son, Johnny, his favorite receiver, are coming to USC. Spring, 1971.

Alabama's Bear Bryant is my best friend in coaching. In 1970 I beat him Down South. This is just before he got even in 1971.

Nothing disturbs my concentration on game day.

Ouch! Dropped passes always hurt—even when we're just warming up.

This crowd looks like it's ready for a street fight. Those are my 1972 national champions around me just before kickoff.

Gripping programs as pacifiers, UCLA coach Pepper Rodgers and I meet before our 1972 Rose Bowl showdown. We won, 24–7.

We call most of the plays on the sideline—and send them in with either backs or ends.

I had a good reason to look worried here. Notre Dame was our next opponent.

Our 1972 defense knocked a lot of backs off their feet. This one played for Stanford, a good team we held to 183 yards. We gained 407.

I may look relaxed, but I don't miss much at practice. I want the players to know I'm watching, and this golf cart helps me get around faster.

I spend at least an hour almost every day drawing plays. Here I sketch one for the sportswriters who cover us.

For ten years we've been bitter but friendly rivals in the greatest intersectional series in football. The man in the dark jacket is Notre Dame's Ara Parseghian.

Defensive back Charles Hinton and I have a good reason to look pleased. We're enjoying the final minutes of our 42–17 Rose Bowl victory over Ohio State. January 1, 1973.

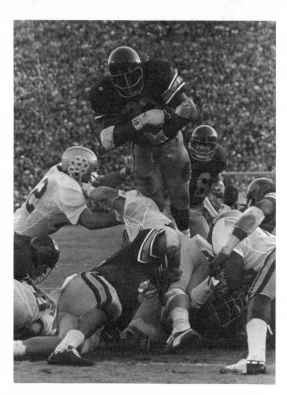

Sam Cunningham's famous dive play. This was one of his four touchdowns in our 42–17 Rose Bowl victory over Ohio State.

There's great joy when you win. Tackle Pete Adams is waving Turd, the unofficial mascot of our 1972 national champions. I had the utmost respect for Turd.

This is the most memorable play of my coaching career. O. J. Simpson cuts to the middle of the field right in front of me (I'm the coach in the middle) and runs 64 yards for the winning touchdown against UCLA in 1967. It won the national championship and put us in the Rose Bowl.

THE GREAT
RUNNING BACKS

*"Why not? It isn't
very heavy"*

WHEN WE PLAYED Texas A&M in 1964, the Aggies
were scared to death of our tailback, Mike Garrett. Every
time the ball was snapped and Mike took a step, it looked
like all 11 members of the defense flowed toward him.

On one play a tackler hit Mike so hard that his helmet
flew off and rolled along the grass. Honest to God, another player tackled the helmet. When he found out
Mike wasn't in it, he slammed it down on the ground.

In some ways not much has changed at USC in the
last decade. Every team in the nation knows that when
they play us they better keep all 22 eyes on our tailback.
He's the young man who stands hunched over, hands on
his knees, behind the fullback. Fans who concentrate on
the tailback will see a lot of action, because he's going
to be in it most of the time.

The workload got so heavy in O. J. Simpson's era
that fans and sportswriters began criticizing me. O.J.

was carrying the ball 35 times a game his senior year and people began to worry about his health.

"Don't you have any depth at tailback?" they asked.

"Simpson IS depth," I said.

"Well, isn't there anything else you can do besides run the tailback? Why is he carrying the ball so much?"

"Why not?" I shot back. "It isn't very heavy. And besides, he doesn't belong to any union."

I began to get weary of the questions. One day I announced to a group of reporters: "We will continue to operate from only two plays which I'll signal to O.J. I'll nod 'Run left,' or I'll nod 'Run right.' "

Well, O. J. Simpson ran left, right and up the middle enough to set new NCAA career and single-season rushing records—and he broke the career record in only two years. It had belonged to Garrett before him. O.J. also won the Heisman Trophy, three years after Garrett won it.

College football yardage has increased dramatically the last three or four years, because of offensive advances and clock-stopping rules, which allow more plays. But we've consistently gained good yardage since the days of one-platoon football. Since we went to my I-formation exclusively in 1962, we've averaged 366 a game in total offense, 217 on the ground. Eight times in 12 years the USC tailback has gained over 900 yards. Six of the eight he's gone over 1,000. In the same period we've won 81 percent of the time. There must be some correlation.

Human beings are naturally jealous, however, and this trait exists in my profession, too. Coaches are not prone to give other coaches credit. So they'll note that Garrett, Simpson, Clarence Davis and Anthony Davis all had thousand-yard seasons and say: "No wonder

McKay's teams gain a lot of yards on the ground. Look at the great runners he's had."

People tend to oversimplify everything, and they've oversimplified the art of running with a football, too. Great runners are not born. Great runners are made.

The physical attributes, like speed, ability to accelerate and cut quickly and good peripheral vision, are natural. But you just can't take this talented young man, hand him a ball and tell him to get in there and go.

He must be taught how to run, where to run and how to challenge the defense. And sometimes against his will he must be forced to become tougher than he wants to be.

In O. J. Simpson's first spring practice he carried against our best defense and couldn't even get to the line. Anthony Davis came along in the spring of 1972, blessed with great ability and great desire, and almost got killed in the first scrimmages. Somewhere between those first steps and the gobs of yardage they gained later, they learned a little more about running with a football.

A few years ago, the coaching staff from Georgia visited one of our spring practices and marveled at how much harder our backs ran than theirs did. They were mystified, because all the Georgia runners were very fast —faster, in fact, than ours were that season.

"Your backs run so hard," they said. "How do you get them to do that?"

"What do you teach your backs besides the plays?" we asked. "What do you know about running?"

"Aren't runners basically born?" they said.

"Let's put it this way. You work several hours a week teaching an offensive guard to pull and block, right?"

"Certainly."

"Why do you do that? Aren't guards just born?"

"Of course not. You have to spend a lot of time teaching them."

"Right. Guards aren't born and neither are runners. You have to teach a back the proper way to run with a football."

You can't make everybody a guard. You can't make everybody a running back. But given certain physical attributes, you can develop them.

USC's backs run hard because we insist they run hard. We're always screaming "Run hard!" We won't play anybody who doesn't. All our drills and all our plays are run at full speed, and we add something extra for backs —a grinding little exercise we call our bag drill. We have the bag drill practically every day in spring practice and early fall. Some of my assistants have suggested eliminating it, but that drill will stay at USC as long as I do.

What we do is organize players and coaches in two parallel lines several feet apart and tell the back to run for his life between them. First he approaches the lineup and cuts off and by a movement of a coach's head, then blows through two potential tacklers and goes down that line. All the way through, players and coaches sling fist-hard bags—about as big as pillows—at his knees and ankles. They throw them as hard as they can.

The average running back wants to loaf through. If he does, he'll get knocked flat. When Simpson first tried the bag drill, we knocked him down every time. But we taught him, by God, O.J., you concentrate you are not going down. You're never down in a game until you're stretched out flat. Keep your legs moving as hard as you can and you've got a chance to get away.

We won't let you shuffle through. When they throw the bags at your legs, kick the damn things. The same is true in a game. You have to challenge tacklers. If you don't, they have all the advantages. Unless you're driving, you've got to go down if a tackler hits you. There's almost never been a great runner who wasn't aggressive.

Too many backs are afraid to hit tacklers. They spend all their time trying to make tacklers miss them. That's why so many trackmen can't make it as running backs, even though they might do the 100 in 9.2 or 9.3. They try and run away from the defense. But the goal line is downfield. Run toward it, don't run toward the sideline. You won't find anything over there but the water bucket.

If a defensive player has committed himself to hit you low, you don't have to be as aggressive. You can move around on him, since he's on a downward plane. But if he takes off high, he's on an upward plane and you should attack a part of his body.

Imagine you are carrying the ball for USC, and we block you through the line. Here comes a linebacker to meet you. Fake him one way, say to the left, and while he's off balance, cut right and hit him with your shoulder pads. In other words, turn his body to your advantage, pop him, slide off and keep going straight downfield.

A tackler will usually expect you to fake either left or right. If you simply cut to the left and he happens to be as quick as you are, he'll follow, and his force and two arms make him stronger than you. If you simply fake left and try and go by on the right, you may fool him or you may not. If you don't, there he is, still in front of you. If you do a little dance, left and right, you're just horsing around and letting the other ten players catch up with you. So we teach our runners how to hit tacklers.

Knowing how to hit a defensive player and good body balance, which the bag drill helps teach, can also keep a runner from getting hurt.

One of the greatest running backs in USC history was Jon Arnett, who played in the mid-1950's, when I was at Oregon. Jon had an extra skill—he was a gymnast. It was hard to knock him down, because he kept his balance so well. We can't make all our runners gymnasts, but we do tell them, "If you start to go down, remember God gave you two hands and you're carrying the ball with only one. Put the other on the ground and push yourself back up." Our runners have done that countless times. But they didn't pick it up by instinct.

We want our backs to be rugged, and our great ones have been. Jump on them, hit them in the face, and they'll run right back to the huddle, come out and carry the ball again.

Many young kids think they'd like to be running backs, because of the glory and excitement, but when they get in big-time football they discover they don't like it anymore. We'll never recruit a high school running back who takes himself out of a game every time he gets bumped hard.

A runner must understand that there's one bad thing about carrying that football—it attracts a crowd. It's like a damn magnet. There's traffic coming from both sides, and everybody's mad. No one takes a pounding like a top running back.

On one of our early teams we had a ballcarrier who stood 6-2, weighed about 205 and had pretty good ability. But he was always tiptoeing around in practice. One day we had all the backs lined up, taking turns running with the ball in a hard-hitting drill.

I noticed this guy kept hiding and never came out to run. I asked him why.

"Coach," he said. "I don't want to. I've discovered I'm just not tough enough."

I shook his hand and let him go. "Finally," I said, "I've found an honest man."

Almost everything else in football is individual—one man against another. Nobody has as many people after him as a running back. When you put two players on a goal line for a kickoff, you can almost sense which one really wants the ball. The other is probably thinking, "I sure hope they kick it to my buddy." We're after the man who wants the ball.

Even if he's not carrying, a back hardly ever avoids contact. He might catch a pass, or fake, or block. If he fakes well he'll get belted. If he blocks, he'll usually block a lineman or linebacker who is bigger than he is.

To play tailback for USC you must be a super athlete who's super-enthusiastic about physical condition. You have to be in great shape, because you'll never get a chance to loaf. And you've got to have a burning desire to excel.

Besides preaching aggressiveness, we preach acceleration. We tell our runners to hit the hole and get moving. Run all out for a first down and don't worry about running 90 yards for a touchdown. When you run for a first down the touchdowns will take care of themselves. And if there's no hole, don't run backward. We might not block well enough for you to gain anything, but we'll block well enough for you not to lose ten or eleven yards.

Sometimes when backs try and break off long runs, they take chances with the ball—which can lead to fumbles. There's a proper way to carry a football and I'm sure every coach in America knows it. Put the ball in against your body, grip it tightly with your fingers and stick your elbow into your rib cage. The farther that elbow goes out, the easier it is for someone to hit you and knock the ball out the backside.

Admittedly, some great ballcarriers don't do this, because sometimes you must take a chance to make a long run. Simpson and Gale Sayers, two of the greatest runners in history, carried the ball "incorrectly"—out away from their bodies. By doing it they could run faster, because they had both arms swinging free, like a sprinter. When you bring the ball in to your body, you've got only one arm swinging free. You're tilting a little and you slow down.

You can put up with this dangerous practice with a Simpson or Sayers. They're like the baseball player who makes an error in the outfield, then hits two home runs. They may drop the ball a couple of times, but they'll also run for three touchdowns. I remember one game when O.J. was having a bad day. My assistants were going crazy on the sideline. "We gotta get him out of there," they said. "He's fumbling the ball, fumbling the ball."

"Let's leave him in a little longer and see what happens," I said.

Whoosh, touchdown. Whoosh, touchdown.

"What do you guys think now?"

"Hey, old O.J.'s coming along pretty good."

So we must weigh the mistakes against the ballcarrier. If he's not a great one and fumbles, we can't put up with him at all. Some backs are just promiscuous with the ball and are basically fumblers, no matter how often they carry. I don't think there's any ratio of fumbles to carries. Certainly if you run 60 times, you have more chances to fumble than if you run 10. But that's no excuse. I don't believe backs get tired and fumble. Sometimes they just take chances. For example, when they get tackled, they must not lunge out with the arm that's carrying the ball. They must turn the ball under their bodies.

Not fumbling simply takes concentration. There's no drill to protect against it. With some players it becomes a psychological problem and the more we yell, "Don't fumble!" the more they do. There's not a damn thing we can do except get them out of the game.

We also look for great peripheral vision in our tailbacks. Obviously, this cannot be taught. You watch a good back flying down the field, a tackler cuts on him from behind, and all of a sudden he zips the other way. How did he know that tackler was there? Good backs just know when people are coming up on them and I don't think they ever sit down to figure it out. They see them out of the corners of their eyes. Sometimes I think it's almost subconscious. They just feel people behind them.

I can walk behind people and tell who has good peripheral vision and who doesn't. Women are just terrible. Many people are in a daze, but I've never seen anyone more in a daze than women. We'll drive the team bus into the parking lot next to the Coliseum and they'll walk right in front of it. The bus weighs four tons, comes up on their shoulder, and they don't even see it. I'm thinking, good God, do they know that if a bus hits them at 10 miles an hour, it'll knock them halfway across the lot?

Many backs don't have that feel either. They run like a horse with blinders on.

Another thing I'll never minimize is the importance of familiarity with the plays and the system. A back can't very well run inside the tackles, for example, unless he practices doing it every day. If a Jim Brown turns up on your team, you can't assume he's so good he doesn't have to practice the plays over and over.

I learned this from my own experience. When I left the Air Corps in 1946 and went to Purdue, I was introduced to the T-formation for the first time in my life. I had always been a single-wing tailback or wingback, catching the ball deep in the backfield or taking it on a reverse. At Purdue, however, the big thing was the quick-hitting dive play.

Suddenly I was taking the ball from the quarterback right on top of the line, and I just wasn't very good at it. I'd hit the line as fast as anybody, but I didn't have any feel for running in there. So I spent most of my time at defensive back.

When I went to Oregon and came back to the Midwest to play Michigan in 1948 as both an offensive and a defensive back, one of my friends saw me and was surprised. "Hey," he said, "John's really improved as a runner." Of course I had, because I had learned how to run from the T-formation. That taught me a big lesson: It takes a player a lot of time and hard work to adjust to new plays or new formations. I've applied that lesson to my coaching.

I became aware of something else, too. Despite adapting to the T, I was convinced the single-wing tailback had the best stance to run from, because he was standing up and could see the defense. In the T the backs were down in a crouch. That distant memory had some influence on me when I designed USC's I-formation.

The first I-formation I ever saw was used by Don Coryell in the early 1950's at a junior college in Washington. Don, who is now a pro coach, ran it for the belly play. This is where the quarterback spins and hands off to the fullback or fakes the ball into his stomach and keeps it to run an option around the end with one of his halfbacks. Don had a halfback lined up behind the fullback, so by the time the quarterback was ready to pitch out to him he had a head start toward the end since he was starting from the middle of the backfield. But both backs were down in the traditional stance. The halfback or tailback wasn't standing. I didn't like this idea or think much more about it.

A little later, Tom Nugent, who coached at Florida State and Maryland, became the first to put all three running backs down in a line, or an I. But again they were all in normal stances with heads down, which I didn't like. Nugent's backs had to line up too far apart, because if they were crowded together each guy would have his head up the rear end of the man in front. They never shifted and it was impossible for them to run outside unless they tried an option. Nugent also couldn't get his halfbacks in the passing attack because they were lined up so deep in the backfield.

Later on, Tom got pretty upset when people gave me credit for developing the I, instead of him. But what he used and what we ran from the beginning are completely opposite. As far as I know I was the first coach to stand a running back up in the T-formation. We had the quarterback under center, the fullback down in his stance several yards behind, and the tailback, hands on knees, standing behind the fullback. We took the other halfback and made him either a flanker or wingback.

And while Nugent had two tight ends, we split one end and flopped our line. In other words, we always have a strong side and a weak side of the line—the strong side being the one where the tight end is, the weak where the split end is—while each set of guard, tackle and end can line up on either side of the center.

As he stands behind the fullback in the middle of the backfield, our tailback has a host of advantages, beginning with a tremendous number of angles to run from. He can run to either side of the center effectively, and the defense can't guess before the ball is snapped which direction he's going. He can get outside on a pitchout more quickly, because he's already halfway across the backfield. In short-yardage situations we can crowd him behind his leading blocker, the fullback, and we can even swing him in motion more easily for passes.

But perhaps the most important advantage of all—which we get by standing him up—is that he can see the defense before the play starts. We teach our tailbacks to study it every time they come out and line up. The phrase "running to daylight" has become a cliché by now, and our backs do it, too. But they have a head start against certain defenses because they know where the daylight is going to be.

If two linebackers are inside, for example, and the tailback starts one way with the ball, he knows the linebackers will flow with him. So he can then cut back against the grain, knowing they'll be a little out of position. When people said, "Boy, Simpson is really thinking fast, because he changed directions so quickly," they didn't realize that O.J. knew ahead of time approximately what was going to happen.

Let's take another example. O.J. comes out of the huddle, lines up and notices that where he's supposed to run—outside one of our guards—there's a defensive tackle playing. We've taught him that in this situation our guard can't block the tackle to the inside, because the tackle is lined up outside of him. So the guard must block him to the outside. So, instead of running outside the guard, where does O.J. make his cut? Inside.

No matter what formation you're in, if you're a back and you have your head down you can't see those things. So our tailback has always stood up. Occasionally in the past we would line up in the I and then shift quickly to a two-back alignment, with the fullback and tailback down, side by side. By shifting, we would force the defense to make last-second adjustments and give us an advantage. In the last two years, however, we've started every single play from the straight I and had great offensive success.

There's no question in my mind that you can run better from the I than from any other formation, except the wishbone, and the I is more versatile than the wishbone, because you can pass better from it. We've gotten fantastic running yardage from excellent backs with our formation, but we've also gotten very good yardage from average backs.

And we can make our offense work with one good runner. The wishbone needs four, including the quarterback. If you play the wishbone we can take your best back away from you, but if we block you can't take our tailback away from us. In our last six games against wishbone teams, including three with explosive UCLA and one with Oklahoma's unbeaten 1973 team, we've allowed a total of 40 points. That's an average of 6.7.

Going into the 1974 season, however, our old I-formation had not been shut out in 70 games, and we had scored under 10 points in only three of them.

We've often been labeled as a running team, because of our tailback-oriented attack, but since 1962 we've averaged 149 passing yards a game, 13 scoring passes a year and completed over 50 percent of our throws. We've gained 60 percent of our yardage from running and 40 percent from passing, which is about what you want. If you're balanced you're always going to run a little more, because you come into more short-yardage situations which call for a running play. Almost every good college team runs well, because it allows them to keep the ball longer, consuming time and taking the pressure off the defense.

We first began using the I-formation in 1961, my second year as head coach, figuring we'd line up that way and then create other formations from it. In 1961 we shifted out of the I about 75 percent of the time. That's why we first called our offense the shifting-T. Other coaches told us we couldn't do certain things from the I, like sweep the ends, and we believed them and didn't try to do very much. We had no pitchout to the tailback, which today is one of our two or three biggest plays.

In 1961, we opened the season using the new formation cautiously and lost to Georgia Tech, 27 to 7, although our quarterbacks, Pete Beathard and Bill Nelsen, passed for 240 yards. The critics in the press box were not thrilled by my new offense. They were amused by it. One of them said "I" stood for "incompetent." Another said it meant "ineffective," and a third said it should be called "intolerable."

The next week we shifted Willie Brown, our first quick USC back, from flanker to tailback, and Willie ran 93 yards for a touchdown as we beat SMU. We gained 285 yards rushing, a lot in those days.

Our first great offensive game at USC came the next week on national television, when we played Iowa, ranked number one. Although we fell behind, 21–0, we exploded for 34 points and lost only in the last minute, 35–34, when our two-point conversion try failed. But we had proved we could move the ball on a good team.

However, the I was still in the early stages of its development—we were shut out twice that season—and so was our defense. Our first great team was a year away.

In 1962, utilizing the new defense we had adapted from Frank Broyles and a more refined I-formation, we won the national championship. We had learned it was easier for the tailback to run than we thought and started plays out of the formation much more often, instead of shifting to two down backs. We sent the tailback in motion a lot, rolled out our quarterbacks and got several cheap touchdowns, because teams couldn't figure out what we were doing. Our point production per game increased from 15 to 24, we went 11-0 and coaches barraged us with questions about the new formation.

Brown was the 1962 tailback most of the time, although occasionally he and the flanker switched positions. But in 1963 Willie moved to flanker for good when Mike Garrett, the first of our great tailbacks, took his first handoff at USC.

Mike was only 5-9 and 185 pounds, but at the time he was the greatest college player I had ever seen. He was a tremendously strong runner, so damn quick you couldn't believe it. He had much better speed than anyone ever thought he had. And when he was surrounded and going down, he could scramble along the ground for more yards faster than some people can run standing up. He was a good pass receiver, a very good blocker, a great faker and ran as well inside as he did outside.

Sensitive and introspective, Mike was the most emotional of all the great runners we've had. I thought it was a crime that he never went to the Rose Bowl. Two of his years we lost out in votes, and the last and most galling time, UCLA knocked us out in the last three minutes of our game—after Garrett had carried 40 times for 210 yards.

Mike was a complete football player who did everything we asked of him—and we asked a lot. There wasn't anything he couldn't do. When he was a sophomore, college football was still basically one-platoon, and he had to play defensive cornerback as well as tailback. He was a very good defensive back.

In his three-year career Garrett ran for 3,221 yards, which was a new collegiate record, averaged 5.3 yards a carry, rushed for 25 touchdowns, caught 36 passes for four more scores and returned 44 punts for an 11.3 average and two more touchdowns. He also returned kickoffs. By the time Mike was a senior, opposing rooting sections stood up and cheered when their teams held him to three or four yards.

In Mike's first season, 1963, he averaged 13 carries a game and gained 833 yards. The last two years we really went to a tailback-oriented attack and he averaged 22 and 27 carries a game for 948 and 1,440 yards. As a senior he averaged 144 yards a game, led the nation in rushing and won the Heisman Trophy.

Garrett's increase in carries was only logical. The more we stayed in the I, the more it followed that our tailback would have to carry the ball more. On most of our plays we needed a blocking leader, and that was obviously the fullback, whose main job became blocking. Except for occasional reverses or counters to the flanker, the only other player who could run with the ball was the quarterback. And our quarterbacks in Mike's last two years, 1964 and '65, did not run nearly as well as Pete Beathard did in 1962 and '63.

Although Garrett and I developed a close relationship, I don't think he feels as close to me today as he used to, because he read years later that I said Simpson was the greatest back I had ever seen. Well, O.J. is the greatest back I've ever seen, but I wish I had never said that in the first place. I never meant to imply anything derogatory about Garrett, because he was a hell of a football player. Simpson was just bigger and faster. God gave him more ability. But nobody ever got more out of his ability than Garrett. And I don't think anyone will ever get more out of his ability than Anthony Davis has the last two years. But I'll never single out my all-time 22 best players, because you hurt too many people's feelings when you do that.

Two years after Garrett left, from San Francisco City College came Orenthal James Simpson, also known as "Orange Juice." He was charming, outgoing, comfortable with people from the beginning, stood 6-2, weighed 210 pounds and ran the 100 in 9.3. He was the perfect physical specimen for the position of tailback. Before O.J. left USC, we said he would be the greatest runner in pro football. Many of the pros scoffed. They said he'd find out it wasn't so easy to run against a lot of big, fast guys.

Simpson is now the greatest runner in pro football. In 1973 he broke Jim Brown's unbreakable, single-season rushing record.

Simpson accelerates like a jackrabbit, but his speed is deceptive, because he seems to glide. You don't think he's going fast until you try to tackle him. But how many big running backs have ever been on a world record relay team? Simpson was. He ran on USC's 440-relay team that shattered the mark.

Most sprinters who become running backs slow down when they put on their equipment. They're not strong enough to carry the extra pounds. O.J. puts on the uniform and other gear and is almost as fast as he was without it.

As a freshman in junior college he played almost entirely defense his first few games and was an excellent defensive back. Then he became a flanker. So when he arrived at USC as a junior he was nowhere near the accomplished runner he became. Each game he played he got better. As a senior he was 30 or 40 percent better than as a junior.

Since the middle 1960's, the number of carries our tailback gets has always depended on his ability and on the strengths of the team. If there are other good runners, or the potential for an excellent passing attack, or the tailback lacks great ability, the number of carries falls off.

But in 1967 and 1968, Simpson's two seasons, we had 5 foot 9 fullback Danny Scott, who could block but couldn't run very well, 5 foot 9 quarterback Steve Sogge, an excellent leader but only adequate passer and runner, very little depth at tailback, and a bad knee. The bad knee belonged to our flanker, Jimmy Lawrence, who got hurt in the middle of both seasons, which further weakened our offense.

So Jay—I called him Jay—began carrying more and more. He was an amazing athlete. There was no doubt about that, because he was never on a team that really dominated anybody physically. He ran behind two pretty good offensive lines, but as a unit they weren't as good as the national championship 1972 line. Often he made yards entirely on his own—with everyone keying on him. He could look bad on a couple of plays and just when you thought he was going to look bad for a third, he'd run for a touchdown. If you ever made a mistake against him, he was on his way to the end zone.

Northwestern's Alex Agase just shook his head in wonder after Simpson shredded his defense. "He approaches the hole like a panther," said Alex, "and when he sees an opening, he springs at the daylight."

As a junior Jay averaged 29 carries a game and gained 1,543 yards as we won our second national title. Before his senior year I discussed my theory of offense for 1968:

"We plan to run O.J. 30 times a game," I said. "Maybe even 35 or 40. You have to let your best player handle the ball most of the time. In 1962, when I had Pete Beathard, the quarterback-rollout offense was the best for us. As soon as I get another Beathard, maybe I'll go back to it. Right now I have Simpson, and I can't think of anyone I'd rather have carrying the ball."

I kept my word. We slipped O.J. the ball so often people said I was sadistic. We had plays for him we've never run since. And he carried USC's offense more than I've ever seen anyone carry an offense. His average number of carries zoomed to 35 and twice reached 47. He also had days of 40, 39, 38, 34 and 33 carries, gained over 200 yards four different times, averaged 171 yards a game and led us to an unbeaten regular season and return trip to the Rose Bowl. We rushed for 24 touchdowns that season, and Simpson scored 23 of them and gained 1,880 yards. Needless to say, he won the Heisman Trophy.

What did Jay think of all that work?

"I enjoyed running that much," he said. "It made me feel like I was in the game. It helped my concentration. Also, I think it helped my running. The more you run, the more you learn."

He kept learning during a game. He had tremendous fourth-quarter endurance and seemed to get stronger while everyone else got tired. Against Minnesota, for example, we were behind 20 to 16 in the fourth quarter on a muddy field. O.J. carried on 11 of our last 12 plays, scored twice and we won, 29–20.

"Simpson," I said, "gets faster in the fourth quarter and I get smarter."

People were always pointing out the number of carries Simpson had, and I kept shrugging them off. "Only 40 carries for O.J.?" I said after the UCLA game. "Heck, he can go out dancing tonight."

Although we went unbeaten in the regular season, critics said we were stereotyped and dull. I ignored them. I've always remembered what Jim Aiken, my old Oregon coach, said. Do what you think is right, no matter what anyone else says. You must believe in yourself and believe totally in your offense.

And consider this: If you had Henry Aaron on your baseball team and the rules said he could take every turn at bat, wouldn't you let him?

As it turned out, I think we influenced quite a few coaches. In the last five or six years, several great runners have averaged 25 or 30 carries a game and gained well over a thousand yards a season. We showed that it was possible, and the I-formation helped make it possible.

In two seasons, O. J. Simpson averaged 32 carries a game, ran for 3,423 yards to break Garrett's career record, scored 36 touchdowns, averaged 5.1 a carry and as a senior tied for the team lead in pass receptions with 26. As a junior he passed for three touchdowns. We never had him return punts, but he ran back 15 kickoffs during his career.

Simpson's closest competition for the 1968 Heisman Trophy was Purdue's Leroy Keyes, but I would have matched Simpson against Keyes in anything, including marbles.

Jay's career ended, and the very next year, 1969, soft-spoken Clarence Davis arrived from East Los Angeles Junior College. His success the next two years didn't surprise me at all. The first time Clarence carried the ball in a USC scrimmage he ran for a touchdown.

Clarence proved a recruiting theory of mine—that you have to study kids very closely in high school and not just look for the obvious. Somewhere you might find an offensive guard who can run like hell. Clarence Davis was a guard in high school.

Davis at 5-11 and 195 was bigger than Garrett. I don't think he ever got the publicity he deserved, because he was a super back, although not in the class of Garrett or Simpson. He averaged 24 carries a game for his two seasons and totaled 2,323 yards with a 4.5 career rushing average. Clarence was a very good blocker, caught the ball real well, returned 16 kickoffs, including one for a touchdown, and like my other top backs, was blessed with great acceleration.

At times Clarence couldn't carry the ball as often as we wanted, because he lacked endurance, but he still ripped off 1,351 yards as a junior and 972 as a senior. I spread the ball around more in his last season, because we had more depth at tailback than we'd had in several years. I didn't think Davis minded that, because he never said anything to me about it. But when he went to the Oakland Raiders he told a sportswriter he wished he had carried more.

In Clarence's junior season we went unbeaten and landed in the Rose Bowl for a fourth straight time, but in 1970, his last year, we had our worst record in eight seasons, 6-4-1, and when we also stumbled in 1971, I sat down to appraise our situation.

I realized we needed more speed on defense, but I was also ready to revamp the offense. I may be stubborn, but I'm not too stubborn to change. So instead of taking a vacation in the summer of 1972, I spent it in the dark looking at USC films.

For three weeks I watched films of our offense and concluded that we had become easier to defense. I felt our offense had indeed become stereotyped. We had changed for Simpson, because we were mostly determined to get him the ball, and we had fallen very heavily into the tailback syndrome. We had been pretty good at it, but rather than develop the rest of our attack, we had stayed with the tailback offense. And stayed with it. And stayed with it.

I knew before the 1972 season that we were going to get good tailbacking again, but that wasn't how I planned to win. We could still make healthy yardage because of our blocking angles and the other strengths of the I-formation, but I wanted to disguise our attack much better. I realized that we weren't shifting and going in motion as much as we used to. We always had the same two wide receivers out—just like the pros. I also decided that there were certain facets of the wishbone which I liked and might try to incorporate in our offense.

So I decided to go back to formations we had run five

to ten years earlier, when instead of just catching passes, our flankers often moved in near the tailback and carried the ball on reverses or counter plays.

We call the flanker our "Z back," and in 1972 and 1973 we had our best one ever, Lynn Swann. So we used him like a chess piece to create different formations. If we moved him in a certain way, for example, we had the same basic setup as the wishbone on one side of the backfield, although the tailback and fullback were still in an I. So I called this my "I-bone." Now we had overloaded one side of the field and planted more doubt in the minds of the defense. And by utilizing more shifting and motion, we became twice as hard to defense.

Before defensive players can react, they must first recognize what formation the offense is in and communicate to each other so they all understand. But we would shift, and the defense would react, and then suddenly we'd go in motion the other way. We gave defenses less time to figure out what we were doing. To do this, we called about 65 percent of the plays from the bench, more than ever before.

What happened in 1972 was what I thought might happen. We ended up with some big mismatches, as in 1962, and scored several easy touchdowns.

In 1972, unlike 1967 and 1968 when O.J. carried so often, we could be more versatile, because we had the personnel to be more versatile. We not only had two good passers in Mike Rae and Pat Haden, but we had three good tailbacks in Anthony Davis, Rod McNeill and Allen Carter and a great fullback in Sam Cunningham. We won our third national title.

Anthony Davis, who has become our latest great tailback, surpassing a thousand yards in both 1972 and 1973, is the closest to Garrett in both size and style of all my runners. Facially, he looks like O.J. so much he could pass as his little brother. I told him when he arrived at USC as a freshman that he could be another Garrett if he ran all out in every practice like Mike did and became an aggressive runner. He did everything we asked him to.

Like Garrett, Davis can literally crawl for yards, and he can stop and cut so fast that when he cuts he's going another direction at full speed. He's only 5-9, 190 pounds, but he's got an unbelievable build. He has a chest like a weight lifter, which I guess helped him pin opponents as an L.A. city wrestling champion in high school.

He has very strong legs, fantastic body balance, long legs for a short man and a unique running style that reminds me of Gale Sayers. He has the ability to split himself like a Russian dancer and keep running. It's astonishing that a back only 5-9 can have a stride that long. But he kicks his leg out and throws tacklers off him. In the 1973 Rose Bowl, an Ohio State defender smacked him, and he just threw his leg right through the guy and burst 20 yards for a touchdown. Davis is a very good blocker, too, which is a skill he learned at USC because in high school he was a quarterback.

A.D.—that's what we call him—is also the most brash of all my tailbacks, so brash that he stopped me on campus one day and needled me about gaining weight. Many of my players see me and avoid me.

As a sophomore, Davis ran for 1,191 yards, averaged 5.8 a carry, returned seven punts and handled a dozen kickoffs. Against Notre Dame he ran kickoffs back 97 and 96 yards for two of his six touchdowns in a phenomenal performance. He scored 19 times that season.

Some coaches won't put a real good back deep on punts or kickoffs, like we do with Davis and have done with our other great tailbacks. They worry he might get hurt. But I feel this is the one time our runners are assured of getting the ball where they have plenty of room to run with it. We don't put all good backs deep on punts, because catching them takes a special skill, but you can drop a kickoff, pick it up and still go a long way because there's more time.

Davis gained over a thousand yards as a sophomore even though he only started the last four games. When the season began, junior Rod McNeill was our first-string tailback. Rod had a lot of ability, but until late in his senior year he was never in the kind of shape it takes to be a great tailback, and Davis went by him.

As a 1970 sophomore, McNeill averaged six yards a carry playing behind Clarence Davis, but he had a pull behind his knee and could never work out until Thursday. Three or four carries in a game and he'd get tired. He looked great the next spring, but then broke a hip and had to sit out the 1971 season. That's a hell of a serious injury to come back from, and although he gained 567 yards in 1972, he wasn't running nearly as well as we thought he could. His hip wasn't strong, and in addition he got two charley horses. It was tough luck for a back with considerable potential.

Davis, meanwhile, kept getting better and better. The last six games he whirled for 926 yards. I loved A.D. from the beginning—even though he wasn't starting. I'm not hung up on who's going to start, anyway, although I guess fans are. I like a player who's ready when we really need him. Although he began as a reserve, Davis ran every practice play like it was against Notre Dame.

After his phenomenal finish in 1972, I guess Davis disappointed many people in 1973. He gained 1,112 yards and scored 15 touchdowns, but his average dropped to four yards a carry and he didn't break off as many long runs. I still thought he had a great season.

He didn't duplicate the impossible by getting six touchdowns against Notre Dame, but he did score five against California, including an 80-yard kickoff return. And he had five 100-yard games, including 145 in our Rose Bowl–clinching victory over UCLA. Besides, we lost the best blocking back I've ever seen, Sam Cunningham, and six of our seven offensive line starters from the national championship team, and it took several games to build a cohesive new unit.

Behind Davis, a stronger McNeill pounded for 763 yards, as we alternated the two much of the time the last few games.

During a game a tailback can learn a lot by standing next to me on the sideline, watching and listening. The back on the field who makes an error usually comes back to the huddle and thinks, "Damn, I wish the guys would start blocking." Yet, if he could watch another runner make the same mistake, I'd tell him, "See what your friend did?" And he'd calmly appraise the play and reply, "Sure, he should have broken outside, instead of inside."

I can't yell advice like that to a player on the field, because the defense would hear me. So I always have a tailback, a split receiver, a quarterback and maybe a fullback walking back and forth with me. They carry in our plays, and they're learning by watching.

We preach to all of our players that they must stay alert off the field, too. We don't want anyone sitting on our bench watching his shoes. It's like being in a class in school. You must stay tuned in to what's going on.

And there will always be a lot going on around the tailbacks. They often get mentioned by the sportswriters more than I do. Back in 1968 I was tempted more than once to sign autographs: "John McKay, friend of O. J. Simpson."

THE GREAT
TROJAN TEAMS

"Intensity is a lot of guys who run fast"

ONE DAY, a few minutes before kickoff, I was working off my nervous energy by pacing behind our bench. The game was a sellout and the Coliseum was jammed with people. But right behind me—on the 50-yard line—I noticed a lady sitting next to an empty seat.

I went into the stands and asked her why no one was sitting there. She said the seat belonged to her husband, who had died.

"Oh, I'm sorry," I said. "But why didn't you give it to one of your relatives?"

"Because," she answered, "they're all at the funeral."

Of course this isn't a true story—at least I've never asked anyone about empty seats—but occasionally I use it to illustrate the popularity of USC football in Los Angeles today, despite all the other diversions and teams in this city. We sold only 23,000 season tickets for my first team in 1960. In 1973 our season-ticket sale had soared to a record 50,001. My thanks to the one person who put us over 50,000.

All those season-ticket holders didn't come out to watch me stand stoically on the sideline. They opened their checkbooks because the Trojans were winning football games.

In the last 12 years, beginning with 1962, our record has been 101-24-6. Six of those teams had a combined record of 61-4-3, and this chapter is their story.

Three of them won national championships (1962, 1967, 1972) and three of them were unbeaten (1962, 1969, 1972). Of course, it's easier for some teams to be unbeaten than others. I've always said the chances of your staying undefeated are in direct proportion to the number of teams you play in the top ten. When you notice that a team hasn't lost, check its schedule.

Several things have to break right for us to win a national title. We not only need the right players, the right schedule and a little luck, but the good teams we don't play have to get knocked off by somebody else. Just going undefeated won't guarantee a national championship. We took it with a loss in 1967, but in 1969 we went unbeaten and wound up ranked behind Texas and Penn State, which were also undefeated. A tie with Notre Dame killed our chances.

It's impossible to define a perfect football team, but we do want a large number of big, fast, alert, fairly intelligent young men with a driving urge to excel.

We often have to sacrifice size for speed, or speed for size, depending on position. It's not enough, for example, to be quick at tackle. But you can be smaller and play linebacker if you're fast.

All of our players not only have different ability, but also different degrees of enthusiasm. Some get by with less desire and more ability. Others make up for their deficiencies with more desire. But the more players with most of those above-named attributes, the better.

It isn't just the players that make a team great, but the mix of those players. How well do they get along? Do they respect each other? Sometimes, after a year passes, you'll replace players with others who are their physical equals, but the team doesn't have the same spirit of unity it did before. In 1972 we not only had tremendous talent, we also had the perfect blend of personalities. Until late in the season when Anthony Davis exploded, there was no one person who was the star.

There's no doubt it was my greatest team. As Nebraska's Bob Devaney said, it will go down as one of the greatest of all time. I know I've never seen a team that could beat it—if the kids played as well as they could play. There was no comparison between the 1972 team and my other top ones. They outscored their opponents by more points than any of my other great teams scored in a whole season. Four of our best ones, including two national champions, scored between 255 and 261 points, while the 1973 team scored 322. In 1972 we reeled off 467, which was 333 more than the 12 teams we beat. We averaged 39 points a game, and that has to be my favorite team. I can't think of a weakness.

The 1972 team was 12-0. The other outstanding seasons were 1962 (11-0), 1967 (10-1), 1968 (9-1-1), 1969 (10-0-1) and 1973 (9-2-1).

Speaking generally, all those teams had one common characteristic. No matter how refined the I-formation was, or who was playing tailback or quarterback, they were all damn good defensive teams.

I can't say enough about the importance of defense. Coaches without a good defense don't sleep at night. With a good one, there's always a chance for victory. With a poor one, there's always a great chance for defeat.

If we have a super offense sitting on the bench all day, it does us no good at all.

But with a solid defense we know we'll have a pretty good season, and maybe we'll get lucky and be better than we hoped. Defense will get us in a position to be lucky.

There's an old saying that there are more ways to score on defense, and counting punt returns, that's true. The defense has to score or set up scores for a team to get 40 or 50 points. In 1972 we beat Michigan State, 51–6, while outgaining them only 390 to 211. Our leading rusher had only 53 yards. Our quarterback threw four interceptions.

But our defense set up six touchdowns with five fumble recoveries and four interceptions, and Lynn Swann got the other by streaking 92 yards with a punt.

I've always said, let me have the ball five times on your side of the 50, and I'll probably beat you by a wide margin. The team that plays on the shortest field will win.

For good defense we need quickness, strength and the urge to get after ballcarriers in what we call "an angry frame of mind." We want intensity, but you won't see much intensity on defenses that are slow. Intensity is a lot of guys who run real fast.

I've always believed that the best defense is the zone. Ten years ago most of the professionals disagreed. Now they're all playing it. It's much better than the man-to-man. Johnny Unitas summed it up best a couple of years ago when he said if pro football really wants higher scores, they should outlaw the zone.

Strategy is as important on defense as it is on offense. We have to ascertain what the other team does best, and then plan how to take it away from them. If they're a tremendous option team, like some of the wishbone teams are, then we want to force them to run inside.

Our players must also understand how to adjust when the offense changes formations. Just like a quarterback audibilizes on offense, the defensive quarterbacks—we have two, a linebacker and a safety—adjust on defense. The linebacker calls the defense up front, and the safety calls the pass coverage. And they must yell loud, because communication on defense is very important.

We also have to make sure our players understand the concept of team, rather than individual defense. This is sometimes difficult for the inexperienced ones. Instead of covering their areas, they want to make the tackle themselves, and they often wind up out of position and get burned. This happens most often against option plays. In those situations we must have complete discipline.

We don't like to gamble much. We always go into a game and hope we can beat people playing straight. We played straight most of the time in 1972.

My first big victory at USC was a defensive one—an upset of UCLA in 1960. Out of it came a new three-year contract, and it occurred when I was very unpopular with USC's fans. Our record was 3-5.

My hiring was a disappointment to many, because I wasn't a "name" coach. In addition, people figured we'd have a great team in 1960, because we were coming off an 8-2 season in 1959 and had people like All-Americans Mike and Marlin McKeever returning. *Playboy* magazine, in fact, picked us number one in the country.

Playboy, however, knows a lot more about the female formation than the T-formation. In 1960 I could outrun our backs, and I was 37 years old. Dave Levy, the first assistant coach I hired, said we might have trouble against the Long Beach Poly team he had just coached to the Southern California prep championship.

I told USC's president, Dr. Norman Topping, that we'd be lucky to win five games, maybe six at the most, despite what the public was thinking. Several good players had graduated, like tackles Garry Finneran and All-American Ron Mix, and fullbacks Clark Holden and Jim Conroy. Another top lineman, Al Bansavage, quit and went to the Baltimore Colts, and still another, Marv Marinovich, later a starter on the 1962 national champions, was suspended by the school for a semester after a dorm fight.

And were we slow! "USC's backs," wrote one sportswriter, "run as if their shoes are too big and laced too tight." Jerry Traynham, our best runner, did the 40 in 4.9 or 5.0. Today that makes you a defensive tackle.

But while we recruited for the future, we were stuck with the present, and no sooner did the 1960 season begin than we were hit with a flurry of injuries. Mike McKeever, who was a guard, was hurt in the third game and missed the rest of the season. Traynham broke a hand and missed several games. In fact, 13 of our top 25 players missed at least four games each. Some of the injuries were hard to believe. One of our players wrecked his toe kicking a locker. Before playing Baylor, I announced that we were so short of players that my son, Richie, one and a half years old, was going to start for us. Richie immediately slipped in the bathroom, cut his chin and had to have four stitches.

We were so short of halfbacks for that game that we started our sub quarterback, Al Prukop, at left half, giving him the job on Thursday.

From that season I learned we would have to be real deep in personnel to play USC's type of schedule.

Meanwhile, we wobbled up to the UCLA game, and

while I cracked jokes to the sportswriters, the alumni growled, "We want a coach, not a comedian."

Although Dr. Topping supported me, my contract was only for a year and I developed the feeling USC might not invite me back because of all the pressure. So it was with much bravado that Corky and I sent out invitations for a post-UCLA game cocktail party at a downtown hotel.

UCLA had a 5-1-1 record and was favored by 12 points. Their single-wing, directed by explosive tailback Billy Kilmer, made them doubly difficult to prepare for.

So I redesigned our defense to stop Kilmer. Marlin McKeever at defensive end was ordered to pressure Kilmer every time he started to roll out on the run-pass option. And every time he rolled, most of our line, linebackers and secondary, rolled with him. Kilmer completed just 4 of 17 passes and ran for only 29 yards. Defensive back Jim Bates broke up two possible touchdown passes, we held them to 171 yards, and we won, 17 to 6.

Bill Nelsen threw a touchdown pass to Marlin McKeever, who also played offense for us, Hal Tobin ran for another score, Don Zachik kicked a field goal, and I was carried off the field to a happy postgame party. The rooting section—this was before war became unpopular —chanted "We killed Kilmer!"

I got my new contract.

Although my first two seasons were losing ones (4-6 and 4-5-1), we were getting better players by recruiting and in 1961 I was fiddling around with the I-formation. Although injuries killed us again in 1961, we could have gone to the Rose Bowl by tying UCLA in our last game. The conference had only five teams that season and we were 2-0-1 in league play to UCLA's 2-1-0. But we lost, 10 to 7. In the third quarter, Carl Skvarna's 38-

yard field-goal attempt for us hit the left goal post and bounced away.

In 1962 it all came together as we won that first national championship. Before the season I told Dr. Topping that I thought we had one of the best teams I had ever been around. We had offensive and defensive speed, two good quarterbacks in Nelsen and Pete Beathard, and I had refined the I-formation and adopted the Arkansas defense.

They improved more than any team we've ever had. It took them a while to believe they were good, and in the early season we were struggling for our lives. Although we beat some teams very easily in going 11-0, we also won four times by a touchdown or less.

Defensively our kids were magnificent. In the regular season we allowed just seven touchdowns, held eight teams to seven points or less and outscored our 10 opponents, 219 to 55.

We were ultimately maligned, because our 42–14 lead over Wisconsin in the Rose Bowl dwindled to a 42–37 victory. But until we started running out of players we played one of the greatest football games of all time. For a while I thought we could have scored 100 points.

That was a one-platoon era, and my Lord, we had a little team compared with today. The offense averaged 203 pounds a man. In 1972, our national champions averaged 218. But the greatest difference was in the line. Not counting the split end, the 1972 offensive line outweighed the 1962 line by 35 pounds a man.

Because we were playing one-platoon ball, we used the three-team system, which Paul Dietzel had popularized at LSU. Any time you're good enough to play a lot of people you'll have good morale, and we did. There were games in which I played the entire squad, but more important there were 33 kids who knew they would probably play in every quarter.

The restrictive substitution rule said any player could enter any one quarter only twice, so we always substituted by teams. We had a unit that could play both ways, which we called our Red Team; a unit that played only offense, the Green Team; and a unit that basically played defense, the Gold Team. Because of the rules, however, the Green and Gold teams could be caught in the game at the wrong time for a play or two. So the Greens also spent some time practicing defense, while the Golds worked on offense.

People referred to Nelsen, our senior quarterback who later led the Cleveland Browns to several divisional titles, as a second stringer, but he wasn't. He was quarterback of the offensive team, because he was too slow to play defense. But he was a fine passer. Beathard led the Red, or two-way, team, because he could play defense. So he saw more action. Pete could do everything. He ran extremely well, which made him effective on rollout passing, and he had only one pass intercepted in 107 attempts, while completing 51 percent.

Willie Brown was another outstanding player who was not only our best runner, but also our best defensive back. He's now one of my assistant coaches. Willie and Dickie James, whom I coached at Oregon in the early 1950's, were the best two-way players I've ever seen. They could do damn near anything—run the ball, catch it, play defense, return punts and kickoffs.

And then there was split end Hal Bedsole, a tremendous physical specimen at 6-5 and 220 pounds with sizzling speed. Unfortunately, Hal's biggest problem during his career was himself. He was immature and temperamental, with a talent for enraging both the coaches and players. But no one could have had a better season as a home-run receiver than he did in 1962, despite the fact he also had to play defense. On 33 catches Hal scored 11 touchdowns and averaged 25 yards a play. He was an All-American, and if he hadn't had knee trouble as a pro, he would have become one of the great ones.

Ben Wilson was a good fullback, a big, strong runner and blocker. Tackle Gary Kirner, I think, was our best lineman. He did a hell of a job both ways, although he only weighed 205. Damon Bame, 5-11, another All-American, was a defensive specialist at linebacker, and he starred at an incredible 190 pounds. Another fine player was tackle Marv Marinovich, who was named the most inspirational member of our team.

There were some milestones that season and many remarkable moments.

Our 14–7 upset of Duke in the opener moved us into the top ten (ninth) for the first time in my coaching career. Our 32–6 fourth-game win over Cal, on a day Bedsole caught six passes for 201 yards and two touchdowns (46 and 79 yards from Nelsen and Beathard), pushed my record over .500 for the first time. And our seventh victory, 39–14 over Stanford, jumped us into the top spot in the UPI poll. Nelsen was hot that day, throwing for two touchdowns and running for another. The next week AP ranked us first for a clean sweep of the polls.

But the biggest victories on the way to the national title and the Rose Bowl were over Iowa, Washington, Navy, UCLA and Notre Dame.

Two of the most remarkable moments came a month apart, against SMU and Illinois.

We played SMU in Dallas on a hot, humid September night, and I addressed the team confidently before the game.

"Gentlemen," I said, "let's show them something down here in the Southwest Conference. If you guys get off your asses up front and block like you should, Willie Brown will take the opening kickoff back for a touchdown."

Willie caught the kickoff on the eight, ran up the middle, cut right and sprinted 92 yards for a touchdown. It took 13 seconds. SMU collapsed, 33 to 3.

At Illinois, we had taken a 15–8 halftime lead on a 73-yard scoring pass from Beathard to Bedsole in the last 48 seconds of the first half, but the Illini were tenacious. Future All-Pro Dick Butkus was playing middle linebacker.

In the locker room I turned prophet again. "When we get the ball to start the second half," I said to the team, "we're going to run a 48-tear play on first down. If you all do exactly what you've been taught, and you, Beathard, get around the end and block Butkus, Brown will go 60 yards for a touchdown."

Willie did not exactly go 60, because the ball was put in play on our 27. But he did run 73 for a score. And Beathard did chop down Butkus. And we won by 12.

The Iowa victory in the third game was important, because it was an upset and the Hawkeyes' first shutout at home in 10 years, 7–0. It proved to me that we just might be on the way to becoming a great team. We didn't give up a single turnover, while our defense forced seven and set up the only touchdown, which Ron Heller of the Green unit scored on a 19-yard run. The touchdown followed a fumble recovery on the Iowa 24.

Our victory over Washington was the eventual Rose Bowl decider and the Huskies' only loss of the season. Since 1959, they had been the dominant team on the Coast under my buddy, Jim Owens. Our common opponent, Illinois, picked the Huskies "because they block and tackle harder."

With that in mind, I decided to play psychologist. Before the game I announced:

"Washington is stronger than us physically. Our only hope is to throw and keep throwing."

We had an explosive passing attack, and that made sense. I guess the Huskies believed me. While they watched for passes, we ran for 247 yards and shut them out, 14 to 0. Our two touchdown drives went 76 and 79 yards and consumed 22 plays, only three of them passes. Brown gained 99 yards, while Beathard ran five for one touchdown and threw a 12-yard pass to Bedsole for the other.

Owens praised us after the game. "I didn't figure anyone could run on my team," he said. To prove it, Washington blanked its next two opponents.

Meanwhile, I was facing a possible personal crisis. Before the Iowa game, when we were only 2-0, my eight-year-old daughter Terri asked me to buy the family a swimming pool. I must have been about the lowest paid major college coach in the country—my salary was only $16,500—and I couldn't have afforded one. But I said, "Oh, sure, Terri, if daddy wins all his games we'll get a pool."

After Washington, when we were 6-0, my son Johnny approached me in the locker room. "Daddy," he said, "Terri says to remind you about the pool."

That week, Johnny, Michele, Terri and Richie were out in the back yard digging with spoons.

After we beat Stanford the seventh week, Terri pressured me. "Dad," she said, "only three to go."

But the McKays and the pool were almost thrown for a loss in the eighth game by unheralded Navy and its astonishing sophomore quarterback named Roger Stau-

bach. Roger's big play that day was one he's made an
art form of since. He goes back to pass, gets trapped,
and then runs like hell. That day he ran like Red Grange.
All told he scrambled for 113 yards and completed 11
of 17 passes.

We helped out by fumbling the ball away four times
and were lucky to win. One of our fumbles was on the
opening kickoff, and one play later Staubach scrambled
18 yards to a touchdown and 6–0 lead. A short scoring
pass from Beathard to Bedsole, a 56-yard touchdown
run by Brown and a conversion gave us a 13–6 lead, but
late in the game we lost another fumble on our 44. Navy
marched to our five with three minutes to play. A touchdown and two-point conversion could win the game.

From the five, fullback Pat Donnelly burst free and
headed for our goal line. Just as he was arriving, Brown
and Beathard hit him and the ball squirted into the end
zone, where Gary Potter recovered it for us.

It was Donnelly's first fumble in 93 carries. And we
held them off, 13 to 6.

UCLA was next, and the pressure of a possible national championship was beginning to tell on our players.
We were 8-0 and voted into the Rose Bowl that week,
but the conference delayed announcement of the vote
until after the game with the Bruins. At halftime we
trailed 3–0.

This time I wasn't sure what to say. I thought of giving
the players a loud harangue on their mistakes, but I figured the polls had them under enough pressure. So I
took it easy, although I admit if I had had an old Knute
Rockne record, I would have played it.

In the third quarter we drove to UCLA's 20 and lost
the ball on a fumble. Later in the period, we got a break,
recovering a Bruin fumble on their 21. We were on the
UCLA three as the fourth quarter began. From there,

Ben Wilson fought to the one on fourth down and missed a first down by inches. The score remained 3–0.

UCLA punted on third down and Brown made the first of two plays that helped save our national championship. The first was a spinning 18-yard punt return that brought the ball back to UCLA's 26.

Two plays, however, gained two yards. On third and eight from the 24, Willie broke open on a pass pattern in the end zone, but Beathard didn't see him and threw incomplete.

I sent Nelsen in to try the same play on fourth down. Willie went downfield again and Nelsen threw for him on the UCLA two-yard line. The pass was very high, but somehow Willie went up a ladder of air and caught the ball just as his legs were jerked out from under him by UCLA defensive back Al Geverink. He came down on Geverink's back, clutching the ball in his right hand. It was an unbelievable catch.

And it destroyed UCLA. On first down, Wilson boomed two yards for the touchdown that put us ahead, 7–3, with ten minutes left, and the Bruins wilted. We drove 82 yards to score again with 35 seconds left and won, 14–3.

Louise Hunter, Corky's mother, hugged me after the game. "Whew, I'm glad that's over," she said. "I couldn't sleep all week, worrying about UCLA."

"But why?" I asked. "I didn't plan to use you."

Everyone breathed more easily the next week as we clinched the national championship by beating Notre Dame, 25–0, in a game I want to get into later.

So we had finished 10-0 as undisputed national champions, because both polls in 1962 concluded their voting before the bowl games.

The kids demanded their swimming pool.

"Well," I said, my fingers crossed, "don't lose interest

in my team now. Root us in once more against Wisconsin in the Rose Bowl, and we'll see about that pool."

A coach detects a difference in his players about three days before the Rose Bowl game when they start walking without their feet touching the ground. I don't think there's a team in the country that wouldn't come to the Rose Bowl, if it was invited. But the pressure, needless to say, is incredible. It hit me the first time I walked out and saw over 100,000 people in those stands.

The 1963 Rose Bowl was a dream matchup. We were ranked first, had an explosive offense and great defense. Wisconsin, with one loss, was ranked second, led the nation in scoring and also had a great defense. The Badgers had played top-ranked Northwestern midway through the season and beaten them by 31. They were favored by two over our national champions.

My God, what a game that was. It lasted only slightly less long than the War of 1812, winding up in foggy darkness. The head official, who had some of the most elaborate gestures I've ever seen, launched a long pantomime every time he assessed a penalty, which ate up a lot of time. At one point the game was even halted by a television technician who ran into our backfield while both teams were lined up. He stopped play for a commercial.

But the length of the game didn't take the edge off the excitement. At first, behind Beathard, who set a new Rose Bowl record with four touchdown passes, we took a great defense and blew it apart. We were leading 42–14 early in the fourth quarter, and every play we really worked on scored. Beathard threw two 13-yard touchdown passes, one on a gambling fourth-down tackle-eligible play to Ron Butcher, and nailed Bedsole with 23- and 57-yard scoring throws. I predicted the 57-yarder.

We were ahead 21–7 at halftime. "Gentlemen," I said, "we will start the second half with a slant-in pass to Bedsole. Hal, I want you to hold up at the line for two counts, take a few steps, cut back inside, and you'll catch the pass and run for a touchdown."

Football isn't that easy anymore. But, sure enough, on the first play Bedsole lined up as the split end on the left, cut inside like we told him, and Beathard rolled left, lobbed the ball to him, and Hal ran straight across the field and down the right sideline for the score.

No team I've ever had played better than that one until the loss of some key defensive players caught up with us, and all of a sudden we almost got beat by the passing of Ron VanderKelen.

Our two best defensive tackles, Kirner and Marv Marinovich, missed the second half. Kirner caught his finger in a luggage rack a few days before the game and almost cut it off. He was in for just a few plays. Marinovich got kicked out of the game late in the first half for a personal foul. Another top tackle, Mike Gale, couldn't play because of an injury in our last regular season game. And that 1962 substitution rule also trapped us with the wrong players in the game on several plays. But it was the loss of Kirner and Marinovich that really killed us.

Maybe we let down, too. Sometimes you ease up and can't turn it on again. We knew the Badgers were a strong fourth-quarter team—and they were. They scored 23 points in the last 12 minutes and lost only 42 to 37.

We kept trying to stop VanderKelen. We shot our linebackers, we ran him to hell and back, but he just went crazy. He completed 18 of 22 passes in the fourth quarter and 33 of 48 in the game for 401 yards. We did intercept three of his passes in the game, and two led to touchdowns.

However, at 42–14, Ron drove Wisconsin to the score that made it 42–21, a 13-yard run with 3:19 gone in the final period. They kicked off to us, but Wilson fumbled on first down, and they were right back on our 29. Five plays later, VanderKelen threw a four-yard scoring pass to make it 42–28 with 6:28 elapsed.

We charged back to their 32, but our drive died, and here came VanderKelen again—all the way to our four. But when he threw into the end zone, Brown intercepted.

On fourth down our center's snap sailed out of the end zone for a safety, and the score was 42–30 with just under three minutes left.

We kicked after the safety, and a long return landed the Badgers on our 43, from where VanderKelen attacked again, scoring in three plays. The third was a 19-yard pass with 1:19 left in the game. That made it 42–37, but we recovered their onside kick and finally ran out the clock.

From the criticism we got as we ran off the field, you would have thought we lost.

"Wisconsin!" I said like a swear word to my players after the game. "That's all they're talking about. In a few minutes the writers will be in here telling you men how lucky you were to pull this one out. Don't you ever believe it. You're the best damn team I ever saw. Our intention was to win today—and what does the scoreboard say?

"Who was picked to lose to the Big Ten powerhouse? We were. Ask the experts which team scored 42 points. You did, and you earned every one of them. Wisconsin was number two, and they lost."

Later, VanderKelen, who had been ignored in the pro draft, was deluged with offers.

I couldn't resist a comment on that irony.

"What a fine coach I am," I said. "Wisconsin's Milt

Bruhn had VanderKelen for four years and all the boy got was a college education. I had him only four quarters and got him $60,000."

And the McKays got their swimming pool. The alumni were so grateful that they bought us one.

But the athletic department wasn't so grateful. For winning the national championship I got only a $1,000 raise. Not until the Los Angeles Rams made their first offer to me in 1965 did I go over the heads of the athletic department to negotiate a separate contract with the president, Dr. Topping. Topping was always very fair to me. When he and I talked contract, he discovered that after six years as head coach, I was only making about $19,000 a year. He gave me a substantial raise.

Football was a different game when we won our next national championship in 1967. The two-platoon rule was back, players were bigger, and the quality of play better. Defense had become more refined, because there were now full-time defensive players. In 1967 our defense allowed only 87 points. Until 1972, it was our best defensive unit.

Our 10-1 record was the beginning of a three-year hot streak, resulting in a 29-2-2 record, final rankings of first, fourth and third and three straight Rose Bowls, giving us a record four straight.

We had also gone to Pasadena at the end of the season in 1966, but a three-game losing streak climaxed by a loss to Purdue in the bowl did not leave us with pleasant memories over the winter.

A new recruit had visited our losing Rose Bowl locker room to try and cheer us up. His name was O. J. Simpson.

Jay said to one of the players he knew:

"Don't worry about this loss. We'll be back next year."

He brought a host of talented players back with him. We had super defensive personnel, like ends Tim Rossovich and Jimmy Gunn, linebacker Adrian Young, middle guard Ralph Oliver and several good tackles. Young and Rossovich were All-Americans and safety Mike Battle was one the next year.

Outland Trophy winner Ron Yary at tackle led the offensive line, which also had two very good tight ends in Bob Klein and Bob Miller. World-record hurdler Earl McCullouch was at split end, Jimmy Lawrence was a versatile flanker, Steve Sogge gave us good leadership at quarterback, and there was Simpson, who simply gave us the national championship with a 64-yard touchdown run against UCLA.

O.J. averaged 154 yards a game rushing in 1967, topping 150 seven times, including a one-game high of 235 yards. When he sprained his foot against Oregon, reserve Steve Grady came in at tailback to run for 108 yards that day and 103 the next week against California. Even without O.J. the old I-formation kept working.

The two biggest games were the 24–7 defeat of Notre Dame, USC's first win at South Bend since 1939, and the 21–20 victory over UCLA that won everything.

But there were also key victories over Texas, Michigan State and Washington. Though I hate to mention it, there was also a depressing 3–0 loss to Oregon State, our last shutout.

Texas was fifth-ranked when the Longhorns came to the Coliseum for our second game, but O.J. rushed for 158 yards and we outfought them, 17 to 13, to move to second and third in the polls.

We became number one after beating Michigan State, 21–17, in the third game. My buddy, Duffy Daugherty, had gone unbeaten with the Spartans the year before, but had been upset in his 1967 opener.

"Duffy, what happened?" I asked on the phone before we met.

"John," said Duffy, "let's just say that against you we'll find out whether we have character on our team or just plain characters."

Duffy's Spartans had so much character that we were lucky to escape with our lives. On a cold day in East Lansing, Sogge hit 14 of 16 passes and O.J. gained 190 yards, but the winning points came in a most unusual way. Simpson threw a seven-yard scoring pass to Lawrence midway through the third quarter.

Michigan State had a touchdown nullified by an offensive interference penalty, but we gave them a free one by fumbling a punt away on our one-yard line.

The Michigan State victory was the first of five road games in seven weeks. Another was the big victory over Notre Dame, which pushed our record to 5-0 and will be discussed later.

After Notre Dame we were on the road the very next week for a showdown with Washington. The 13th-ranked Huskies were 4-1 and had not allowed a touchdown in the second half.

The crowd noise in the Seattle stadium was incredible as the game began. Washington's band was pounding drums, it was drizzling, the field was slippery, and on our first series Simpson ran 86 yards for a touchdown. The noise level dropped.

Two field goals cut our lead to 7–6 by the late third quarter, but two field goals were all the points our defense allowed. And shortly after, Battle's interception set us up on Washington's 32. From there we moved to the Husky ten, where on the second play of the fourth quarter, Simpson made one quick cut and ran the ten for another touchdown.

For the afternoon O.J. carried for 235 yards and also

wound up the scoring with a 16-yard pass to McCullouch. We won 23-6.

We were 8-0 when we were dealt that 3–0 upset by Oregon State. The ground-hugging Beavers had lost twice, once in and once out of the league, but in the last three weeks they had first upset unbeaten and second-ranked Purdue and then tied unbeaten UCLA, the new second-ranked team. We had to play them in Corvallis, Oregon, where it had rained most of the week. It was before the development of artificial turf, and there had been no tarp covering the field.

After missing a game and a half with his sprained foot, O.J. slithered for 188 yards in the mud but no touchdowns, and we lost on a second-quarter field goal. In our other ten games, including 49–0 and 30–0 victories, we averaged 26 points, but none of them did us any good that day.

"We performed well most of the game," I told the press. "But they performed better. Yes, the field was wet, but if we had been the better team we would have won."

On the way home many of the players were crying on the plane. Some of them swore the Oregon State field goal was no good.

"Listen," I said. "If the referee puts both hands over his head, he's not praying to the Lord. And the referee put up both hands after that kick."

Danny Scott, our fullback, came over to me and asked if I thought we still had a chance for the Rose Bowl and the national title.

"You'd better believe it," I said.

The same afternoon UCLA had smothered Washington, 48 to 0, to become the nation's top-ranked team. We fell to third. Next week would be the showdown. It was USC against UCLA for the national championship, the Rose Bowl and ownership of Los Angeles. And we had lost two in a row to the Bruins. They were 7-0-1 and we were 8-1.

UCLA was a versatile team, led by Heisman Trophy winner Gary Beban at quarterback, and All-American linebacker Don Manning on defense. The Bruins went into the game with two big advantages: they could clinch the Rose Bowl with a tie, and they had a tremendous long-distance kicker in Zenon Andrusyshyn.

As we studied films, however, we discovered that Zenon's soccer-style place kicks were line-drive, low-trajectory shots that barely cleared the line of scrimmage. So by game time we had adjusted our defense against his kicks, overloading with five men on the right side of our defensive line that he had to aim through. Whenever he kicked 6–8 Billy Hayhoe leaped up in the path of the ball. The tackles and middle guard were instructed to charge through the gaps in the Bruin line with their hands up and keep them up, even if they were on the ground or blocked. The linemen who didn't rush joined Hayhoe in jumping with their hands in the air.

On that memorable Coliseum Saturday afternoon, Hayhoe blocked one of Andrusyshyn's field-goal attempts, Tony Terry knocked down another, and the rattled Bruin kicker missed still another. More important, Hayhoe slightly tipped Andrusyshyn's third conversion attempt, which sailed wide to the left.

Of all the great games we've had with UCLA, this one remains my favorite. The lead changed hands four times, and the score was tied twice. Both teams played fanatically.

For example, Jimmy Gunn, our sophomore defensive end, tore ligaments in his knee in the first quarter—he later needed surgery—and sat out most of the game. Although he had trouble running, we didn't realize how badly he was hurt, and when he insisted on returning in the fourth quarter with us ahead by a point, we sent him back in. On that bad leg Gunn rushed Beban and threw him for losses three times in the last five minutes as UCLA struggled to catch up.

Although Beban—who was playing with torn rib cartilage himself—passed for 301 yards and two touchdowns, we sacked him for 80 yards in losses. And, on the last play of the first quarter, cornerback Pat Cashman picked off Gary's pass in the left flat and ran untouched 55 yards to score for a 7–7 tie.

In the second quarter I called a play I felt would surprise UCLA. It was a reverse to McCullouch, who had been switched to flanker for the injured Lawrence, and Earl ran 52 yards to set up the first of Simpson's two touchdowns. Number one by O.J. was a 13-yarder that some coaches have said is the greatest run they've ever seen. When Jay took Sogge's handoff, he disappeared into a crowd of blue Bruin jerseys, but he broke six different tackles to make the end zone. So we led at the half, 14–7, and I thought we had established momentum. We had taken away their running game. In fact, they rushed for only 43 yards all day.

Beban's passing was another story. He struck back with a 53-yard scoring bomb in the third quarter and a 20-yard touchdown pass with 3:19 gone in the fourth quarter for a 20–14 UCLA lead. It was after that last touchdown that Andrusyshyn, assisted by Hayhoe, missed the conversion.

The Bruins kicked off, and I sent senior Toby Page in at quarterback to replace Sogge. I wanted to shake some life into our attack. Simpson, who was to gain 177 yards on 30 carries, had been having a good day, despite a curious ploy by UCLA. Every time the Bruins tackled Jay they helped him up immediately. I guess they didn't want him to lie on the ground and rest.

"That didn't bother me," said O.J. later. "I was glad they helped me up. I was getting a little tired."

Not too tired to win a national championship.

A minute after UCLA's final touchdown, we were faced with a third-and-eight play on our 36. I called a pass, but ordered Page to audibilize to Simpson if they double-covered our receivers. Toby lined up the team, looked at UCLA's defense, and handed off to Simpson.

A good back might have made the eight yards for a first down. O.J. made it to the Rose Bowl.

He faked to the right side, then cut left, getting good blocks from guard Steve Lehmer and tackle Mike Taylor. He twisted through a crowd of Bruins as end Ron Drake and center Dick Allmon also threw blocks, shot down the left sideline dodging more tacklers—he almost fell once—and then, right in front of me, exploded toward the middle of the field and was gone. McCullouch went with him, screening off UCLA's safetyman, who tried in vain to pursue.

As O.J. touched the end zone after running 64 yards, my mouth fell open. "That's the damndest run I've ever seen," I whispered to myself.

Rikki Aldridge kicked the extra point, we held UCLA off, and we won the national championship, 21 to 20.

After UCLA the Rose Bowl was somewhat anticlimactic, as we dominated an Indiana team that was 9-1, winning 14–3. We outgained the Hoosiers by 128 yards, and it was an impressive win because we had lost three starting linemen before the game and two more in the game itself.

Nevertheless, we choked off Indiana's fine quarterback, Harry Gonso, with only nine completions in 25 attempts, and were on our way to breaking the game apart early in the second quarter when fullback Danny Scott lost a fumble at the Indiana goal line when we had a 7–0 lead. After that we seemed to lose our offensive momentum.

It was a modest afternoon for O.J. He scored both touchdowns from two and eight yards out and ran for 128 yards.

Since the alumni had given me a swimming pool for winning USC's last national championship, I was asked what I expected now.

"I am hoping," I said, "to get the light fixed on the front porch."

I have always preached that it is vital during a game to keep calm. Our coaches don't rant and rave when we're behind, and so the players stay cool, too. This coolness is supposed to be one of the positive things young men get out of competitive sports. You continue to do the job, rather than going to pieces.

It's human nature when you fall behind to start trying wild plays. But we know what we've practiced all week will work best, and we think it's a mistake to come out of the huddle throwing crazy punches. We just keep doing what we've done in practice.

This Trojan calmness was never more evident than in 1968 and 1969 when our teams won 19 games, lost one, tied two and went to the Rose Bowl two more times. But we won or tied 12 times with fourth-quarter rallies. We had to come from behind in seven of our ten last-quarter victories. In the other three we broke ties.

Our players got as much out of their ability as any group of guys could have, but they had to work like hell to do it. We even received a new nickname, "Cardiac Kids."

The Cardiac Kids gave fans the most heart trouble in 1969 when they won twice in the last minute, once in the last two minutes and once with three minutes left.

They kept their poise, didn't panic and didn't beat themselves.

1968 was O.J.'s final year for the Trojans, and we had only 15 lettermen to go with him. It was the youngest team I had ever fielded.

Since we had virtually no one to carry the ball but Simpson, we fed it to him 35 times a game, and he responded with 171 yards a game, 23 touchdowns, 26 pass receptions and won the Heisman Trophy.

Normally, we don't want one player to do everything, and O.J. wouldn't have carried so often on our 1972 team, for example. But in 1968 I knew that if he didn't do it, it wasn't going to get done. We planned to try and overpower people with a fantastic athlete and good blocking.

Despite the attention focused on Simpson, there was no jealousy on the team. O.J. lifted the other players up. He helped them get more publicity, inspired them, and convinced them they were good. Once you're on top, you don't want to fall.

With the threat of Simpson freezing the defense, Sogge threw enough to keep opponents loose and did an excellent job, completing 59 percent of his passes for 1,454 yards. He spread them around to Simpson, Lawrence, Terry DeKraii, Bobby Chandler, Sam Dickerson and tight ends Bob Klein and Bob Miller.

The last half of the season we were ranked number one again, until we rallied to tie Notre Dame in the final game and fell to second. We finished up 9-1-1, after losing in the Rose Bowl.

But mostly it was the story of Simpson. Minnesota coach Murray Warmath summed up the exasperation felt by other coaches, after he had watched Jay run for 236 yards, score all four touchdowns and catch six passes, as we came from behind to win, 29–20. Informed that Simpson had carried 39 times, Warmath looked up wearily and said:

"I thought it was 400 times."

We also came from behind to beat Stanford (27–24) and Oregon State (17–13) and broke ties in the last five minutes to beat Washington (14–7) and Oregon (20–13). We had to stop Washington inside our one-yard line, before starting our winning touchdown drive. Oregon wound up on our eight in the last few seconds, missing three straight passes in the end zone.

Our biggest intersectional victory, ironically, came easily, as we beat Miami, 28 to 3. We had a lot of motivation for that one. In 1966, Miami had given us a pretty good kicking around—when we were unbeaten—and we just stood there and took it. Not only did we lose, but eight of our players got hurt, including punter Rich Leon, who had his leg shattered when Miami players crashed into him.

In 1968 Miami, like USC, had won the first two games, allowing only 1.5 yards a rush. They had a super defensive end, Ted Hendricks, who had broken up all our sweeps in 1966. Ted was listed at 220 pounds, which was nonsense. He must have weighed 220 at birth.

So I installed a new formation to stop him. Instead of using two wide receivers, we replaced one with Klein, whom we moved in as a wingback. I had noticed that if blockers played close to Hendricks, he could ward them off with his long arms. But if the blocker hit him from a couple of yards away, he could get to his legs.

Klein popped Hendricks on every play and tied him in knots, O.J. ran for 163 yards, Sogge completed 11 of 17, and we breezed.

Then there were the victories over Stanford and Oregon State. Stanford, our fourth opponent, had future

Heisman Trophy winner Jim Plunkett, who waged a tremendous battle with Simpson. Plunkett passed for 247 yards and built leads of 7–3, 17–10 and 24–17, before O.J. brought us back.

Simpson came into the game with a very sore left leg, and had been held out of practice all week, except for light jogging. When he emerged from the locker room the leg was tight, and he was limping so badly that two assistant coaches helped support him.

Therefore, what he did bordered on the incredible. He ran 47 times for 220 yards, ripped off scoring dashes of 3, 4 and 46 yards and threw the 15-yard pass that set up Ron Ayala's winning field goal in the fourth quarter, as we won, 27–24.

"How do you feel, Jay?" I said after the game.

"Coach, the leg feels a lot better now," he said. "But it did seem to throw my timing off early in the game. Sometimes I was stuttering around out there."

Some stutterer.

We clinched the Rose Bowl bid when we were 7-0 by beating 1967 nemesis Oregon State in the Coliseum. The Beavers had lost a pair of nonconference games by a point, but were 4-0 in the league, had won six straight games and had a fullback named Bill Enyart, a thousand-yard rusher. Bill had acquired the nickname "Earthquake."

But our defense held Enyart to 68 yards, while Simpson, lugging the ball 47 times again, gained 238, including a 40-yard touchdown sprint that wrapped up the victory.

We were behind 7–0 going into the fourth quarter, making it seven straight quarters the Beavers had blanked us. But early in the period, Gerry Shaw intercepted a pass and returned to their 36. From there we moved to the 22, where Sogge passed to Terry DeKraii for the tying touchdown.

It was some play by Terry. One of his hands had been split open by a line-drive pass in practice, and it took 14 stitches to close the cut. He grabbed that ball with his hand all taped up and bleeding.

An Ayala field goal and O.J.'s long run made it 17–7 with 1:20 left in the game. But on the first play after our kickoff, Beaver quarterback Steve Preece dropped back and threw a perfect 74-yard touchdown pass. We had to recover their ensuing onside kick—which seemed to bounce around forever—to win, 17 to 13.

The Rose Bowl was another classic matchup. Our opponent, Ohio State, was also unbeaten, and thanks to our tie with Notre Dame, had edged us for first in both polls. But since we were second, a victory would give us two straight national titles, at least according to AP, which votes after the bowls.

Unfortunately, Simpson was under heavy pressure before the game. His wife had presented him with their first child, a baby daughter, and then he missed much of the practice period flying around the country collecting awards. When he returned home after two weeks of travel, he admitted he was tired.

Ohio State was an excellent team with a lot of sophomores that kept improving. It was the quickest Big Ten team I had seen to that time—especially on defense.

We jumped off to a 10–0 lead, the touchdown coming in the second quarter, as Simpson took a pitchout around left end and cut back against the flow of tacklers to go 80 yards for a touchdown.

But Ohio State tied us by halftime and won, 27 to 16. We were miserable in the second half, turning the ball over five times. Fumbles by Sogge and Simpson led directly to Ohio State scores, as Rex Kern took advantage of the mistakes to throw two touchdown passes.

If we hadn't given up the ball so often in our own territory, I think we would have beaten them. But when you do that, you get beat.

Simpson's remarkable career at USC ended with 171 yards on 28 carries and eight pass receptions.

The 1969 team belonged to sophomore quarterback Jimmy Jones, tailback Clarence Davis and an aggressive defensive line known as the Wild Bunch. This was perhaps my most interesting team and a pretty good one, although I believe it just wasn't any better than many of its opponents. Yet we went unbeaten, powered past Michigan in the Rose Bowl for a 10-0-1 record and wound up as probably the most maligned unbeaten team in history.

We had one of the better defenses of the decade, but the second version of the Cardiac Kids were too hit-and-miss on offense and often found themselves in a hole. Six of our victories were by 10 points or less.

But those kids did something very impressive. They were 4-0-1 against other schools in the nation's top 15. They beat Michigan and UCLA, which were in the top ten, tied Notre Dame, another top-ten member, and beat Stanford and Nebraska, which made the top 15.

Although he was a sophomore, I thought Jones did an outstanding job at quarterback. Of course there were those who said if we'd had another quarterback maybe all those games wouldn't have been so close. We'll never find out. But when the games were on the line Jimmy didn't panic. Under pressure he threw extremely well. Of his 88 completions, 13 went for touchdowns.

And Davis, our new tailback, rushed for over 150 yards four times and totaled 1,351.

Two members of the Wild Bunch, end Jimmy Gunn and tackle Al Cowlings, were 1969 All-Americans, and the other end, Charles Weaver, made it in 1970. Other members of the unit were middle guard Bubba Scott and tackle Tody Smith, Bubba Smith's younger brother.

The "Wild Bunch" nickname just happened, inspired by the movie of the same name. Assistant coach Marv Goux, who handles the defensive line, looked at his guys one day in practice and said they were the meanest and wildest group he'd ever seen.

"That's us, coach," grinned Cowlings, "the Wild Bunch."

Jones, Davis and the Bunch had to come from behind to beat Stanford (26–24), Georgia Tech (29–18), California (14–9) and UCLA (14–12), all in the last three minutes. They also broke a tie in the fourth quarter to beat Washington (16–7).

They did beat Nebraska on the road more easily, 31–21, in a season opener that was memorable, because it was one of only two Cornhusker losses in three years. Playing in his first varsity game, Jones threw a pair of touchdown passes and built a 28–7 lead.

I remember the game was marked by an extraordinary number of penalties against us, and I was furious as I walked off the field at halftime, even though we led. Nebraska's coach, Bob Devaney, came up on my right side.

"Hey, John," he said, as he strolled past, "how do you like my brother's officiating?"

The Stanford game, our fourth of the season, topped even the 1968 duel between Simpson and Plunkett. The lead changed hands seven times, and this time Plunkett passed for 296 yards and two touchdowns, as we fell behind 6–0, 12–0, 15–14, 21–20, and finally, 24–23, before we beat them on a last-second field goal, 26–24.

One of the passes Plunkett wished he hadn't thrown was returned 57 yards by Tyrone Hudson for our second touchdown just before halftime.

But Jim's 67-yard pass late in the game set up the field goal that gave Stanford the lead with a minute and three seconds left. The Stanford players thought they had won. They danced and hugged each other all over the field. It looked like a love-in.

This was the game I referred to in the first chapter, when I sent Davis off tackle on a fourth-and-five play at our 20 with 41 seconds left. He made seven for a first down, and Jones completed passes of 28, 17 and 11 to set up Ayala's 34-yard field goal with no time left. It was a brilliant game for Clarence, as he squirmed, twisted and hurdled for 198 yards on 39 carries.

There was an interesting play in our come-from-behind defeat of Georgia Tech. We were down by three points with three minutes left, when Jones faded to pass at our 45. Immediately he was in trouble. He scrambled and scrambled and scrambled and finally threw a 55-yard touchdown pass to Sam Dickerson that won the game.

In the dressing room I asked Jimmy when he had seen Sam break open.

"I didn't," he said. "I just knew somebody had to be open on that side of the field, so I threw."

The following Saturday we beat California with only 57 seconds left, when Davis dove a yard to culminate a 55-yard drive by Jones. Jimmy set it up with a pass to Bobby Chandler, who held the ball even though he had a broken left hand.

In a dramatic repeat of 1967, the season came down to the UCLA game. Both teams were unbeaten, with 8-0-1 records, but this time we could have clinched the Rose Bowl with a tie because the Bruins had a league tie, and our league record was perfect.

Unlike us, they had beaten most of their opponents with relative ease—Tommy Prothro called it his best team—and were favored by two. Sharp-shooting Dennis Dummit, who passed for 2,000 yards that season, was the quarterback.

Three minutes into the first quarter, Dummit pitched out to halfback Greg Jones on a third-and-one play, and Jones threw a 41-yard touchdown pass. Since he couldn't afford a tie, Prothro gambled for a two-point conversion, but Weaver knocked down Dummit's pass.

For the next 54 minutes the Wild Bunch dominated the game. They were devastating. The Bunch threw Dummit for losses nine times, including three in a row at one point, intercepted two of his passes, broke up two more, caused three fumbles and forced Dummit into three other interceptions. Previously he had only five interceptions in nine games. He really hated Cowlings, who sacked him five times.

We weren't moving much better. Jones missed all nine of his first-half passes, and we scored just one touchdown, a 13-yard run by Davis. Ayala's conversion gave us a 7–6 halftime lead.

It was 7–6 for a long, long time. With only five minutes left in the game, Dummit suddenly connected on a 57-yard pass, and with three minutes left, he threw a seven-yarder for a touchdown. UCLA led for the Rose Bowl, 12 to 7. Dummit again tried to pass for two, but the Wild Bunch broke it up again by sacking him.

So we were behind, as usual, and, as usual, Jones found his arm. He completed three passes in a row, and we had a first down on the Bruin 43. Jimmy narrowly missed a bomb to the end zone, but on fourth down we were still at the 43. His desperate pass for Dickerson on fourth down sailed over Sam's head at the 32.

As it did, however, a Bruin cornerback tackled Dickerson, and as he fell, so did the referee's handkerchief for interference. The Cardiac Kids had a reprieve on the 32. And a first down.

I knew what play I wanted. All season Dickerson had been our most explosive receiver, averaging 20 yards a catch. Sam's best pattern was a simple streak to the corner of the end zone.

UCLA figured we might try the play, and they shot both linebackers to Dickerson's side on first down. But fullback Charlie Evans knocked down one, and Davis picked up the other. It was one on one, Dickerson and a UCLA safety deep in the corner of the end zone, and Jones laid the ball up in the darkness. Sam made a tremendous catch at the back of the end zone, just before going out of bounds, and we had exploded again for a 13–12 lead with 1:32 left.

Our team went crazy. They all ran to the end zone, where they were jumping up and down, hugging Sam, dancing and yelling. I was yelling too—yelling for a time out. This was no time for a celebration.

UCLA still had Zenon Andrusyshyn as a kicker, and I wanted to tell my players to go for two points, instead of one. We could have lost on a field goal, 15 to 14.

But the kicking unit lined up automatically, without hearing me, and Ayala kicked the conversion for a 14–12 lead. I settled for 14–12, because we won with it—our third straight victory over UCLA.

"I've checked my heart," I said to Corky after the game, "and I don't have one."

So we headed for our fourth straight Rose Bowl, where Michigan, which had upset the so-called super team, Ohio State, was waiting and favored by four. We were 9-0-1 and ranked fifth. The Wolverines were ranked seventh and had an 8-2 record.

We went into the Rose Bowl game without our All-American offensive tackle, Sid Smith, who injured a knee against UCLA, but Michigan had to play without its coach, Bo Schembechler. Bo had suffered a mild heart attack a couple of days before the game.

Certainly Bo's loss must have affected his team, but I don't know if anyone could have dented the Wild Bunch that day. To counter Michigan's running attack, which had been averaging 277 yards a game, we added Tony Terry for a six-man line, and held the Wolverines to 162 on the ground.

We beat a team that had been averaging 35 points a game, 10 to 3, when Jones threw a 33-yard touchdown pass to Bobby Chandler with two minutes left in the third quarter. The ball was thrown just over the middle, but Bobby spun away at the 20 from the only Michigan tackler who had a shot at him.

Afterward, our unbeaten team, which finished up third in the country, attracted the attention of President Nixon, who phoned his congratulations. I offered him the Wild Bunch.

"If you ever need any bodyguards," I told him, "I'll send my five guys to you."

It was a long way from the Cardiac Kids of 1969 to the national champions of 1972, who averaged 39 points a game and never trailed in the second half. USC, 1972, was a great team to coach. They absolutely refused to make a mental mistake, never had a down game and were behind only three of 12 opponents.

Our closest margin of victory was nine points over Stanford. Only two college teams in the previous 25 years did better than that.

In going 12-0, our kids scored 467 points, averaged

432 yards a game, intercepted 28 passes, limited their opponents to an average gain per rush of 2.5 and never gave up a run longer than 29 yards.

We were so dominating that I found myself in an ironic situation. In 1968 and 1969 I defended the team because we didn't beat people easily enough. In 1972, I was accused of pouring it on—particularly when we scored over 50 points in three straight games.

But I wouldn't consciously run up a score. Even if I disliked the coach, I don't hate the other team's players. I'm a father, and they're all 18, 19 or 20 years old, like my son. Scores mount, because the other team's offense gambles and makes mistakes, particularly interceptions, or because the other defense gives up when it feels it has no chance to win.

If a defensive back picks off a pass with a clear path to the end zone, I can't stop him. I can't stop one of our eager young runners from trying to go all the way either.

In 1972 we had the perfect blend of experience and youth, with great leadership from the seniors.

We had super quarterbacking with senior Mike Rae and sophomore Pat Haden. Rae, the starter, did as good a job as anyone I've ever had, completing 57 percent of his passes for 1,754 yards. Haden came off the bench to throw seven scoring passes, led us to victory in a game when we were deadlocked and was tremendous for team morale. Pat, who is now the best passer I've ever coached, always performed when asked and didn't say a word when he didn't play.

Anthony Davis was a fantastic sophomore tailback, and there were Rod McNeill and Allen Carter besides. All-American fullback Sam Cunningham was the best blocking back I've ever seen and startled everybody with the easy way he dove for touchdowns. No defensive line was too high for Sam to dive over.

We had our best offensive line ever, including All-Americans at tight end in Charles Young and at tackle in Pete Adams. Five members of the line had been together for three years. There were several skilled outside receivers, including Lynn Swann, sprinter Edesel Garrison and sophomore Johnny McKay.

Our defense was the quickest I've ever watched, college or pro. All-American tackle John Grant was so smart he could come out of the game and explain exactly what the other team's offense was trying to do, right down to the theory. The other tackle, Jeff Winans, and cornerback Charles Hinton, an ex-running back, were the two most improved players on the team. There were half a dozen excellent linebackers, including All-American Richard Wood, who runs the 40 in 4.5 and catches halfbacks from behind, and a quick, ball-hungry secondary, including safety Artimus Parker, who was an All-American the next season.

Despite the talent, I was a little worried about our defense before the season, because only four starters returned. So we kept it simple.

Our biggest intersectional victory was our first, a 31–10 "upset" of fourth-ranked Arkansas in the opening game at Little Rock. At the time it was Arkansas that was talking of a national title, but I had a feeling we might surprise them.

On a hot and humid night we began badly, fumbling the opening kickoff, and they recovered and kicked a field goal. But the next time Arkansas scored, we were ahead, 24 to 3.

Rae completed 18 of 24 passes in his first start, kicked the first of his eight field goals, scored a touchdown and handed off to McNeill for two more. Returning from a year out for hip surgery, Rod rushed for 117 yards.

Arkansas's fine quarterback, Joe Ferguson, made a

prophetic statement after the game, which I read on Sunday. "If USC doesn't go undefeated," said Joe, "then something's wrong."

I wasn't about to agree with that, but I do admit a coach can tell after one game if he's going to have a good team. The next week I told the press:

"We have as good a chance as anyone to win the national title."

We were immediately ranked first in one poll and second in the other. After our 51 to 6 victory over Oregon State in the second game we were ranked number one in both polls for the rest of the season.

A memorable play in the Oregon State game was my son Johnny's first college scoring catch. He bounced all the way from the end zone to the sideline where he jumped into the arms of Craig Fertig, who had recruited him. Johnny had a very fine sophomore year, catching 26 passes, and I don't think he dropped a ball all season that he should have caught. He played even better than I expected—and I expected a lot. We both realized he had to convince the rest of the squad he deserved to play.

Before Michigan State, another 51–6 victory, a rumor circulated that Rae had broken his leg. Since Mike had completed 69 percent of his passes the first three weeks, this would have been a big story.

As I left the practice field, a reporter rushed up and asked me if we were hiding the injury.

"I just watched Mike run the offense for 90 minutes," I said, "and if he has a broken leg, he's hiding it well."

Rae never was hurt, and we had just one serious injury all season—the loss of starting offensive tackle Allen Gallaher early in the year. The lack of injuries was another big plus in 1972.

Besides Arkansas, the only other teams we were behind were Illinois, 7–0 and 14–7 (we won 55–20) and Stanford, 7–0 and 10–7. The Stanford game was the most controversial of the season.

It was our fifth, and both teams were unbeaten. They had defeated us twice in a row and gone to the Rose Bowl both years. But it seemed like every time we had beaten them in the past—and we won ten straight times —I'd read where some Stanford player said we were lucky and not that good.

In 1965 we won, 14 to 0, and their quarterback, Dave Lewis said, "There's no doubt, whatever, that we were the better team."

I didn't see how we could lose if we weren't scored on—unless they put a new rule in the book.

It happened again in 1972. We led 30 to 13 with two minutes left and won, 30 to 21. We outgained them, 407 yards to 183, and had 12 more first downs. So, right after the game, a Stanford defensive back said:

"SC ain't shit—and you can put that in the paper."

Because of statements like that over the years, plus treatment we had received from Stanford players and fans, I made one of my more infamous statements after this game.

"I'd like to beat Stanford by 2,000 points," I snapped. "They're the worst winners I've ever gone up against. They have no class."

People really jumped on me for that. They said *I* was the worst winner of all time. But I had a good reason to be furious. It went back a few years.

I had been going to Stanford as a player and coach since 1948, and one thing had always remained the same. Because the dressing rooms are about a mile from the stadium, the players would meet for pregame and half-time talks right there in the stadium. The visitors went into a room back in a tunnel, where fans couldn't bother them. The home team gathered in an area that was more out in the open.

In 1970, when we played at Stanford and lost, their team took the tunnel, and we had to meet out in the open. We were told the meeting areas had been changed. When I tried to talk to my team before the game, the Stanford band stood next to us and played. I had to shout to be heard. The same thing happened at halftime, and we might just as well have sat there and eaten oranges. After the game, members of the crowd threw rocks at us.

I felt the harassment by the band had to be planned. Their coach, John Ralston, must have been trying to gain an unfair advantage by cheap, off-the-field tactics. The game should be decided from goal line to goal line. But here they were putting our team in danger and encouraging a riot.

In 1971 Stanford came to Los Angeles and I learned later that when the two teams filed in and out of the Coliseum, some of their white players made racial insults to some of our black players.

So I was already mad as hell when we went north in 1972. Before the game we were out in the same damn meeting area. First the band blocked our path to the field. Then they played again when I tried to talk. They blocked an end zone when we tried to warm up. I had to stop assistant coach Marv Goux from charging them. At halftime, while USC's band marched on the field, Stanford's stayed next to us and played again.

After we had won the crucial game, 30 to 21, I felt our team might be in for some trouble if we stayed in the stadium. So I decided we would leave and walk that mile to the dressing rooms. It was an uneasy decision.

In the old days, when we had the room in the tunnel, we simply sat there and waited until the crowd filed out.

But as we walked this time, fans swore at us viciously:

"You no-good, nigger-loving, son of a bitch, McKay. You win because you've got all the niggers."

My youngest son, Richie, was walking next to me crying. Our players were seething. But we held our tempers. I didn't explode until I met the press.

No one, I thought, is going to say those things about my players. If I don't say anything, why should they ever stick up for me? But I was so mad I didn't explain it well, and it came out like sour grapes. So everyone up and down the Coast wrote and said I was at fault.

Swann, who is black and was walking about four yards away from me, said later:

"Coach, I don't hate people, but when they act like that it causes you to hate them. And I don't want to hate anyone. Why are the fans up here so belligerent? Why can't they just leave it as an athletic contest?"

Well, from now on when we go to Stanford we'll dress at our hotel, bus to the stadium, demand the meeting room in the tunnel, get on the bus at the end of the game and return to the hotel to dress. I won't have my players insulted by fans like that anymore.

I never held the players or Stanford's new coach, Jack Christiansen, responsible for those statements in 1972. They were no more responsible than we're responsible for our fans and alumni.

In fact, I like Christiansen, and in 1973 when we beat Stanford in the last few seconds in the Coliseum, some of their players came to our locker room to congratulate us. Relations were good that season, and I hope it's a good omen.

The two games after Stanford in 1972 were quiet, easy

victories, but the eighth game—against my alma mater, Oregon—was a little nervous. Haden and Davis saved us. It was the day A.D. emerged as a superstar.

In Eugene, rain had made the AstroTurf as slick as ice, and the game was a sliding match. The wind was blowing, the ball was wet, the air was cold, and Rae fumbled five times and lost three.

The score was still 0–0 with nine minutes gone in the third quarter—the latest stage all year in which we hadn't taken the lead for good. I sent Haden in at quarterback and he lined up the team on the Oregon 48. On first down he pitched to Davis, who began a power sweep to the left. Cunningham and reserve flanker Dave Boulware threw big blocks, Davis brushed off a couple of tacklers and suddenly he was in the clear. It was a footrace and he won, going 48 yards for a 6–0 lead. Young led a swarm of Trojans who embraced him in the end zone.

On our very next play—after Oregon failed to move —we got the ball on our 45. Again Haden pitched to Davis going left, and this time Anthony turned the end, got another block from Cunningham, cut across field and sprinted down the right sideline for another touchdown. After running 55 yards, he bumped the wall at the back of the end zone and fell exhausted. He wasn't injured, but Oregon was dead at 12–0. We won, 18 to 0, and Davis finished with 206 yards on 25 carries.

When we destroyed a good Washington State team, 44 to 3, with an almost perfect performance the next week, Cougar coach Jim Sweeney said:

"John, you're not the number one team in the country. The Miami Dolphins are better."

With a 9-0 record we had two weeks to prepare for still another Rose Bowl showdown with UCLA. In the intervening week, the Bruins were upset by Washington, but still took an 8-2 record into our game. Under conference rules they could have gone to the Rose Bowl by beating us.

UCLA was a great challenge for our defense, which had yielded just one touchdown in the previous three games. We were allowing 75 yards rushing a game and UCLA was averaging 361. They were also averaging 35 points a game, and their wishbone had broken off nine touchdown runs of 30 yards or longer.

Before the game a sign was posted in our locker room which read: "Can UCLA Beat USC By Running?" Underneath, someone had scrawled, "No!"

And they couldn't. They gained 198 yards on the ground, but every time James McAlister or Kermit Johnson would break clear for a step or two, Richard Wood or Charles Anthony or James Sims or Dale Mitchell would catch them almost instantly. The tackles, John Grant and Jeff Winans, and middle guard Monte Doris closed off the middle. They could never block Grant. And the defensive backfield charged up quickly to help out. UCLA's longest run was 20 yards.

Davis almost outgained their backfield by himself, rushing for 178 yards with nine runs in double figures, including a 23-yarder for our first touchdown in the 24–7 victory.

Rae quarterbacked the team smoothly, completing 7 of 12 passes, running for one touchdown and kicking a field goal. McNeill scored the other touchdown. It was 17 to 7 at halftime, and the defense never let up.

This was an exciting night for the seniors, who were finally going to the Rose Bowl, after two successive failures. Young paraded around the locker room with a long-stemmed rose.

Two weeks later we beat Notre Dame, 45 to 23, to

clinch UPI's version of the national title. Since AP now waits until after the bowl games to pick its national champion, Woody Hayes of Ohio State, our Rose Bowl opponent, said his team should be number one if they beat us.

I got fed up with Woody and everyone else who argued that point. Although Ohio State (9-1) was ranked third, they had lost by a touchdown to Michigan State, a team we had beaten by 45. Everyone else in the country had at least one loss, including second-ranked Oklahoma, and I just couldn't see how losing the Rose Bowl game could deprive us of anyone's version of the national title after the kind of year we had had. Only if several undefeated teams go into the bowls does a late poll have any real meaning. Besides, I already had flown around the country accepting awards like the MacArthur Bowl for winning the national championship, in addition to the UPI award.

Woody Hayes is an excellent coach, but he's so damn cantankerous. He does exactly what he wants and ignores everyone else. At the traditional Rose Bowl luncheon a couple of days before the game, Woody was introduced first. After he spoke and answered a few questions, I was introduced. As I walked to the microphone, Woody walked out of the room.

"I have to go back to work," he snapped. "Put John's words on tape for me."

I figured he might do something rude like that. It was a stupid ploy to shake me up. But he didn't have to tackle me. He had to tackle Davis.

The game also took on greater significance because of a statement I had made, and the inevitable criticism that followed. I said playing in the Rose Bowl is a reward for our efforts all season, and we'll treat it that way. We're not going to scrimmage before the game—we once

lost a starting guard in a pre–Rose Bowl scrimmage—
and we'll practice just once a day and use only 13 of our
allotted 16 practice days. I said I wanted to win, but if
we lost, it wouldn't be the most important defeat of my
life.

According to my experience—and this was my sixth
Rose Bowl—this was the best way to approach the game.
All teams over the holidays are flat anyway. They're
thinking of Christmas and girl friends and don't start
getting edgy and ready to play until December 26. I gave
my players three straight days off for Christmas.

But the angry mail poured in. Fans screamed that I
wasn't taking the game "seriously." My friends were
worried. Our new president, Dr. John Hubbard, was
worried.

"We're going to play well," I assured them all.

I knew full well that if we didn't the criticism would
hit me like an avalanche.

I knew, too, that although we were 14-point favorites,
we were facing an excellent Ohio State team which ran
well, passed pretty well and had a strong, quick defense.

My friend, Duffy Daugherty, who had beaten the
Buckeyes, lectured me. Duffy said we couldn't run outside on them, because their defense reacted so quickly
and pursued so well.

"Duffy," I said, "we'll do what we do well and not
worry about Ohio State. Running outside is a big part of
our game. We have to run outside and we will—even if
Woody stations his defensive ends on the sidelines. We'll
play the way we have all year."

On January 1, it was a hard-fought first half. Rae
threw a scoring pass to Swann for a 7–0 first-quarter
lead, but they tied us at 7 by intermission. The Buckeyes
were running pretty well and putting heavy defensive
pressure on Rae. Statistics were about even.

I knew we'd play well if we got scared, and at half-time our kids were scared. I told the offensive line to stop trying to finesse people and just fire out and hit them. We didn't make any fancy adjustments in the second half, we just hit harder.

We took the second-half kickoff and drove 57 yards, mostly on Rae's passing, to a two-yard touchdown dive by Cunningham. Ohio State countered with a field goal to cut our edge to 14–10. Then, in one 18-minute burst, we outscored them, 28 to zero.

Some of the moves Davis put on the Buckeyes were astonishing. He dashed for 157 yards, and it was his 20-yard scoring run that broke the game open. Three more marches ended with Cunningham diving over the line to score from the one, giving him a Rose Bowl record four touchdowns. Sam made the dive famous in 1972. Whenever we needed a yard or two for a first down or touchdown, he moved from fullback to tailback and simply flung himself over the line like a diver going into a swimming pool.

Rae's passing was a major factor in our explosion. Mike completed 18 of 25 for 229 yards, with no interceptions.

The defense was just as mean as it had been all year, with interception runbacks by Charles Hinton and Charles Phillips setting up scores. Phillips also recovered a fumble to set up our first touchdown.

With time running out and the score 42–10, I cleared the bench and put everybody who hadn't played in on defense—even reserve offensive players who weren't sure where to line up. Against them, Ohio State marched 88 yards in 14 plays to score with 57 seconds left.

And so our greatest season had ended with my 100th coaching victory, 42 to 17, and I admit I was a little salty after the game.

"I wonder," I said, "is there anybody else the Associated Press would like us to play?"

Everyone says you shouldn't look backward, but it's human nature to do that, and you can't take human nature out of football. For much of the 1973 season our team was looking back—to 1972.

Following one of the greatest teams in football history, our kids played under intense pressure every week. The coaches felt it, too. Everybody was shooting at us, and for what we did in 1973 we didn't always get credit. After 1972 almost everything was a disappointment.

Certainly, the season wound up with one of my most disappointing losses, when Ohio State got even in the Rose Bowl by coming from behind three different times and then exploding for a 42–21 victory. No team should have beaten us by that score.

Still, in going 9-2-1 we had an excellent year. We had lost 12 regulars from the national champions, but earned our seventh Rose Bowl bid, stretched our unbeaten streak in league play to 18 games and held an unbeaten Oklahoma team that averaged 39 points in its other ten games to a touchdown in our 7–7 tie.

Our victory over UCLA in the Rose Bowl showdown is one of my most satisfying wins ever, and the one-point win over Stanford is one of the most incredible. It rekindled memories of the Cardiac Kids.

In his first season as the starting quarterback, Pat Haden completed 56 percent of his passes for 1,832 yards and 13 touchdowns.

Flanker Lynn Swann, one of five All-Americans, caught 42 passes to give him a new USC career record with 95.

All-American safety Artimus Parker had a super season. He had a bad finger half the time and it hurt like hell to catch the ball, but he still intercepted eight passes to give him a new league career record with 20.

Our kicker, 5-5, 130-pound Chris Limahelu, connected on 14 of 18 field goals, although I could never pronounce his name. Whenever I sent him in, I always said, "Hey, you."

Anthony Davis had his second straight thousand-yard year, rushing for 1,112, although we had lost six regulars in the offensive line, and it took weeks for us to get a cohesive running attack.

But Booker Brown at tackle was as fine a blocking lineman as I've ever had, and both he and the other offensive tackle, Steve Riley, made All-American teams.

Even so, you could see a mental difference between the 1972 and 1973 teams early. The national champions didn't always drive right down the field and score, but if they failed, the offense usually came off the field laughing, "We'll get them next time."

In our second 1973 game, a 23–6 win at Georgia Tech, we took the opening kickoff, drove immediately to Tech's 29, and then on fourth and three, Davis was hurled for a five-yard loss when the blocking collapsed. Several of the kids came out moaning, "Oh, we can't do anything right."

I had to get them relaxed by the next week. Coming to Los Angeles was wishbone power Oklahoma, and both our 14-game winning streak and number one national ranking were in danger. The Sooners had an advantage, because they had played one game and had a bye, while we had played twice. They not only had two weeks to prepare for us, but also an extra chance to scout us.

"We're going to the Rose Bowl no matter what happens tonight," I said to our players before the game.

"So relax, go out and have fun and knock the hell out of them."

There was a lot of knocking, but not much scoring. In a mistake-filled game, we took a 7–0 halftime lead on Haden's 15-yard touchdown pass to my son Johnny. Davis had injured his ankle on his first carry, however, and sat out the whole first half. He returned to run for 55 yards in the second half, but his temporary loss really hurt us.

In addition, we also had a first-quarter, 42-yard touchdown pass from Haden to tight end Jim Obradovich nullified when Jim jumped offside. Ironically, I think he would have beaten the defensive back covering him worse if he hadn't jumped. It was a first-down play, and the defender was creeping up. But when Jim started to run, the guy began to back up.

After a while I really thought Oklahoma wouldn't score, but they tied it at 7–7 on a two-yard run after a long third-quarter drive.

Later, the Sooners popped off that they were the better team, because they outgained us by 178 yards and had nine more first downs. But when they got the ball with 2:28 left in the game on their own 16, they played for the tie.

They never called time out, tried seven running plays and threw only one short pass, as they ran out the clock. That broke our winning streak.

Several weeks later Notre Dame snapped our unbeaten streak at 23 with a 23–14 victory, but we approached the Stanford game, our ninth, more worried about the Rose Bowl. So was Stanford, because they had a chance to go, too.

Favored by a ridiculous 25 points, we made a bundle of mistakes. Three lost fumbles and an interception set up 20 of Stanford's points. In addition, I watched in awe as their kicker, Rod Garcia, boomed four field goals, including three of 59, 52 and 42 yards. We trailed by as much as 23–10 in the fourth quarter.

At this point Swann made a fantastic play for us. It was third and 13 on the Cardinal 26, when Haden scrambled and lobbed a pass to him on the two. Lynn outjumped two defenders for the ball, came down, was hit by a third defensive back and carried him into the end zone.

Swann made us believe in miracles, and we needed one to win. We were still behind, 26–17, with 3:10 left, when a 42-yard interference penalty on a Haden-to-Swann pass set up Haden's ten-yard scoring run with 2:10 to go. That made the score 26–24.

When we kicked off to Stanford, they made one quick first down with 1:40 left, and we looked beaten. But middle guard Monte Doris tackled their fullback on three straight plays and held him to five yards, and they had to punt. We got the ball on our 30 with 33 seconds left.

In 26 seconds Haden completed three straight passes, 24 yards to Obradovich, 4 yards to Davis and 25 to Obradovich, to drive us to the Cardinal 17. We had no time outs left, so Obradovich had to fight his way out of bounds to stop the clock with seven seconds remaining and set up our field-goal attempt.

The ball was snapped, placed down and three seconds were left as Limahelu's winning 34-yard field goal cleared the crossbar. Until then, we had never led.

Coincidentally in 1969, when we beat Stanford with no time left, Ron Ayala's field goal had also come from 34 yards out.

Two weeks later was our Rose Bowl showdown with UCLA. While we had nosed out Stanford, 27–26, the

Bruins had beaten them, 59–13. Since losing their opener to Nebraska, they had averaged 49 points a game to lead the nation, while we had struggled in several of our games. Their wishbone had rushed for an unbelievable 54 touchdowns and averaged 415 yards a game on the ground. Since they had a better season record (9-1 to 8-1-1), they could clinch the Rose Bowl with a tie. Oddsmakers picked them by four.

There's no doubt this was the strongest UCLA offensive team we had ever faced. They had dominated people so easily that a coach could look at their films and think, "There's no way we can win."

"But damn," I thought, as I watched Bruin movies, "we should be able to play better defense than that. Are they that good, or are people just playing them wrong?" I liked the challenge.

In our last five games against the wishbone, we had been very successful, yielding just 27 points. It wasn't the wishbone that worried us; it was Kermit Johnson, James McAlister and the other swift Bruin backs who were running from it.

Our defensive philosophy against UCLA was the same as it is against everybody: we wanted the ball inside. For UCLA we moved one of our deep backs up on the line to play as an extra linebacker, giving us five altogether. The idea was to tie the Bruins down to running at the middle guard and inside linebackers, because there were so many people on the outside waiting for them.

But we had to defend against the pass, too. Some teams had gambled everything to stop UCLA's running attack, and the Bruin quarterbacks had surprised them with bombs. The receivers were wide open. If we were going to get beat on a pass, it wasn't going to be because we didn't have anybody on the guy.

Our defense played a super game. Middle guard Monte Doris, who led all tacklers with 18, joined inside linebackers Richard Wood, Charles Anthony and reserve Kevin Bruce to handle all that pressure UCLA threw at them. And we got tremendous play out of tackles Art Riley and Gary Jeter, outside linebackers James Sims, Dale Mitchell and reserve Ray Rodriguez and our entire secondary.

We also beat the Bruins with ball control. They didn't make a first down on their initial series, and we marched 68 yards to score the first time we touched the ball. Davis, who ran for 145 yards, swept in from the four.

The Bruins retaliated with a field goal, but on our second possession, Haden took us 80 yards and got another touchdown when he scrambled and threw 16 yards to Johnny in the end zone. It came on a third-and-nine play and gave us a 14–3 lead.

"All three of our receivers were covered, but I knew when that happened Johnny would break for the corner of the end zone," said Haden. "He did it 100 times in high school. Sure enough, there he was, waving his arms."

Said my son: "It was the biggest thrill of my life."

UCLA cut our lead to 14–10, but Haden, who completed seven of his first nine passes, took us 74 yards for the first of Limahelu's three field goals and a 17–10 halftime lead. Davis set up the kick with a 48-yard run.

We didn't make one turnover in the game. But we recovered four Bruin fumbles and intercepted two passes. We played conservatively in the second half and won, 23 to 13.

Ohio State (9-0-1), our Rose Bowl opponent, was even better than the 1968 Buckeye national champions.

Ranked number one most of the season, they came to Pasadena ranked fourth after their tie with Michigan. In the previous Rose Bowl I knew that unless we fell on our faces we should win. This time I knew we had to play as well or better than we did against UCLA to win.

The Buckeyes had outscored their opponents, 371 to 43, with four shutouts. I hadn't been more impressed with an opposing defensive team in years. It was the best Woody Hayes had ever had.

But we remembered that Mike Rae's passing had broken open the last Rose Bowl, and we figured we could get receivers open on them again. We decided to throw much more than we normally do, planning to maintain ball control that way.

And we did. We kept the ball 82 plays, 15 more than Ohio State, gained 406 yards and had seven more first downs than they did. But our receivers dropped too many passes, we jumped offside too often, and we didn't play good defense in the middle. So we lost.

Despite the drops, Haden completed 21 of 39 for 229 yards. I thought he was the best player on the field.

The score doesn't indicate how close the game was. Just like the previous game, it was tied at half, this time 14–14. We also led 3–0, 14–7, 21–14 and 21–20. Limahelu booted 47- and 42-yard field goals, and Davis dove a yard for one touchdown and took a lateral and passed ten yards to Johnny for another.

After the Buckeyes had charged ahead, 35–21, in the fourth quarter, we rallied, but with seven minutes to go, Swann dropped a perfect pass on the Ohio State 13 that would have given us a first down. On defense we got desperate, started grabbing for the ball, and Archie Griffin escaped 47 yards for their final touchdown. He had a 149-yard day.

With just over a minute left, Haden completed a pass to freshman flanker Shelton Diggs on the Ohio State five, he fumbled the ball away, and we were thwarted one last time.

But it was a team defeat, and Ohio State certainly deserved the victory. I left Pasadena looking ahead. If we're fortunate enough to come back next year, we'll play better.

NOTRE DAME

"Kiss me, I'm Irish"

WHEN I GREW UP as a Catholic in West Virginia I loved Notre Dame and its football team. The Fighting Irish were the first team in any sport I rooted for. I think they've always had that fascination for young Catholic kids, and today I still cheer for them—except when they play us.

Notre Dame has lent a lot of dignity and tradition to college football, and I am fond of most of the people there, including Father Theodore Hesburgh, the school president, and Ara Parseghian, the coach. The enthusiasm of their student body is tremendous, their fight song is inspiring, and I get goose bumps when I go back to South Bend and see the leaves falling and the Golden Dome shining in the sunlight.

From the stadium you can see the huge mosaic of Jesus Christ on the front of Notre Dame's library. They've dubbed him "Touchdown Jesus," because both his arms are upraised. There's also a statue of Moses, who is holding the Ten Commandments in his left hand, with one finger of the other hand pointed skyward. Moses, the Irish fans say, is simply signaling "We're number one."

I've said it a hundred times and I'll say it again. There's no greater thrill in football than playing in South Bend. I get keyed up and ready to play myself, but thank God that won't happen. I always hope my kids are as keyed up as I am.

There's no intersectional rivalry that compares with USC–Notre Dame, because it has nationwide interest. It captures the Midwest, the West and the East, and—unlike other intersectional series—it's been an annual event since 1926. The two schools missed playing only three years, all during World War II. We've met Notre Dame 14 times since I became head coach, and the outcome has either determined or helped determine who was national champion nine times.

By percentage, Notre Dame is the winningest college team in history, and USC is eighth. The Irish have had far and away the most All-Americans, Heisman Trophy winners and national champions. The university with the second highest number of All-Americans is USC.

Our series began with a handshake in 1921. Howard Jones, who later won a pair of national titles at USC, was coaching Iowa that year and led the Hawkeyes to a 10–7 victory over Knute Rockne and the Irish. It snapped Rockne's 20-game winning streak.

When the two great coaches met at midfield, Rockne said, "Howard, you've got to give me another chance."

"Okay," said Jones, and they shook on it.

Jones took over at USC in 1925. In 1926 he kept his word by adding Notre Dame to his schedule. Rockne got even in the rematch, 13 to 12, and the series was an immediate sensation. In 1927 an estimated 120,000 fans watched at Soldier Field in Chicago. In 1929 the two teams returned to Chicago and drew an official 112,912. In 1931, when USC ended Notre Dame's 26-game winning streak on Johnny Baker's field goal, the Trojans were given a victory parade through downtown Los Angeles. Incredibly, 300,000 people jammed the streets to cheer.

We're now scheduled to play the Fighting Irish through the late 1980's, which is as far ahead as our schedules go. It amuses me that coaches say they'd like to play Notre Dame, but when it comes time to schedule them few teams stand in line. Ohio State hasn't taken a chance since 1936. The Buckeyes tried twice and lost twice. UCLA played the Irish twice in the early 1960's, lost twice, and that was the end of that series.

Pick any year. The Irish will be as good or better than any team we'll play. I tell our kids that if you don't get up for Notre Dame, you must be dead.

When I was a boy my family listened to all the Irish games on the radio. When they lost, it was like a funeral in our house.

Darkness had descended on the Coliseum late in the afternoon of November 26, 1966. All the fans who watched that day's football game had scattered to homes, bars and parties. Only the cleaning crew remained in the giant stadium. One by one, the lights blinked out.

But I was still there. I was sitting in the USC dressing room with assistant coach Dave Levy, staring at the floor.

My USC team, used to winning, had been beaten by Notre Dame, 51 to 0. As the score got worse, I wanted to walk out the stadium tunnel and keep on going. When I finally did leave the field, an arm around the shoulder of my 13-year-old son, Johnny, an angry USC fan threw a bottle that narrowly missed us. Johnny has never forgotten it. It scared him and made us both even more bitter.

But I had other worries that day. Ahead of USC in the near future was the Rose Bowl, and we were going in as 51–0 losers. Ahead of me in the next couple of hours was a speech to our biggest athletic donors, who were gathered in a hotel eight or nine miles from the stadium.

Finally, after all the lights went out, I looked up wearily at Dave and said, "Let's start walking." We left the dressing room and walked a couple of blocks through the darkness to Vermont Avenue. Quietly, we turned up Vermont and walked four miles to Wilshire Boulevard. We turned on Wilshire and kept going, feeling like everyone driving by was watching us and knew who we were.

After we had walked about five miles, I stopped. "Okay, Dave," I said. "Let's get a cab."

The reality of that loss was something we had to live with, and I was determined to learn from it. For the next year I took the films of that game out at every opportunity. I watched that 51–0 destruction at least once a week and sometimes every day. The mood would descend on me and I'd walk down the hallway in our old athletic office building to the tiny film room and watch it alone. At times during the film, I would call for my assistants and point out our mistakes—over and over.

It was the only game I've ever coached that I've replayed in my mind long after it was over. I still have that film and once in a while I'll watch it again.

As important as many of our 14 games with Notre Dame have been, that's obviously the one I remember most. It has helped us since against the Irish more than just about anything else, and it will stick in the minds of the coaches who were there for a long, long time.

Notre Dame was going for the national championship —and this game won it for them—but I looked up at the scoreboard with two minutes left in the game, the score 51 to 0, and they still had most of their top players in. They were still trying to score. The first-string defense played the whole game, because they were determined to shut us out.

Irish fans have claimed I vowed never to lose to Notre Dame again, but I did not. I wouldn't vow not to lose to Siwash. But I'll tell you, they'll never out-tough us again. I think they won some of our early games that way, but they'll never do it again. They stuck it to us pretty good, and we ate a lot of humble pie.

The first seven times we played Notre Dame they won five and outscored us by 94 points. After 51 to 0 in 1966, we won four and tied twice in six years, and they didn't beat us again until 1973. I still feel like we beat ourselves in 1973.

I usually let my assistants have quite a bit of freedom at practice, but the week of that momentous game they'll do less and I'll come out of my golf cart and get more active in the practices.

If you're a team member and the season has moved along consistently for several weeks, and suddenly you see me becoming more involved at practices, you can't help but snap to attention. The week we play Notre Dame I'm much more vocal. And loud.

To beat Notre Dame you must make big plays. Ball control won't win for you. Because of their big, tough defense, you won't make a first down that consistently. You'll get all psyched up, run off tackle and make an inch. Usually, when we've beaten them we've passed well or broken off a long run.

Under Ara Parseghian they're difficult to defend against, too, because they have countless formations. They also use a lot of motion and faking. They'll pull their guards to the right, and then run left. Next time they'll pull the guards right, and run right. Because they're a multiple-offensive team, if you make a mistake you can give up an easy touchdown.

Before they reversed their policy against appearing in bowls, the Irish often considered USC as their bowl game. More inspiration was all they needed.

When I first became head coach, we were scheduled to play Notre Dame the week after UCLA, home and away every year. Playing your two biggest rivals back to back is a hell of a difficult situation. After the UCLA game we're usually highly elated or extremely depressed. Besides the crosstown rivalry, the game often determines whether or not we go to the Rose Bowl. And then to turn around and play Notre Dame. . . .

But I didn't mind that as much as I minded the weather in South Bend in late November or early December. The first time I went back there was 1959, when I was an assistant to Don Clark. We took a team that had won eight of nine games to play an Irish team that was only 4 and 5.

We boarded the plane in Los Angeles where it was 82 degrees and walked off in South Bend where it was 9. On game day it was maybe up to 15, and there was slush all around the field. As I watched our players get ready I knew we were going to lose. They were more interested in staying warm than playing football. Some of them wrapped themselves in so much clothing there was no way they could tackle anyone.

And we got frozen, 16 to 6.

I decided this was a very bad deal for us—playing in conditions we hadn't been exposed to all season. So I switched the game at South Bend, every other year, to mid or late October. It's still always cool, gray and wet, but at least we haven't frozen like we did in 1959.

Emotionally, this midseason game is still difficult for

us, because it means taking a week off right in the middle of the Rose Bowl race. Beating Notre Dame won't put us in the Rose Bowl. And when we play in Los Angeles in alternate years, the game is still held right after UCLA as the season finale.

My first game with the Irish as a head coach was in 1960, and as luck would have it, it rained in Southern California. In fact, it poured so hard that the players and coaches had to walk onto the field across boards spread over the mud and water. The field was rimmed with miniature lakes. At midfield, where vegetable dye had been used on the grass, there was green mud, a good Irish omen.

On the first play of the game, Notre Dame halfback Angelo Dabiero, who was only 5-8, ran a sweep, was tackled and slid into the pond in front of our bench. It was four or five inches deep and he damn near drowned before we fished him out.

It turned out to be the Trojans who drowned. This was the week after my first big win, that 17–6 upset of UCLA, and maybe we let down as teams sometimes do after emotional victories. Parseghian would not become Notre Dame's coach for several more years, and the 1960 team had lost eight straight. But they outgained us by 232 yards and shut us out, 17–0.

It was such a rotten day for USC that Jim Maples caught a 19-yard pass on the last play of the game and fumbled it away as he was tackled crossing the Irish goal line.

In my second season we played Notre Dame the week after our wild, one-point loss to top-ranked Iowa. But the Irish did nothing to boost our spirits. We went to South Bend and got shut out for the second straight time, 30–0.

Notre Dame has an incredible pregame rally in South

Bend. They invoke all the ghosts: Rockne, the Gipper and all the rest. The campus is ablaze with the colors of fall, which is all very pretty, but it's also festooned with welcoming signs calling on the Irish to kill, crush, hammer or bloody the Trojans. Any or all of those things.

There are also mock religious signs, such as "God Made Notre Dame Number One," or "Hail Ara, Full of Grace."

Others are personal greetings, like "On Saturday McKay Will Pay."

Many invoke history, including "When Irish Eyes Are Smiling—51–0."

Others refer only to the ominous present: "Enough's Been Said. The Time Is Here."

Notre Dame recently became coeducational, inspiring this sign:

>"1973 Means More Girls,
>Means Less Frustration,
>Means Victory Over USC."

In short, no phrase is left unturned.

And, as a matter of policy, if we have a great tailback, the Irish student body will hang him in effigy.

On Saturday afternoon their compact stadium, jammed with 59,075 people, creates an enormous strain on visiting teams. The constant roar of the fans drowns out your offensive and defensive signals, intimidates your players and charges up the Irish to superhuman heights. Some visiting teams run out on the field and fold during warmups.

In the last decade, Notre Dame has won games in South Bend by such scores as 64–0, 58–8, 56–7, 50–7, 51–10, 56–6, 48–0, 47–0, 44–0, 40–0, 41–8, 46–14, 45–12 and 35–0. I could keep going on, but I think you get the idea about what can happen in South Bend. The Irish have lost only 53 games at home in 85 years.

I've always thought the best way to prepare our young players for their first trip back there would be to take each one down to the basement and have three of our biggest players sit on him. Notre Dame's big guys are liable to sit on him anyway. And then, while he's down, a corps of drummers will move in and beat their drums directly over his head.

In 1961 we were drummed right out of the stadium. Willie Brown missed the game with injuries and Hal Bedsole scarcely played. They held us to a minus four yards rushing, while Daryle Lamonica ran for two touchdowns and passed for another. Notre Dame was much the bigger team, grinding out 322 yards rushing. I began to realize that we were going to have to recruit bigger players if we were going to play the Irish every year.

The 1962 meeting was crucial for us. We had just slipped by UCLA for our ninth straight victory and were on the way to our first national championship—if we could only beat the Irish. They came to Los Angeles with a four-game winning streak, and Lamonica had completed better than 50 percent of his passes.

I felt like the poker player who's won all the money —nine games and the Rose Bowl—and then is challenged to a showdown: all or nothing. As I pointed out to our fans, Notre Dame had shut out my first two Trojan teams.

"You bet we want to win," I said. "But first we're going to try to score."

Bedsole had a spectacular season in 1962, snagging 11 touchdown passes and averaging 25 yards a catch, but he made me furious that week in practice as we prepared for Notre Dame. Our manager blew the whistle one day to call the team over, and when that happens I expect all the players to sprint to me. Bedsole walked.

I sent everybody back and had the whistle blown again. Bedsole walked over again—and I threw him off the field and off the team. The only way he was coming back was to apologize and admit he was wrong.

The players were worried, because they figured they needed Hal to beat Notre Dame. I was a little worried, too. But the next morning he came into my office and apologized—and I think this helped our team. Everybody realized that no one man was more important than the whole team.

By game time I was very confident, even though we were favored by just six points. It turned out to be our best game of the season, and we won our first national championship, 25 to 0, before 82,000 in Los Angeles.

This still ranks as one of my biggest wins.

Our big fullback, Ben Wilson, who had been nagged by injuries all season, was healthy, and the way he ran in practice seemed to inspire the rest of the team. Ben pounded away at the Irish for 72 yards on 16 carries and scored twice. We outgained them by 150 yards, never let them inside our 20 and held Lamonica to 7 completions in 20 attempts.

We scored on our first series. On the third play, Pete Beathard threw a swing pass to Willie Brown, and Willie bounced off two tacklers and ran 34 yards to the Notre Dame 18. Wilson slashed for eight yards, and three plays later leaped over a stack of bodies at the goal line for a touchdown.

In the second quarter, Beathard ran 28 yards on a broken-pass play, Brown sped around end for 21, and Wilson got eight and five and finally one for his second score. We led 13–0 at halftime and scored twice more in the fourth quarter. Notre Dame could never sustain a march.

We took great pride in postgame comments made by defensive halfback Tommy MacDonald, the leading pass interceptor in Notre Dame history.

"In South Bend the feeling had existed for years that USC teams didn't like to play tough football," MacDonald told a sportswriter. "The team we played today destroyed that idea. They really put it to us."

In 1963 MacDonald helped put it to us. No USC team had won in South Bend since 1939, and we couldn't do it in 1963. Although we were the superior team—we had a 7-3 record that season and Notre Dame was only 2-7—we lost, 17–14. But with a few less dropped passes we might have won by as much as 30 to 7.

The weather, for once, was marvelous. The sun was shining from a cloudless sky, the temperature was in the 60's, and with ten minutes gone in the first quarter Beathard lobbed a pass to Bedsole in Irish territory. It was a little high and Hal tipped it in the air, from where it was rescued by MacDonald, who ran 62 yards for a touchdown.

We tied it at 7–7 and then 14–14 by halftime on 74- and 92-yard marches.

On the last play of the third quarter, Beathard rolled out at the Notre Dame 26 and hit Bedsole with a perfect pass on the three. Hal was wide open, but he dropped it. That was the game's turning point.

In the fourth period a 33-yard field goal with 6:28 left beat us. By coincidence, both teams gained 283 yards.

Our 1963 team narrowly missed out on a repeat invitation to the Rose Bowl, losing the vote to Washington, which beat us. But we had a better record for the season.

The 1964 Notre Dame game, played in the Coliseum, however, was to be the center of a major Rose Bowl controversy.

On the previous Saturday we beat UCLA to run our seasonal record to 6-3 and conference mark to 3-1. Oregon State also had a 3-1 record, but we didn't play them that season. The Beavers had finished their year with an 8-2 mark, while the best we could do was 7-3. But our schedule had been much, much more difficult, including a game with then second-ranked Oklahoma, whom we beat, 40–14. Our only league loss was by a point to Washington, and we had also overcome the loss of 13 starters by injuries for all or part of the season.

There was still no mathematical formula for choosing the Rose Bowl representative. Again it was up to the various schools to decide by vote.

On the Monday after we beat UCLA, representatives of all eight league universities met and voted to postpone their decision until after we played Notre Dame. I based my hopes for the Rose Bowl on that action. I did not consider myself lucky in votes, however, remembering 1963 and also 1948 at Oregon, when we lost out to California.

But thoughts of the Rose Bowl stirred us up for Notre Dame. It was some challenge. This was Parseghian's first season, and he had turned Irish football around. They blitzed nine straight opponents and came to Los Angeles ranked number one. They had outscored their victims, 270 to 57, holding seven of them to a touchdown or less. Not only were the Irish nearly impossible to run on—they led the nation in rushing defense—but they also attacked passers like a swarm of bees. They poured eight men through after the quarterback—four linemen and four linebackers—and all eight were big.

The offense was balanced and explosive. They ran well, and quarterback John Huarte, the Heisman Trophy winner, had passed for 15 touchdowns and more than 1,800 yards in nine games. Jack Snow had caught 50 of Huarte's passes. We were 12-point underdogs.

Needless to say, I was inspired by the challenge. People asked me if I was scared.

"A hernia operation couldn't make me call it off," I said.

What about that tremendous Notre Dame defense?

"Well," I said, "I've decided that if we play our very nitely make a first down."
best and make no mistakes, whatsoever, we will defi-

But I did believe we could move on them. We had a good passer in Craig Fertig, two excellent receivers in Rod Sherman and Fred Hill, and, of course, Mike Garrett at tailback. Somehow we had to loosen them up with passes, so Garrett would get room to run.

Since they were shooting eight men at the passer, I figured that if we sent out two or three receivers, we would be outmanned, and our quarterback would end up on his back like everyone else's had. Notre Dame had won nine games playing the same defense, so we didn't figure they'd change for us.

On Thursday afternoon, I called backfield coach Dave Levy and Fertig over to the fence surrounding our practice field.

"The hell with Notre Dame," I said. "If they're going to rush eight guys, we'll block all eight. This is what we're going to do."

Right there on a little blackboard on the fence I designed a new pass offense. We would keep nine players in to block, including Garrett and fullback Ron Heller, and send out only one receiver, Sherman or Hill. The receiver had three alternate routes, and Fertig would drop back, wait for him to break free and throw to him. We called it "the Notre Dame pass."

Saturday arrived, and just as I thought, we moved the ball well in the first half. But at halftime we trailed 17 to 0.

It was frustrating. At 10–0 Fertig overshot an open receiver in the end zone, and at 17–0 he threw a perfect pass to Hill in the end zone, but Fred dropped it when a Notre Dame tackler jarred him.

Meanwhile the Irish machine had cranked out 17 on Ken Ivan's 25-yard field goal, Huarte's 21-yard pass to Snow and Bill Wolski's five-yard run.

I heard later that Parseghian went to the blackboard in the Notre Dame dressing room and scrawled on it: "JUST 30 MORE MINUTES."

Thirty minutes to a national title. Thirty minutes can be a long time.

In our dressing room I didn't feel we were out of the game. We'd moved the ball, and there was no question we should have scored two or three times. But we hadn't.

"I told you before the game we could beat Notre Dame," I said to the players, "and I'm just as confident as ever, even more so. You can win it—if you go out there and block and tackle. I want you to take that second-half kickoff and go right in for a touchdown.

"And one other piece of advice. If you don't score more than 17 points, you'll lose."

The team took the second-half kickoff and went right in for a touchdown, driving 66 yards. To run the ball we attacked their big tackles with two backs going in to blast a hole for Garrett, and Mike squeezed through enough holes for 79 yards in the game. Heller ran for 44. And, just as I had designed, we often sent out one receiver, with nine men blocking and Fertig throwing.

When they dropped the linebackers back to help against the pass, we'd run Garrett. Fertig, Garrett and Heller brought us to the Notre Dame one, and Garrett scrambled into the end zone to make the score 17–7.

Notre Dame retaliated with a drive to our nine, but Huarte threw a wild pitchout and we recovered. Early in the fourth quarter they marched again, scoring on a one-yard plunge. It was nullified by a holding penalty. The score remained 17–7.

For the game, Fertig completed 15 of 23 passes for 225 yards and no interceptions, and he was hot now. We took the ball on our 12 and flew 88 yards, 78 on passes. Craig threw for 28, 13, 14 and finally, 23 yards to Hill for another touchdown. We missed the conversion, but with 5:09 left we were behind only 17 to 13.

Right then, I knew we had Notre Dame. The momentum was all ours. And in a situation like that, the number one rating is a fairly suffocating thing.

The Irish had lost their aggressiveness because they were trying to defend their ranking. Again they couldn't move—and we got another break. Their punter kicked to our 23, but another holding penalty forced him to punt again from his own 19, and he kicked just 27 yards to the Irish 46. It was returned to the 40.

The big Coliseum clock showed 2 minutes and 10 seconds left.

Fertig threw to Hill for 23 yards, and we were on the Notre Dame 17. Garrett took a handoff, but he was swarmed after a two-yard gain. On second down Fertig threw to Hill in the end zone as 84,000 people screamed, and he caught the ball—but just out of bounds. On third down, Fertig was incomplete again.

Now we were faced with fourth and eight. Sherman, who was our leading receiver in the game with seven catches, insisted he could get open. He said he could beat their halfback on his side. I sent him in with the play.

After delaying at the line, Sherman faked to the outside and turned cornerback Tony Carey the wrong way. Then he cut down the middle and Fertig laid the ball right in his hands on the three-yard line. Carey reacted quickly, spinning to get an arm over Sherman's shoulder, but he never touched the ball. Sherman whirled and slipped away into the end zone. Carey, whose number, appropriately, was 1, fell down as Sherman scored. The clock showed 1:33 left. And we won, 20 to 17.

It was pandemonium. The crowd went stark raving mad, and there must have been 10,000 people on the field as the gun popped. I almost got killed getting off. In the dressing room our players sprayed each other with soft drink bottles and threw me in the shower. Garrett embraced me and we jumped up and down.

When the Midwestern sportswriters came in, I kidded them, "We always play like that. It's in my contract."

And then Father Hesburgh showed up to congratulate me. He shook my hand. "John," he said, "that wasn't a very nice thing for a Catholic to do."

"Father," I said, "it serves you right for hiring a Presbyterian."

We were ecstatic not only because we had beaten the top-ranked team, but because we had convinced the conference we should go to the Rose Bowl. Or so we thought.

Two hours later came the stunning announcement. Oregon State, which included a 10–7 victory over hapless Idaho in its eight victories, had been selected to go to the Rose Bowl instead.

I found out while celebrating at a downtown hotel. Our players heard the news at a restaurant where they were holding a victory party. They and their wives and girl friends ate in silence.

At the time I was shocked, but I tried to be generous.

"I hope Oregon State does a real fine job," I said. "They're a well-coached team, and I hope they justify the conference decision that they're better than we are. I'm not mad at them. I'll root for them in the Rose Bowl. I guess I'm just not very lucky at votes. That's the third time I've lost one for the Rose Bowl."

But I was still mad. Apparently, the conference vote had ended in a 4-4 tie, and, since we had been at the Rose Bowl more recently, we lost out. In case of a tie, the team which had been away the longest got the nod.

I thought it was a tremendous miscarriage of justice, and I still do. I didn't mind so much that Oregon State was going to the Rose Bowl, but I minded like hell the way the conference handled it. They could have voted a week earlier and ended the suspense. But they left it up in the air and led everyone to believe they were holding off to see how we would do against Notre Dame. We told our players they had an excellent chance to go to Pasadena if they won. They did win and they didn't go.

Parseghian, I'm sure, felt even worse over the loss of the national championship. There are many opportunities for USC to go to the Rose Bowl, but a national championship may come along only once in a lifetime. Before we met, Ara said this was going to be Notre Dame's bowl game. As it turned out, I guess it was ours, too.

A few days later I looked at a film of the game and saw something that surprised me. I noticed one of our injured players who was standing on the sidelines in street clothes, and he was bouncing up and down like a pogo stick. It looked like he was going ten feet in the air. He also ran back and forth yelling encouragement to his teammates.

It was one of our best linebackers, who had been side-lined because of a freak accident. He had walked through a plate glass window that week and cut his Achilles tendon slightly, besides suffering other gashes all over his body. Our doctor ruled him out of the game.

Damn, I thought, if a guy could jump that high in street clothes, I wonder what would have happened if he had played.

None of our players jumped for joy when we met Notre Dame next season. It was back to South Bend, and the Irish didn't forget the team that knocked them out of the national championship.

The year was 1965, and we were unbeaten (4-0-1) and ranked fourth. Notre Dame was ranked seventh and had a 3-1 record. We flew to Indiana off successive shut-outs of two excellent conference opponents, Washington and Stanford. In our first five games Garrett had run for 852 yards and scored eight touchdowns.

When we arrived on Friday, I sent Fertig, now an assistant coach, to a Knights of Columbus meeting as guest speaker. The Knights remembered Craig and his winning touchdown pass in 1964. I think some of them wanted to tackle him. When he got up to talk, the room shook with boos. Then they wadded up their napkins and threw them at him. Later that night Craig knocked on my hotel room door, and his face was scared-white.

The team, student body and other fans were crazy to get even with USC. And Parseghian had the previous weekend off, giving him two weeks to prepare for us.

Saturday morning, as we bused to Notre Dame Stadium, I looked up at the name tag over the driver. It said: "Your bus driver today is Fred Loser." That figured.

We went into our dressing rooms, went out to warm up, and came back for the final pregame talk. The referee pounded on the door. "Five minutes to go," he yelled. Five minutes later he came and got us, so we left.

As we ran out, there were screaming Notre Dame students all over the field, the wind was blowing, and it was raining. The temperature was 39 degrees.

"Where's Notre Dame?" I asked the referee.

"Back in the dressing room," he said.

We waited out there 20 minutes. I've always been a great believer in not showing fear of the weather before a game—no matter where we are—so I hadn't ordered any parkas for our team. Our kids stood there, shivering in the cold, watching Notre Dame fans carry a coffin around the playing field. Draped on the coffin was a jersey with Garrett's number. It was smeared with catsup.

The crowd kept chanting, "Remember . . . Remember . . . Remember." The wind reached 20 miles an hour and there was a hail flurry. Still we stood there.

Suddenly, the Fighting Irish took the field, and the sound could have broken windows.

We won the toss and elected to receive. Our deep man was Mike Hunter, who stood 5-7 and weighed 150 pounds. The noise was incredible as the kickoff sailed toward him.

Hunter caught the ball on the eight and streaked five yards to the 13, where he slipped and fell flat on his face. For a couple of seconds he lay there without moving.

"Christ," I said. "They shot him."

It was a horrible start. Hunter wasn't hurt, but the team soon was. On the first play, Garrett was thrown in the backfield for a two-yard loss. We made one first down, but quarterback Troy Winslow was pinned for a 15-yard loss, and we ended up punting from our 14. The ball rolled dead on our 45.

Immediately Notre Dame marched for a touchdown,

with fullback Larry Conjar ramming over from the two.

Our next six plays netted five yards, we punted twice, and Notre Dame marched for touchdowns twice. Conjar got them both. He also scored their fourth touchdown and gained 116 yards as the Irish swept by us, 28–7.

Notre Dame played a great game, both offensively and defensively, but we were as bad as they were good. Their offensive line play was outstanding, and no defensive line all year penetrated into our backfield like theirs did. Garrett was gang tackled and held to 43 yards in 16 carries. Mike made some great runs just getting back to the line of scrimmage.

By halftime, they had outgained us, 226 to 23, out-first-downed us, 13 to 1, and led 21–0. It reached 28–0, before Winslow threw a touchdown pass for us in the final quarter.

We didn't quit; we kept fighting. But we couldn't over-come that horrible start. In the second half we outgained them, 137 to 101, but it was too late.

Next year was that damn 51–0 game.

It was the worst one I ever coached in my life, and it happened because we tried to win a game we couldn't win. We were trying to regain our honor.

The week before we had been upset by UCLA, 14–7, which caused everyone to assume the Bruins would go to the Rose Bowl for the second straight year. They had finished 3-1 in league play to our 4-1 record—we still weren't playing a full conference schedule—but since they had beaten us, people automatically elected them.

Los Angeles also made a big thing out of the fact the Bruins had won without star quarterback Gary Beban, injured the week before. But they had a week to prepare with second stringer Norm Dow. What everyone forgot was that we lost our own quarterback, Winslow, who had started for two years, in the second half of the UCLA game.

In addition, Don McCall, our best running back now that Garrett had graduated, scarcely played. McCall, who had speed and power, could have been one of my great runners if he hadn't been plagued by injuries and occasional lack of endurance. But he was our leading rusher in 1966 and limited by injury to only eight carries against UCLA.

No one considered we were a little destitute ourselves. Two bad teams played, and we got beat.

Before the game I said the conference champion should go to the Rose Bowl, and by virtue of one more win we wound up as the conference champion. On Monday after the UCLA game we were picked for the Rose Bowl. For the first time I had won a bowl vote. But the press crucified us.

I didn't think UCLA should have been chosen over us, but I have eyes and ears, and the criticism got to me. I panicked. I decided that since everybody was mad, it was important that we make an impressive showing against Notre Dame. I decided to gamble.

Unfortunately, the team I gambled against was one of the greatest in football history—and it had tremendous motivation to beat us badly. A big victory over USC might convince the pollsters to award the Irish the national title. They had played a 10–10 tie with Duffy Daugherty's great Michigan State team the week before, the only blemish on either squad's record. Michigan State, ineligible for the Rose Bowl, had concluded its season, so the Irish had one more chance to beat out the Spartans for number one.

For the season that Notre Dame team had six shutouts and outscored its foes, 362 to 38. They had nine present or future All-Americans and had us outmanned at every position. As I look back, I realize there was no way we could have beaten them.

But we were going to try. We wanted to shut the critics up. I knew we couldn't run consistently on the Irish, but I figured we could pass pretty well, although we had to go with our second quarterback, Toby Page, and our third, Steve Sogge, who was only a sophomore then.

I went against every principle I believed in. We passed deep in our own territory, we didn't punt on fourth down, and practically everything we tried that we normally wouldn't have tried turned into a touchdown for them. We could probably have held the score down to something respectable, like 24–0, if we had just run the ball and punted more often. But we threw 38 passes, including eight on 14 first-down plays.

Tom Schoen ran one pass back 40 yards for a touchdown, and Dave Martin took another back 33 yards for a score. On offense, Coley O'Brien, who had rallied the Irish for their tie against Michigan State, threw two touchdown passes to All-American Jim Seymour, another to Dan Harshman and completed 21 of 31 for the game. Seymour caught 11.

We gambled wildly on defense, too, shooting our linebackers 80 percent of the time, but we couldn't get through to O'Brien.

It was 31–0 at half and 44–0 after three quarters. They gained 273 more yards and had 16 more first downs. And they won the national championship.

I took a lot of abuse after that game, and so did my team. But afterward I told my players:

"You didn't play well, but you didn't play poorly enough to get beat 51 to 0. I got you beat that badly, and I'll never make that mistake again. But we'll come back in the Rose Bowl and play a good game."

And we did, barely losing to favored Purdue and Bob Griese, 14–13.

It was a long winter. Everywhere I went I was reminded of 51–0. If Notre Dame has as many students and alumni as I met that year, the school must have an annual enrollment of about two million.

I was aware, too, that our next shot at Notre Dame would be in South Bend, where no USC team had won since 1939. We had been told since I had been at the university that we couldn't win in South Bend—and many people believed it.

But I have never believed in jinxes. We should be good enough to play football anyplace and win. I was getting tired of the South Bend mystique.

When it came time for the game we had a 4-0 record and were ranked number one. O. J. Simpson was now the tailback, Sogge was at quarterback, and our defense, quick and aggressive, was the best I'd ever had.

Notre Dame came into our game with a 2-1 record, having been upset by Purdue. But the week before the Irish tuned up for us by beating Iowa by 50 points. They were ranked fifth in the country and favored over our top-ranked team by as much as 12 points. Clearly, the oddsmakers believed in the jinx.

For all of us at USC it was a very emotional week. For a year there wasn't a night I went to bed or morning that I awoke when I hadn't thought about 51–0. It was still stuck in my throat.

You could feel the electricity building in our team all week. For added inspiration I turned to linebacker Adrian Young, born in Dublin, Ireland, a player with great ability and enthusiasm. Young led some of the most spirited calisthenics we'd had in years. But I didn't want the team too keyed up. When I saw them getting a little tight, I kidded them.

Notre Dame in 1967 did not have the great running attack of the 1966 national champions, but it was good enough, and the passing attack with Terry Hanratty and Coley O'Brien throwing to receivers like Seymour was dazzling. We had to find a way to stop it.

On Tuesday, about midnight, we coaches were walking through the campus, discussing the game in the dark. How would we defend against Hanratty and O'Brien?

Suddenly I stopped everyone. "Levy," I said, "you and Fertig line up like wide receivers, and I'll pretend like I'm Hanratty. The rest of you coaches get over there on defense. This is how we'll play them."

A fan had given us a bottle of champagne for a good luck toast, and I put it down in the campus street as the ball. Under the moon I designed a new defense by moving all my coaches around. It would look like a normal zone, but would actually have seven men deep to protect against the pass. Both cornerbacks and three linebackers would play man to man on all the ends and backs, and two safeties would play deep to protect them. All the players in man-to-man coverage would thus be helped out from behind. I named it "Trojan coverage."

As usual, the Irish had a good defense, too, with seven starters back from 1966. We had to find a way to counter them, to give Simpson more running room. So we put in a new formation. We moved our flanker, Jimmy Lawrence, in tight as a wingback to force their wide defensive end more inside, and force them to play a linebacker outside, which they didn't like to do. As I've said, no one likes to change a defense.

My last night at home Corky and I ate dinner together. "Corky," I said, "I don't know what the score is going to be Saturday, but we sure as hell aren't going to get beat 51–0."

And so we flew to Indiana, the seniors remembering

they had been outscored by Notre Dame, 79–7. The juniors had been scarred by you know what. Eight of our defensive starters, in fact, had played in that game. One of the few people with no bitter memories of the Irish was O.J. Perhaps that was a good omen.

When my mother visited the coaches' meeting before the game to wish us luck, she said, "Jack, if you win, I'm going out tonight and get loaded."

She'd never taken a drink in her life.

Before we left for the stadium I had my mind made up about two important pieces of strategy. First, we weren't going to let their howling crowd drown out our offensive signals. I told Sogge—and I've told all my quarterbacks since Steve the same thing: "If you can't be heard, walk away from the center. Under the rules, the head official has to call time. Don't snap the ball. If they want to penalize you, let them penalize you all the way to the end zone, and then walk on through. You have a right to be heard."

Second, I had decided we weren't going on the field and stand around like we did in 1965, taking abuse from the crowd while we waited for Notre Dame.

"Kickoff time," I said, "all depends on Notre Dame. We won't show up on the field until they do. We won't go out until the students get off the field, either. I don't care if it takes until midnight. I guess 59,000 people are going to feel mighty foolish sitting in that stadium if they don't get to see a game."

I may dislike pep talks, but I'll admit I was a little emotional before we left the dressing room.

"Not many people can say they've ever played in a USC–Notre Dame game," I told our players. "It will be heard all over the world. No matter where you go the rest of your lives, you will remember you played in this game. To lose it would be a crime. You're too good.

This time you're better than Notre Dame. And if you lose, you'll know you lost to an inferior team."

The referee warned us to be on the field in five minutes. I snapped that we weren't going out until Notre Dame did. He said he could call the game.

"What does that mean?" I asked.

"It means Notre Dame wins 2–0 on a forfeit," he said.

"That," I answered, "would be the best deal we've ever gotten in this stadium."

But we waited. And Notre Dame did take the field first. Then we charged out. I was the first one through the door.

Because we had waited, the game started five minutes late. The tension was obvious, because both teams played a sloppy first half. "It was unbelievable," said Parseghian after the game.

We couldn't score. We tried to double-team Notre Dame's massive left end and left tackle, Kevin Hardy and Mike McCoy, and all they did was grunt. We tried to pass, and Sogge threw three interceptions in the second quarter. One was grabbed on our 19 and returned to the three. Hanratty rolled out and ran in for a touchdown, and we trailed at half, 7 to 0. We had stopped their passing, but the jinx still held.

"You're still too good to lose this game," I insisted at halftime. "If you just hang in there, something will happen. You're gonna beat them."

Again we waited for the Irish to take the field first. And something good happened on the second half kickoff. Notre Dame's deep man fumbled, and Steve Swanson recovered for us on the Irish 18. It took six plays, but we moved to the one, and from there Simpson hurtled into the end zone. Rikki Aldridge tied the score with his conversion.

With just over four minutes left in the third quarter

we moved to Notre Dame's 36. Sogge pitched back to O.J., who swept left end, and with an explosive burst of speed he was gone. His 36-yard sprint gave us a 14–7 lead.

Notre Dame was stunned. A short punt set us up again, and Aldridge kicked a 22-yard field goal with a minute left in the third quarter for a 17–7 lead.

Meanwhile, our defense was tremendous. For the game we intercepted five of Hanratty's passes and two of O'Brien's. Young, the real Irishman, had four interceptions himself. We held Notre Dame to 15 completions in 40 attempts and 93 running yards in 37 carries.

Our defense set up the final touchdown. Just after the fourth quarter started, safety Mike Battle ran an interception back to the Irish 17. Sogge and O.J. took us to the three, and Simpson whipped around left end from there for his third touchdown. We won 24 to 7, and I was carried off the field.

Simpson had carried 38 times for 150 yards. Young had made 12 tackles, and his linebacking partner, Jim Snow, made 14.

It was my biggest win as a head coach up to that time.

When I met Parseghian after the game for the traditional handshake, he said, "Those defenses you set up were amazing. How did you do it?"

"I'll write you a letter about them," I grinned. "In invisible ink."

Back in Los Angeles, 3,000 fans welcomed us at the airport, many wearing green Irish hats. O.J. stepped off the plane wearing a big round button which said:

"Kiss me, I'm Irish."

We went on to win our second national championship.

By the time Notre Dame arrived in Los Angeles for the last game of the 1968 season we were unbeaten at 9-0 and hopefully on our way to our second straight national title. We had been ranked first in both polls most of the season. Late in the year, however, we topped only one poll. Unbeaten Ohio State was first in the other. Again the Notre Dame game took on monumental importance.

The Irish had lost two of their nine games that season, but they were still averaging a stunning 511 yards in total offense and 39 points a game. They were to finish the season ranked fifth in the country, and, although we were unbeaten, we were favored by only two points.

Parseghian had a bye to help prepare for us, and he spent much of it preparing for Simpson, who averaged 171 yards rushing a game that year. While he was getting his defense ready to contain O.J., Ara spent his free time praising him.

"Simpson should be an actor," Ara said. "He gets up slowly after being tackled and then trudges back to the huddle. You see him barely getting back there and you think, 'We've got him now.' Then he runs 40 yards for a touchdown. You'd think he would get a bad bruise somewhere, sometime, which would stop him, but there he is ready to go, play after play. He's just a tremendous athlete, the best I've ever seen."

Ara was impressed all right. He assigned four defensive players to our tailback. He called it his "bubble defense." Wherever O.J. went, four of the Irish were sure to go. And they stopped him. For the afternoon, Simpson gained just 55 yards in 21 carries. At the half he had only 23, and we were shocked to be behind, 21 to 7.

Playing before 83,000, the Irish had rolled up 324 yards and held us to three first downs in the first 30 minutes.

Hanratty was hurt, and Notre Dame had started an inexperienced sophomore named Joe Theismann at quarterback. After only 40 seconds had elapsed in the game, Joe threw a pass over the middle and Sandy Durko intercepted and sprinted 21 yards for a touchdown.

But Notre Dame came right back with an 86-yard drive to tie the score on a three-yard run. And then, just before the first quarter ended, halfback Bob Gladieux burst into a hole the Notre Dame band could have marched through and went 57 yards to score.

Twice we desperately stopped them on our five with interceptions, but the Irish scored again with 30 seconds left in the half. Theismann pitched out to our old nemesis Coley O'Brien, now a halfback, and O'Brien lobbed a pass back to Theismann for a 13-yard touchdown.

At halftime, we were really in trouble. All season we had played with a limited offense, which depended mainly on the running of Simpson. Simpson had been stopped. And our defense had been pushed all over the field.

I looked at our players. "It's obvious you're not going to win this game for yourselves," I said. "In that case, would you consider winning it for the coaching staff's eight wives and 23 children?"

They loosened up and we made adjustments. We decided that if four players were going to flow with Simpson, then Sogge should fake to him and throw to Sam Dickerson, Terry DeKraii and Bobby Chandler.

The defense was just going to have to dig in and stop Notre Dame. They had the potential to do it.

Sogge gave it all he had. And so did the defense. In the game Steve completed 17 of 28 passes with no interceptions, and in the third quarter three big completions moved us to Notre Dame's one. Simpson dove into the end zone, and the score was 21–14.

We played our best defensive football of the season

in that half, shutting out the Irish and holding them to 118 yards. One of those defenders, Gerry Shaw, set up the tying touchdown early in the fourth quarter with his second interception.

From the Notre Dame 40, Sogge fired a perfect pass to Dickerson on the goal line for the touchdown that gained a tie at 21.

There were still ten minutes left in the game, however, and both teams had chances to win. Notre Dame missed two field goals, while Sogge had Dickerson open in the last minute, but couldn't reach him with a long pass. The game ended 21–21.

Parseghian seemed happy. "Give SC credit for coming back," he said. "And you have to say one thing for us. We didn't lose to number one."

I was disappointed. We had lost our number one ranking, and I despise ties. I would rather have played all day and all night to settle the game. Ties are what men get at Christmas and never wear.

But a tie with Notre Dame was what we got again in 1969, this time 14 to 14.

Once again we flew to South Bend unbeaten and 4-0, but this time we were ranked third. The Irish were 3-1 and ranked tenth, having lost again to a good Purdue team. We were coming off our frantic, last-second win over Stanford, with Jimmy Jones, Clarence Davis and the Wild Bunch leading the team.

The oddsmakers never flinched. Notre Dame and South Bend, they decided, should be favored by three.

In 1968 I felt we tied Notre Dame. In 1969, they tied us.

On a very cold afternoon, the Irish stopped our tailback again. Davis gained just 75 yards on 30 carries. But in the first quarter Clarence made two good moves and ran 15 yards for a touchdown. A very questionable holding penalty nullified it. On another occasion we drove to their eight, but fullback Charles Evans fumbled the ball away. It was 0–0 at the half.

The way the Wild Bunch played that day against Notre Dame it was a damn shame that we didn't win. At the half the Irish had netted 35 yards, only 5 on the ground.

Finally, in the third period, Theismann moved his team 74 yards for a touchdown, and they went ahead, 7 to 0.

Jones took us 75 yards to tie, gaining the touchdown on a 19-yard pass to DeKraii, and the third quarter ended 7–7.

Early in the final period Tyrone Hudson ran an interception back to the Irish 15, and from the 14 Jones threw to Dickerson for another touchdown and we were in command, 14 to 7.

We hadn't counted on a defensive tackle destroying our lead. But Mike McCoy did. A unanimous All-American at 6-5 and 274 pounds, McCoy looked as if he came out of a dinosaur egg. With eight minutes left in the game, he crashed through two blockers at our 33 and blocked our punt. The ball skipped crazily back to the seven, where Irish defensive end Walt Patulski fell on it. From the one, halfback Denny Allan squirmed over and we were tied again, this time at 14. The clock showed 6:51 left.

One thing we did poorly in this game was catch passes. Jones hit our receivers in the hands often enough for us to win, but several of his passes were dropped. In the last few minutes we couldn't put together another scoring threat.

But with two minutes left the Irish had a chance to win. They drove to our 31, stalled and Scott Hempel lined up for a 48-yard field-goal attempt.

The second the ball jumped off his foot you could tell it was hit well. And it was hit straight. It looked like it was going through the goal posts, and I jerked my head away and didn't watch.

Just after Hempel kicked, Theismann, the holder, jumped up and hugged him and the two of them did a little dance.

But the ball hit the crossbar square in the middle and bounced back on the field. I exhaled deeply.

"God," I said, "was a Trojan on that kick."

As he had in 1968, Parseghian said he was proud of his team and not unhappy about the outcome. I figured Notre Dame's reaction was the best thing about this game. It was nice to know we had reached the point where it was a big deal for the Irish to tie us. When the game was over, their fans acted as if they had won.

Once again, however, the tie killed our chance for the national title. We went unbeaten and won the Rose Bowl game, but wound up ranked third.

In 1970, it was our turn. We wrecked Notre Dame's national championship bid for the second time in seven years. The Irish flew to Los Angeles unbeaten at 9-0— just like in 1964—ranked third, and on their way to the Cotton Bowl. In the Cotton Bowl they beat Texas by two touchdowns and snapped the Longhorns' 30-game winning streak. Had they not lost to us, they would have been ranked first by the Associated Press after the Cotton Bowl. Instead, they finished second, and Nebraska, a team we had tied early in the season, finished on top.

We may have bothered Notre Dame and Nebraska, but we didn't do much else in 1970. After losing just two games in three years, we collapsed in midseason and arrived at the Notre Dame game with a 5-4-1 record. The previous Saturday we lost to an average UCLA team,

45–20, in perhaps the worst defensive game a team of mine has ever played.

But back to the Irish. Not only did they have an explosive offense with Theismann running and throwing and Tom Gatewood, who caught 79 passes, catching, but their defense had only allowed 6.5 points a game. They weren't as good as everyone said they were. They were better. The oddsmakers tabbed them by 11.

Game day dawned dark and overcast and got darker. It drizzled in the first half. Late in the half the drizzle turned into a downpour.

The game began predictably with Notre Dame taking the opening kickoff and ripping 80 yards to a touchdown, which Theismann scored on a 25-yard run.

Then Jimmy Jones got hot. He directed us to three quick, long scoring drives in the first quarter, with Davis getting two touchdowns on five- and three-yard runs. Jones and Dickerson also teamed up on a 45-yard scoring pass.

Theismann flipped a 19-yard touchdown pass in the second quarter, but Ron Ayala countered with a field goal and we led 24 to 14 at halftime.

That we were leading was remarkable enough. What happened in the first five minutes of the second half was merely incredible.

Theismann was having a fantastic day. Throwing in the rain, he was to complete 33 of 58 passes for 526 yards, shattering Notre Dame's record and barely missing the NCAA mark. But we limited the Irish running game to 31 yards and put so much pressure on Theismann that he fumbled the ball away twice and threw four interceptions. Defensive end Willie Hall, one of the survivors of the Wild Bunch, sacked Joe five times.

On the first play of the second half, Hall forced an

Irish back to fumble, and our Kent Carter recovered on the Notre Dame 17. Through pouring rain we drove to the one, where reserve tailback Mike Berry fumbled into the end zone. Tackle Pete Adams recovered for a USC touchdown. The luck of the Trojans. We led 31–14.

Exactly 42 seconds later, Theismann retreated under heavy pressure and backed up all the way to the end zone, where Hall embraced him and stripped him of the ball. It rolled free, and defensive tackle John Vella flopped on it for another touchdown.

Astonishingly, we led by 24 points, 38 to 14. Theismann produced two more touchdowns, but they weren't enough. We had spoiled their perfect season again, 38–28.

Texas coach Darrell Royal, visiting to scout Notre Dame, summed up the game:

"Emotion was the difference," said Darrell. "When that adrenaline flows, you get there faster, you jump higher, you dive deeper, and you even come up drier."

Parseghian was crushed. "How much chance could anyone give USC after that performance against UCLA the week before?" he said. "But pride is a great motivating force."

The win didn't stun me. I had said at the beginning of the year that we were one of the outstanding teams in the country, and I still felt we had the potential to be one. As disappointing as the year was, our offense still averaged 31 points a game. Our defense had failed us. But beating Notre Dame made the winter livable. And 50 years in the future our seniors could sit around the fireplace and say they had never lost to the Irish.

We upset Notre Dame again in 1971 and began a 23-game unbeaten streak, longest of my career. The 1971 victory is very high on my list of most satisfying wins, because our slump had continued and I was humiliated, angry and depressed. Our record was 2-4, we had lost three straight, and the team was split between quarterbacks Jimmy Jones and Mike Rae.

Notre Dame was unbeaten again, this time 5-0, and ranked sixth as we flew into South Bend. The Irish were two-touchdown favorites. The point spread might have been bigger, but their offense was not nearly as strong as it was in 1970. They had a monstrous defense, however, which had allowed only 16 points to five teams and not given up a touchdown for 14 quarters.

The week before we had been eliminated from the Rose Bowl race, and I decided to alternate Jones and Rae on every series.

Before the game I gave one of my infrequent pep talks. And it was an impassioned one.

"We've been disgraceful this season," I said, "and it's a crime. If we're gonna play, let's for once play as well as we can. For one day, let's forget about who should be the quarterback and put all this nonsense about which player likes another behind us. Forget about yourselves and just play as a team—like men. And if you don't, it may be the last goddamn time some of you guys ever get a chance to play—if I have to play nobody."

Then I began to feel sentimental.

I told the players what the Rams had offered me the previous winter—a 15-year contract that began at $90,-000 a year—and why I had decided to remain in college football, the game I loved. I reminded them I had met all their fathers and mothers when they were young boys, and that I had promised to take care of them.

"And now," I said, "we're back here together in the greatest hotbed of football, Notre Dame, and this is the game that typifies college football. This is what it's all about. This is what I've believed in since I was a little kid. And I still believe in it."

For one of the few times in my life I got tears in my eyes and had to turn away. I couldn't say anything else.

It was like an old Knute Rockne scene. The players jumped up and tried to break through the door four at a time.

It was the afternoon that junior split end Edesel Garrison, who was first-string ahead of my son the next year, had the greatest game of his life. A 9.5 sprinter, Edesel caught five passes for 127 yards, scored twice and set up a third touchdown. He made four of his catches against Irish All-American cornerback Clarence Ellis.

On a typical gloomy South Bend day, Bruce Dyer intercepted a first-quarter Notre Dame pass and returned it to the Irish 48. In two plays we were on the 31. From there, Jones threw to Garrison, who caught the ball on the three as Ellis slipped and fell on rain-soaked grass. Garrison turned and stepped into the end zone.

Notre Dame retaliated with a 66-yard kickoff return that set up the tying score.

Having seen how it was done, Charles Hinton returned the next kickoff 65 yards for us to the Irish 35. From the 24, Rae threw a strike to that man Garrison in the left corner of the end zone, and we led, 14–7, after one period.

We had to keep passing, because no one ran on the Irish that season. They allowed their opponents an average of two yards per carry. Meanwhile, we had returned to our old defense, which we had abandoned for a year and a half. Instead of four down linemen, we used three, with four linebackers. And we stopped the Irish on the next series.

A short punt set us up again, and with only 2:12 gone in the second quarter, Jones fired another bomb to Garrison, who took the ball away from Ellis for a 42-yard gain to the Notre Dame four. Three straight dives by

Sam Cunningham got another touchdown for a 21–7 lead.

The next Trojan to touch the ball was Dyer, two minutes later, as he intercepted his second pass and raced 53 yards down the sideline for another touchdown. We had them beaten, 28–7, and won, 28–14.

I've always respected Notre Dame's players, and most of our games have been hard-hitting but clean. On this afternoon, however, we had a hell of a fight. The officials triggered it by blowing a play. Rae fumbled in the second quarter and we recovered, but they awarded the ball to the Irish.

Our players were furious and insults were exchanged. A Notre Dame player jumped on John Vella's back, John punched back, and both benches emptied in a flash.

The coaches raced out to calm everybody down. My assistant, Marv Goux, brought down one Notre Dame player with a flying tackle that was reminiscent of his days as a USC linebacker.

I wound up pushing their All-American tackle, Greg Marx, who was 6-4 and 250 pounds. If he would have hit me he would have killed me. I looked up at him and got the hell away. If I fought anyone it would be Parseghian, not Marx.

In 1972 it was Notre Dame that had the opportunity to play spoiler. Our victory over UCLA two weeks earlier had boosted us into the Rose Bowl, our record to 10-0 and our unbeaten streak to 15 games. A victory over Notre Dame would give us the national championship, and we were favored by 14, far and away the biggest spread for anyone over the Irish in a decade.

Not that the Irish were so bad off. They had an 8-1 record, were ranked 11th, and Los Angeles was their last stop before the Orange Bowl. A young team, they had averaged 431 yards a game.

Our players had faced few strong challenges in that perfect season, but I had no illusions.

"I'm definitely up for the game," I told the team. "If you're foolish enough not to take Notre Dame seriously, you'll get beaten—and badly. They are far and away the best team we've played."

It was a game of great sweeps. We began like we were going to run the Fighting Irish right out of the Coliseum, but then spent a quarter scrambling for our lives. Finally, the flying feet of Anthony Davis made the difference.

Davis scored six touchdowns, including two of 97 and 96 yards on kickoff returns to tie an NCAA record. No USC player has ever scored more points in a game.

Notre Dame was led by a versatile sophomore quarterback, Tommy Clements, who threw three touchdown passes and took the Irish on a field-goal drive. They were the only team all year to outgain us—by 40 yards.

From scrimmage, the Irish contained Davis pretty well, limiting him to 99 yards on 22 carries, but they couldn't find him on kickoffs. He caught the game-opener on his three, cut to the left sideline, and with great blocking flashed all the way for the longest Trojan return in history. Ed Powell and Charles Hinton teamed up to wipe out the last defender. It took 17 seconds.

By the end of the first period we were ahead 19–3, as Davis carried the ball into the end zone from the one and swept in from the five.

Clements retaliated with a five-yard scoring pass to cut our edge to 19–10 at half, but we jumped ahead 25–10 early in the third quarter. Hinton's interception set us up on the Irish 41, and we moved to the four. From there, Davis shot in for his fourth touchdown.

You can only push Notre Dame around for so long.

First the Irish marched to our one, but lost the ball on a fumble. Then they chased Mike Rae all over the field and forced him into successive interceptions by Mike Townsend, the nation's leader.

Townsend's first interception was turned into a 47-yard scoring drive, with Clements firing an 11-yard pass to cut our lead to 25–17. The second ignited a 42-yard drive, and Clements struck again with a ten-yard touchdown pass. The Irish tried for two points, but failed.

Suddenly, with 1:19 left in the third quarter, we were ahead only 25 to 23, and our national championship was hanging by a shamrock. Our players were quiet, while the Irish whooped it up on the sideline.

Notre Dame eagerly lined up for the kickoff. Since the opening touchdown by Davis, Parseghian had ordered his kicker to squib the ball to keep Anthony from touching it. The kicker squibbed it again, but squibbed it out of bounds. Now he had to kick again, this time from the 35, and Ara ordered a deep kick. He didn't want us to get the ball near midfield. We didn't.

As the kickoff team huddled, Davis reminded everybody to set up a wedge quickly. Once again, as he caught the ball on the four, we opened a lane on the left, and once again he took it. Down the sideline he flew, leaving ten Irish players behind at the 50. Notre Dame had a man right in front of him, however, as the two met at midfield next to the left sideline. But A.D. held the ball in both hands, did a little dance in and out, and blew right by the Irish safety who got one futile hand on him as he went past.

Davis had improved his running time. This trip took only 12 seconds, and all the air went out of the Irish. We led 32 to 23.

"No team had run a kickoff back for a touchdown against Notre Dame since I've been here," said Parseghian later. "And Davis did it twice. TWICE! He killed us."

In the final period, an interception set up A.D.'s sixth touchdown, an eight-yard run, and then Sam Cunningham dove a yard for the final score. The 45 points we scored in our 45–23 victory are the most ever against a Parseghian team at Notre Dame.

At the end of Davis' second scoring return all of his teammates leaped from the bench and ran to the end zone where they hugged him.

"What did they say to you, A.D.?" I asked later.

"What could they say, coach?" he answered. "They said, 'We love you.' "

There was little love for Davis in South Bend. For days before the next game the following year, the Irish student body prepared for his arrival. They taped his picture on sidewalks—so they could walk on him. They hung him in effigy—life-size. They denounced him in signs, many of which were slashed with the word "Remember."

They even called for divine assistance. One sign pleaded:

"Our Father Who Art in Heaven, Don't Let Anthony Davis Score Seven."

And they called upon recent history for further inspiration. We had gone six years without losing to Notre Dame. Said another sign:

"Six Years Is Too Long."

During the game the student body shouted over and over with clenched fists: "Revenge! Revenge! Revenge!"

And back home in Indiana, on a drizzly day, my longest unbeaten streak died at 23 games. It was the fifth time since 1946 that Notre Dame had snapped somebody's streak of 23 or more without a loss, as they got the Trojans, 23 to 14. That was the key Irish win in an unbeaten season that landed them in the Sugar Bowl. There they beat Alabama, and this time they won the national championship.

Ranked eighth when they played us, Notre Dame brought a 5-0 record into our game, while we were 5-0-1, having tied Oklahoma, and were ranked fourth. For the first time in a decade we were favored at South Bend— by a point. I guess we missed the spread.

I was asked later if the law of averages had finally caught up with us in 1973. After all, how long can anyone keep beating Notre Dame? But although some weird things happened in that game, I don't think it was the law of averages. We lost to a very good team because of the complete failure of our kicking game. The key to the first half was our failure to punt more than a few feet. In the second we were nailed with an illegal fair-catch penalty on one punt and jumped offside on another to help sustain an Irish march.

We also lost, I think, because we played without two defensive regulars, outside linebacker James Sims and tackle Art Riley. Sims, who could run the 40 in 4.6, had to watch with a sprained ankle. Riley had trouble even watching. He lost his contact lenses on the eighth play of the game and had to sit out the rest of it.

Except for one play—Eric Penick's 85-yard touchdown sprint, which was the first run longer than 31 yards against us in almost two years—we probably played better defense than we did in 1972 when the Irish scored the same number of points. Penick might not have run 85 yards, either, with Sims on the field.

But we just kept giving them good field position, and you can't stop a team as powerful as Notre Dame on four downs, unless they gamble or you make a real big play.

And so they dominated the statistics, outgaining us by 161 yards and running off a remarkable 85 plays to our 48. They were well prepared, and they didn't make mistakes.

Three field goals by Bobby Thomas were the actual scoring difference. Thomas had kicked two out of ten in the previous five games, but the three he kicked against us may still be in flight.

The Irish didn't stop Davis on kickoffs with signs and banners. They stopped him by booting long, low line drives to his right or left, and then gang-tackling him. He returned none farther than our 35. And they stopped him from scrimmage, too. A.D. netted only 55 yards on 19 carries.

In the first half, Jimmy Lucas, our young punter, was too slow getting his kicks away, and when he did, they sailed only 15, 33 and 22 yards. The Irish got the ball on our 28, their 41 and our 47, and scored every time. Two field goals and a one-yard scoring sneak by Clements gave them a 13–7 halftime lead.

But they had to come from behind. Late in the first quarter we took a 7–3 lead when a 65-yard drive ended in a one-yard dash around right end by Davis. We still led 7–6 with about a minute left in the half when Clements faded to pass and threw right to Richard Wood, our All-American linebacker. But Wood slipped on the rain-soaked grass and fell, and an Irish end caught the ball on our 14. They scored their first touchdown shortly after that.

There were events like that all afternoon. On Notre Dame's final field-goal drive, which began when we seemed to have momentum and gave the Irish a nine-point lead, there were three big breaks in succession.

First we forced them to punt, but a defensive tackle jumped offside to give them a first down on our 47.

From there, they moved to our 38, where on fourth and one Clements took the ball from center but had it squirt out of his hands. Fullback Russ Kornman picked it out of the air and kept going for six yards and a first down—as if the play were planned.

Finally, one of our linebackers bumped a teammate

and dropped an interception on the goal line. That drive was late in the third quarter and made it final, 23–14.

I was proud that we had come back after the way the second half had started. The first scrimmage play was Penick's long run. It was a reverse, and the Irish gave their halfback great blocking to spring him, but then he ran right out of the arms of one of our cornerbacks on his 35 to go the rest of the way untouched. That put us behind, 20 to 7.

We snapped back immediately to go 70 yards in five plays, three of them passes from Pat Haden to Lynn Swann, the final one a tremendous catch by Lynn just inside the end zone. That made the score temporarily 20–14.

In the fourth quarter, when we trailed by nine, Haden marched us 66 yards, but with nine minutes left an Irish defender grabbed Davis' arm and knocked the ball loose on the Notre Dame 16, where they recovered.

With five minutes left, Haden threw a 23-yard pass to Johnny McKay, but he fumbled that away on the Irish 40.

This time it was USC that had made too many mistakes.

They told me the celebration in Notre Dame's locker room was wild. "Because Southern Cal's 23-game unbeaten streak began here at Notre Dame," said Parseghian, "I think it is appropriate that it has ended here as well."

As for me, I hummed the Notre Dame fight song softly after the game. I've known it a long time. Someone in our locker room asked me why I was doing that.

"There is," I said, "nothing else to hum."

PAIN: LOSING AND CRITICISM

"You just go nuts"

As I'VE INDICATED BEFORE, losing really gnaws at me. I take defeat as bitterly as anyone—maybe more so. It's the worst part of coaching. After a loss, I want to crawl in a hole and pull it around me so no one can get at me. Naturally I can't.

In 1971 our losing had reached the crisis stage. After tremendous success we suddenly lost four games in both 1970 and 1971. We rebounded in 1972 to win the national championship. But if 1972 had been like the other two years, I would have quit my job.

Aside from the 51–0 loss to Notre Dame, the middle of the 1971 season was the low point of my career. Slumps seem to happen to all coaches, but when they do they're devastating to your ego.

Bob Devaney was so discouraged he was ready to quit at Nebraska a few years ago—just before he won his two straight national titles. Darrell Royal and Bear Bryant were stunned by slumps in the 1960's, too. Bear told me he couldn't figure out what he was doing wrong, and that makes a coach desperate.

From 1967 through 1969 our record was 29-2-2, and we extended that streak to 32-2-3 until the middle of the 1970 season. We promptly lost eight of the next 13 games. I felt like I couldn't justify my pay.

Although I sometimes kidded in public—"I've told my assistants to get dark glasses and move around as low as possible during daylight"—I was dying on the inside.

A coach can sleep when he can put the finger on what's wrong with his team. If I review a game film and realize that an official caused us to lose by making a mistake, I can keep my sanity. Or, even though I base my life on being a good judge of talent, I don't feel stupid if I understand poor talent is our problem. If you can pinpoint it, you can correct it. But I couldn't pinpoint what was wrong. When that happens you really start doubting yourself. You just go nuts.

In the middle of the 1971 season, I called the assistants into my office.

"If we can't perform better than we are, I'm going to quit," I said, "and I suggest the rest of you should, too. There's no sense in us continuing to play football as poorly as we are now. We have enough talent to do a hell of a lot better than we are.

"So there must be something I'm doing wrong. And if I'm doing something wrong, there must be something you guys are doing wrong. Therefore, if this is going to continue to happen, we should leave. I have no intention of continuing to embarrass the university."

Before the Notre Dame game that year we lost three straight games, the first to explosive Oklahoma, which went 11–1, and the last two, which were the most depressing, to Oregon and Stanford.

Against Stanford we did the poorest coaching job of my career. And losing to Oregon hurt me tremendously not because I had played and coached there: It hurt me because they weren't that good.

We had several linebackers injured, but we took a 23–14 lead on Oregon, and they had to play their second-string quarterback the entire game. He was all of 5 feet 8, but he overtook us with his passing for a 28–23 lead. Still, we were going to win. With 26 seconds left, Jimmy Jones threw a 77-yard touchdown pass to Edesel Garrison.

It was nullified, because our flanker, Mike Morgan, lined up wrong. He lined up on the line as an end, instead of in the backfield. This made the tight end who was on the inside of him an ineligible receiver when he ran downfield.

Morgan was a senior. If we hadn't yet taught him to line up right, it was our fault. We were doing a damn poor job. But we hadn't exactly been stingy on defense either. Oregon gained almost 500 yards.

After we lost, I sat in the dressing room feeling about 100 years old. Our record was under .500 for the first time in a decade.

"If we can't beat Oregon," I said, "we don't deserve to go to any bowl. Not even the Marshmallow Bowl."

Stanford was next, and they began the game with a new formation for them, the power-I. But we should have recognized it. We had invented it. But we couldn't even line up right against our own formation. They outgained us by 140 yards in the first half and had us down 17–0 before we knew what hit us. We lost, 33–18. It was a sad joke. Stanford dominated us by running our own formation against us.

Since we had also lost our opener to Alabama, our record was now 2-4. What the hell had happened? Had the game passed me by? Had we gotten fat and lazy? People were all excited about the wishbone formation that season, but Nebraska was still using our I-formation and was on its way to a second straight national championship. What was the matter with us?

The morning of the Notre Dame game, seven days after Stanford, I finally realized what had gone wrong. I called a meeting of our coaches.

"The reason we haven't been winning," I said, "is that we are playing the wrong people. And our biggest weakness is that we don't have anybody else to play. We're playing people who do not run fast enough to play this game—and we're the slowest on defense. Any time we play a team with real good speed, we get outrun. And offensively, all the backs we have fumble too much."

I realized we had not been selective enough in our recruiting. We began to think, heck, we've been winning like crazy, and we're just going to keep winning, and that's all there is to it. When you assume you're always going to win, you ease up in your recruiting without even knowing that you're doing it. We'd think, "Ah, this player's all right. He can play. He's a lot like old Joe who played here when we had O.J."

Only we didn't have O.J. now. And all of a sudden a coach gets six or eight of these marginal players, and if he gives only 20 scholarships a year, like we do, he's in trouble. You can't give 20 scholarships and make eight mistakes.

I made up my mind that we weren't going to play defense anymore with players who weren't exceptionally fast—particularly on the outside. Most college offenses are option oriented, and with the success of Oklahoma in 1971 we felt more and more teams would be going to the wishbone. I decided that if anyone was going to beat us, they weren't going to outrun us.

The solution was to recruit a large group of freshmen and junior-college transfers who could fly.

I had actually begun to realize we were too slow in 1970, when our defense yielded 21 points a game, far and away the most of my career. So we recruited a brilliant group of freshmen, which included defensive players like All-American Richard Wood, Charles Phillips, Dale Mitchell, Ed Powell and Marvin Cobb and offensive players like Anthony Davis, Allen Carter, Pat Haden and my son, Johnny. But 1971 was the last year freshmen were not eligible, so they couldn't help us yet.

We thought we had improved the varsity too, but we hadn't. We had not recruited enough good people from junior college who could play right away, and we had not made enough defensive changes among the people we had. We were too stubborn. We continued to think that some of the players who couldn't perform in 1970 could do it in 1971—and they couldn't.

So that day at Notre Dame, besides alternating our quarterbacks, we went back to our old defensive alignment—three down linemen and four linebackers—made a couple of personnel changes and upset the Irish. We finished with four wins and a tie in our last five games.

But we still needed vast improvement, so we not only recruited more quick freshmen, but also nabbed some top JC transfers like offensive lineman Booker Brown, a future All-American, and linebackers Jimmy Sims and Ray Rodriguez.

And our 1972 defense was the fastest I had ever seen. The longest run those kids allowed in 12 games was 29 yards, and seven of the starters were new. The defense has been fast ever since.

In 1971 Oklahoma had run for 516 yards and 33 points against us. In 1973 the unbeaten Sooners ran for

330, passed for 9 and scored one touchdown. The 7–7 tie was their only blemish.

Whether a season is successful or not, however, I worry about fatheadedness among the older players every year. One of the things that hurts all coaches, like it did us in 1971, is waiting too long to make changes. We're all wishful thinkers and tend to hesitate to put in younger players for older ones who were good before, but are failing now. It's a little lame to say, "But remember he did it for us two years ago," when you're getting your tail beat now.

I warned our seniors before the unbeaten 1972 season: "Gentlemen," I said, "for two years we have not done as well as we should have. You know I prefer seniors over anybody else, but this is your last opportunity. If we start losing again, I'll go the rest of the year with younger players."

If older players have had great success before, such as winning a national championship or going to the Rose Bowl, they might give up if they lose a game or two early. This happened in 1970 when a loss to Stanford kicked off our slump. If a team is coming off a national title, how do you convince them that 9 and 2 is respectable?

Of all my teams, I'm most proud of the 1965 bunch for not giving up. That was an excellent team which had four shutouts, but it didn't make the Rose Bowl. The record should have been 8-1-1, but it was 7-2-1, and it was a damn shame.

Those kids had two very disappointing losses and rallied both times.

After beginning the season with four wins and a tie in five games, we lost to Notre Dame by a stunning 21 points. But the team shrugged it off, won the next two games and had UCLA practically knocked out in the third, with one foot in the Rose Bowl. That's when the Bruins struck on Gary Beban's two late bombs, and we came up with nothing.

The next week Mike Garrett won the Heisman Trophy, but he told me, "I'd trade it all if our team could play in the Rose Bowl."

But minutes after losing, Mike had gone to the UCLA locker room, tears in his eyes, to congratulate their players. When sportswriters asked him later how he felt, his answer, considering his disappointment, was remarkable:

"I'm mostly sorry for so many USC fans," he said. "That's what hurts more than anything . . . so many people suffering with me. UCLA came back. That's the sign of a good team. We played hard and I thought we deserved the game. But you always get what you deserve."

The next week, by a quirk of the schedule, we closed out our season with a meaningless game against Wyoming. And once again, our team came back. Garrett ran for 112 yards, Troy Winslow passed for four touchdowns and we beat a good team, 56 to 6. Garrett went out like a true champion.

Mike's response after the UCLA loss fulfilled a precept of mine. Win or lose—do it with dignity. Losing may help you grow up, but more than that I think you should shut up. I've never felt there's any reason to stand around and explain a defeat. I tell the players, "If you want to sound off, join the debate team."

If we win, I don't want to spend a long time discussing the game either. If I review the strategy, I feel it makes me sound arrogant, like I'm saying we won because we outwitted them. I'm interested in winning, not outwitting people.

But I am sensitive, and I was furious for a long time after that UCLA game in 1965, because people in Los Angeles implied that UCLA's Tommy Prothro won because he outwitted me. Damn, I thought, we outgained them by 135 yards, had nine more first downs, dominated play for 56 minutes, but lost five fumbles and got beat on two late bombs after leading all day. Did Prothro plan it that way?

We beat them so badly that I thought we should never lose to a Prothro team. They couldn't run on us that day because they didn't know to block a running play. They were never able to block a running play correctly. Their linemen sat back on their haunches.

But when we lost to UCLA the next year by a touchdown, I became classified as the stupid coach in town. And Prothro was the genius. Nobody called me a genius when I beat him three straight times from 1967 to 1969, and no one in Los Angeles said I was a genius when we beat UCLA three straight times before Prothro got there.

However, if we lose, I feel I should be man enough to accept the loss and not show my frustration—except to people who are close to me, like my wife and my assistants. We'll all gather in a hotel room after I speak briefly to one of our support groups, have a drink by ourselves and discuss the game. After the coaches go home, I'll sit alone and rehash it.

And, trapped with my thoughts, this is when I think, "God damn, I wish we hadn't tried this."

I usually get to bed about 12 or one, win or lose, and I'm up by five, thinking about the game again. If we lose often, like in 1970 and 1971, it eats at me. I'll sit and brood, looking for an answer. But sometimes in a particular game there are no answers. The players are human and they make mistakes. The players on the other team could play beyond themselves. Sometimes—and I know it's hard for the alumni to believe this—the other team is simply better.

But you have to come back from defeat. We did it in 1965 and we did it in 1966 when our team was humiliated by Notre Dame, and then rebounded to play a tremendous game against favored Purdue and Bob Griese in the Rose Bowl. We went in as 13-point underdogs.

But Winslow and our leading rusher, Don McCall, who had been hurt the last two weeks of the season, were both healthy, and we outgained Purdue by 80 yards. McCall led everybody in rushing with 92 yards, and Winslow completed 12 of 17 passes. With two and a half minutes left, his touchdown pass to Rod Sherman cut Purdue's lead to 14–13.

Losing may scare the hell out of me, but we didn't settle for a tie. I never have, before or since. We gambled for two points, Winslow threw an interception in the end zone, and we lost.

Fans were amazed that we didn't kick. After all the criticism we had endured for being voted into the Rose Bowl over UCLA, I guess they figured a tie would be a moral victory. But there was no question in my mind. For a month I had told my players they could beat Purdue. When the opportunity came, how could I take the chance away from them? I think they all agreed with me, but I didn't have time to hold a convention.

The only time a coach should ever play for a tie is when something bigger than the game itself is at stake. For example, there have been times we could have clinched the Rose Bowl bid with a tie, although none of the games ever came down to that.

People asked me after that Purdue loss if I wasn't worried about the bitter taste in the mouths of our fans —it was our third straight defeat. But I don't think we should worry about the taste in other people's mouths. We worry about our team and what we preach. And our philosophy is to go for the win.

Win or lose, I have always said a coach must learn to accept criticism, but I still hate it. I don't mean I can't take it myself, but I am concerned about the way it affects my family. When I first became USC's head coach, the oldest of my four children, Michele, was only seven. Critical remarks made by newspapers and by the public were picked up by other children and repeated to my children. This happens with the sons and daughters of all coaches, and we know there are no crueler people in the world than young kids. They'll flat out tell your children that their father is stupid.

I read everything that's written about our football team in the newspapers, and I think over the long haul I've gotten the most wonderful treatment from sportswriters of any USC coach in a long time. But I have complaints. And when I think something written is wrong, I'll tell the writer off.

The writer I despised most worked several years ago for the *Los Angeles Times*. Sid Ziff. He was unfair and never asked a question to determine what the truth was. He just stuck it to people.

A coach expects to be criticized on his won-lost record, but no one should ever do what Ziff did to me in 1962. He crucified me. He wrote that one of our kids played with a broken neck—and then said I had the audacity not to let him stay in the team hotel several weeks later, before the Rose Bowl.

The young man was a defensive tackle named Mike Gale, and he broke his neck tackling Notre Dame quarterback Daryle Lamonica in the last game of the regular season. Mike said later his neck felt a little funny at the time, but he just thought he had pulled a muscle in his shoulder and so he kept playing. He played 28 minutes. He said it didn't even hurt.

But after the game X-rays revealed he had a fracture dangerously close to the spine. Gale was told if he had hit Lamonica just a fraction harder he might have been killed. It was a very freakish injury.

Mike was to recover fully, but his football career was over. He was placed in a body cast from the hips up. A few weeks later we were preparing for the Rose Bowl and Ziff came to our practice, where he encountered Gale, who was watching. Sid talked to Mike and wrote a column about him. It was headlined "No Room for Gale." In the middle were these words:

"Mike's name and picture will appear in the Rose Bowl program and he'll have a seat on the bench. When the team goes to Disneyland, he'll be along. But he won't be with the team when it checks into the Sheraton-West for the final week before the Rose Bowl game. They told him there wasn't a room for him. In the holiday season, the hotel is usually crammed.

"I suppose I ought to keep out of it, but I think somehow or some way I would manage to find a room for Mike Gale."

Ziff didn't even ask Gale if he wanted to come to the hotel, and he didn't have the courtesy to call and ask me about it either. He was a big-time sportswriter for the city's largest paper, and in his eyes I was a nothing young coach.

When an article like that is written, clippings of it wind up everywhere and I get flooded with letters, all of which imply that I'm a mean son of a bitch. And the angry letters poured in.

I liked Mike Gale—I saw him in Hawaii a couple of years ago and we laughed about the story—but there was no reason to take him to the Rose Bowl hotel. If we were a Big Ten team coming, say, from Michigan to California, I would have brought Mike and put him in another section of the hotel. Then he could have seen California. But it was silly to bed him down in a Los Angeles hotel, three miles from campus. What exciting new places was he going to visit?

If he had come and stayed with the team, instead of sleeping in another part of the hotel, he wouldn't have had any holiday fun. Our Rose Bowl rule was, and still is, that after we move into the hotel on December 26 we do everything together. All the players and coaches get up at the same time, eat at the same time and work at the same time, so we stay united. If not, we'll have five players doing one thing, five doing another and 25 or 30 doing something else. Then we're no longer a team. We're a bunch of individuals.

At Rose Bowl time we can't make excuses for someone who is injured, or someone who is married, or someone who has a girl friend. If we don't all do the same thing, the team's concentration is disrupted. Why should I put Mike in the hotel to tell him to go to bed every night at nine?

He got everything else—medical care first, of course, and then a Rose Bowl watch, and trips with the team to Disneyland and the prime-rib feast at Lawry's.

When I complained about the first column, Ziff produced another headlined, "Now It's Up to Gale." He wrote:

"Coach John McKay says that was his decision not to take injured tackle Mike Gale to the hotel with the rest of the Trojan team for the final week before the Rose Bowl game, but if Mike feels strongly about it, they would have a room for him.

"Gale broke his neck in the Notre Dame game and

will be in a surgical cast for another three months. He'll never play another game of football.

"McKay says his policy always has been to take no one that's hurt to the hotel. His reasoning is that anyone not actively in the game will not be as interested in the preparation and tend to horse around a bit.

"He agreed that a boy with a broken neck would hardly fall into that category.

" 'However,' he said [here Sid was quoting me], 'any time there's a boy hurt it isn't as much fun for him at the hotel. About all it amounts to is one meeting after another. And I only want people who will be in the game at the meetings.

" 'Truthfully, I think he would have a better time not living at the hotel. Basically, he'll get all the rewards of the rest of the team. He'll get to come with us to Disneyland and Lawry's.

" 'One of the rewards of the game, in my opinion, is not going to the hotel. I would have to enforce the same rules for Gale that apply to all the others. No phone calls. Nobody gets to go home. Nobody sees anybody. There'll be no distractions of any kind.

" 'But in Mike's case I wouldn't want him to feel badly about it and promise that I'll have a talk with him. We'll waive the rule if he feels strongly about it.' "

Ziff never asked Gale if he wanted to come. When I did, he said, "Coach, I don't want to."

In this second column, Ziff admitted Gale hadn't indicated he wanted to go to the hotel, but I was still his target. The column continued:

"Mike didn't tell me that he wanted to go to the hotel. He simply stated as a matter of fact that he wasn't on the list.

"It was my thought that *a boy who had played in the Notre Dame game with a broken neck* deserved all the honors and privileges his school could bestow upon him.

"I admire McKay. I think his team is wonderful, and he's the coach of the year. I think he muffed this one. I wouldn't leave it up to Gale. I'd want him along. I'd even have a seat for him at the head table."

So despite everything I said, I was stuck out to dry. I realize public figures risk criticism. But the critics should make sure what they say is warranted. If I'm a bad coach, explain why. I've won this many games and lost this many. If the team plays poorly, write that. I'll probably agree with you. I know when the team plays poorly. But don't imply that I'm heartless, because I decide not to take a player with a broken neck to the team's hotel.

My assistants who are away from home half the season aren't even allowed to bring their wives. I don't bring Corky until New Year's Eve.

But when I came to Los Angeles from Oregon, I was very cynical about Southern California sportswriters. There were several in the 1950's who were responsible for the formation of what's called in Los Angeles "the gutty little Bruin syndrome." Without question, I feel that USC has not gotten enough credit for winning in the last 20 years, compared to our crosstown rival, UCLA. This was true when I was at Oregon, and it's been true ever since I've been at USC.

I used to laugh when I was at Oregon, but I don't laugh anymore. The routine is always, "Boy, SC sure has all the players." I get so damn tired of that. If we win it's because we should anyway, and if we lose it has to be because we're stupid.

It all began when Red Sanders was the coach at UCLA and Jess Hill, who was later our athletic director, was the coach at USC. When Jess got the job in 1951, two years after Sanders came to UCLA, the press and the alumni didn't want him. Some of them figured they'd put him in his place.

Sanders had a better winning percentage than Hill, but not that much better (.776 for nine years to .722 for six years). Sanders lost two Rose Bowl games in as many tries, while Hill won one and lost one. The game Jess won was the only time the Pacific Coast Conference beat the Big Ten in the first 13 years of their current pact.

But all of a sudden Sanders was a messiah and Hill wasn't worth a pile of beans. The writers always said—and Sanders fostered the myth—that Red had the poor, struggling little kids, "the gutty little Bruins," while Hill and USC had the big guys. We used to sit up in Oregon and shake our heads. My current assistant coach, Marv Goux, was one of Hill's best big guys. He was the team captain, center and star linebacker in the middle 1950's at 5-10, 185 pounds.

Poor SC couldn't beat us at Oregon. They were 3-4 against us when I was there, including the first two years of Don Clark's tenure after Hill. At the same time UCLA was 7-1, losing only in 1957 when Oregon went to the Rose Bowl. SC was supposed to beat Sanders every year and they couldn't beat Oregon. In the years that Sanders and Hill coached against each other, Red had nine All-American selections and Jess had five.

What had happened? The Los Angeles sportswriters loved Sanders—Ziff, Braven Dyer and Dick Hyland of the *Times* and George Davis of the *Herald*—because he was their drinking buddy. Hill would hardly ever drink with them, and they resented him.

I would drive down from Oregon to recruit and occasionally join Sanders and the writers in their favorite hangout. I admit I liked Red and he liked me, but when I listened to those writers drinking and talking with him,

I realized Hill was going to have to win 77 to 0 to even get a pat on the back. Hill was straightlaced and Sanders was a regular, down-to-earth guy. He couldn't lose.

But Jess Hill was dead in the press. The average person would read the papers and think he was a poor coach and not much of a person.

Hill and I had our differences later at USC, and he did things as a coach that I would never do, but God, don't criticize him because he wouldn't buy drinks and spend all night with you because he couldn't stand you. I watched it happen and I was appalled.

Although I was never criticized as an Oregon assistant coach, I would get mad when the press knocked Len Casanova, if I thought it was a cheap shot. But there was one writer I admired and respected a lot in the early days, George Pasero of the *Oregon Journal*. George is still a sportswriter and a friend of mine. I'd trust him forever. He does one thing that many writers find difficult: he quotes the person he's interviewing accurately.

When I first became USC's head coach, the guys who were the nicest to me were Paul Zimmerman of the *Los Angeles Times* and Bud Furillo of the *Los Angeles Herald-Examiner*. I was a nobody, but they listened to me and respected me. Paul was with me when Ohio State whacked us in Columbus my first year. I was a rookie and he was an experienced sports editor. He came over to my table, put a bottle of booze down on it and talked to me.

"Paul," I said, "we're gonna get us some players and we're going to win and continue to win." He and Furillo believed in me. Ziff was determined to make me a failure from the beginning.

Today, *Los Angeles Times* columnist John Hall is another man who's become a friend of mine. John has been a tremendous booster of college athletics. And Bud

Tucker, a freelance sportswriter, is living proof that I can get along well with some newspapermen. Bud once lived in my house for three months. He had changed jobs and was in the process of moving his family from San Diego.

But, for example, Georg Myers of the *Seattle Times* never writes what I say. He'll turn my answers to his questions around to make me sound arrogant.

Newspapers can easily convey the image they want to. When we flew into Seattle in 1967 the *Seattle Times* had a headline which said something like "Mighty Trojans Come to Town."

They sent a photographer out to shoot the mighty Trojans, and the photographer asked for the starting backfield. It included O. J. Simpson, Steve Sogge, Jimmy Lawrence and Danny Scott. O.J. was the only player over 5-10.

So help me, the photographer looked at me and said, "Don't you have any bigger players?"

"Well, you asked for the starting backfield," I said. "This is it."

"We want some bigger players," he said. He spotted Ron Yary, our 6-foot-5 All-American tackle, and asked me to send him over. Then he took a picture of me looking up at Yary. That's the one they ran Saturday morning before the game. They had their picture of the big Trojans.

Wells Twombly of the *San Francisco Examiner* wrote something about USC in 1972 that made me furious. He said in his paper that our players were so stupid that they couldn't get into reform school. Then he sent me a letter to explain why he had done it. He said he wouldn't have written that if he worked in Los Angeles, but I must understand that sportswriting is just show business.

When he says our players couldn't get into reform school, that's just show business.

Well, one of those players was my son. How the hell could Twombly make a statement like that in a publication read by hundreds of thousands of people? And then tell me that if he were in Los Angeles he'd write the same about Stanford? It is not show business for a leading writer to insult college youngsters.

The same year, when we beat Stanford in Palo Alto and were cursed by fans, another Bay Area writer ripped me unfairly. It happened after I had said, "I'd like to beat Stanford by 2,000 points."

After I had sounded off in the locker room, Dick Friendlich of the *San Francisco Chronicle,* whom I have known for 20 years, came over to me. Everyone else had left. He sat down and had a cigar with me and asked what had happened. I told him. He was the only writer that day I told exactly what had happened.

"Dick," I said, "I was most mad because they insulted my kids. I guess I'm paid to be insulted, but not my kids."

"You know," he said, "you're right. I agree with you. I believe in what you say."

The next day he ripped me in his paper worse than anyone—and I got ripped pretty good by a lot of people. He called me "a vindictive old man" after saying he agreed with me.

I've always opened my dressing room to the press immediately after games, instead of locking everybody out for 30 or 40 minutes like some coaches. I've gone out and drunk with the writers and talked very candidly with them. I've prided myself on the fact that I could lose 51 to 0 and walk into my dressing room and face the press and say the best team won, and that's it. I'll answer all your questions. No locked doors. No running out. No alibis. I don't always say a lot, and sometimes I'm keyed up and irritable after a game, but I've always tried to be a good winner or loser.

That one day at Stanford, however, made me a bad guy. Automatically I was guilty in the eyes of the press, because I sounded off after a win. If I live to be a thousand I won't forget it, because I resent having tried to be fair for years and then winding up being treated that way. I've never been that friendly in dressing rooms since.

I discover, too, as I go into my 15th year as a head coach, that I'm getting more and more tired of answering the same questions over and over, some of which are very inane. I feel most comfortable on Tuesday mornings during the season when I casually sit around with several writers I trust and discuss football over coffee and rolls. We usually ramble on for two hours and have gone as long as three. In this setting they'll ask probing questions and I'll give in-depth answers, some of them off the record. But they've always respected my confidence. The session usually ends with me diagramming plays.

Loel Schrader of the *Long Beach Independent,* another writer I consider a friend, is such a glutton for football that he often comes out of that long session, writes his story, and then watches us practice, scooting around the field on my golf cart.

I feel those Tuesday morning sessions are sensible and civilized, but dressing rooms after games are getting more and more crowded and frantic. First the sportswriters surround me, and then some radio announcer sticks a long microphone right up to my mouth and asks what I thought of the game. When I start talking, some man in the back always yells, "Please speak up!" If I spoke up, I'd eat the microphone.

Rose Bowl dressing rooms are really small, and it's

virtual chaos in there with the people and the TV cameras and cables and lights. Half the time I get pinned right against a locker.

Many of the writers will go talk to the players, which is a modern trend—when I was a player no one asked me any questions—and then they'll come back after I've spoken for several minutes to their colleagues. I'm about to leave and here comes the second wave. The same questions come up again. There's no perfect system, but I'd love to answer a question once and not 15 times in the same interview.

Of course, it's not easy for writers and announcers either, pushing through the dressing room to track down players, stumbling over equipment and sliding on the wet floor. With all the showers going and the people packed in there, the room becomes like a sauna. Writers say they get as sweaty as the players.

Most sportswriters are very nice people, and as I've said, I consider many of them my friends. I think the ones in Los Angeles today are probably the best in the city's history. But there are still one or two I don't trust. There are some who put that tag behind their name and think that they're God. Well, they aren't God. I have never believed that sportswriters can hire or fire me. Only my record will do that.

IN DEFENSE OF
MY GAME

*"Football: the college
whipping boy"*

COLLEGE FOOTBALL has great value. Take the USC-UCLA game, for example. We get 80,000 people together, 40,000 of them knowing who one coaching idiot is and 40,000 knowing who the other idiot is. I mean, they have decided on two idiots. That's got to be great group therapy.

But many people in this country do not consider college football as therapeutic. They see it as a gigantic waste of time. The complaints are as diverse as the critics. Some contend that universities should stick to education, and there's nothing educational about football. Others complain that players don't graduate, that they're favored over other students or conversely that they're exploited, that college ball is merely a free farm system for the pros, and, finally, if nothing else, that it's too expensive.

Most of the critics don't know one damn thing about

football. They're always popping off with clichés like "All football players are dumb." You almost question *their* intelligence. People who haven't competed in football have no idea what anyone can get out of it, and they have no idea what the players are like.

To begin with, I don't believe anyone can set himself up as an authority on which endeavors are important and which are unimportant. I doubt you could get the world to agree on the importance of as many as two things. I would never presume to be an expert on other departments at USC, such as English or engineering, so I resent it when everyone is an expert on the athletic department.

But you know what happens in America. People all want the best. And they've fought to have the best English department, the best engineering department and the best football team. Much of the criticism started because the football players got more publicity than the engineers.

While I want to defend football, I don't claim to be building character, or moral fiber, as a coach. Character should be built in the home and church. The way some coaches talk you would think no one can be any good unless he plays football. That eliminates half the people in the world. Half of them are women.

But there are values football can help impart. It teaches the players discipline, self-sacrifice, the ability to accept criticism, how to perform under duress and the importance of teamwork.

I think football is more liberal than, say, engineering, because you learn to get along with your fellow man to work for the common good. Isn't that the foundation of society?

Football helps cure boys of selfish attitudes—not all of them, but many of them. It teaches them that no matter how talented one individual is, he's still one individual, and he's going to accomplish very little that way. But if these men block well, this man fakes well and that man handles the ball well, then O. J. Simpson can run for a touchdown. There has to be cooperation among people to get something done.

I thought this concept was explained very well last year by Rich Horton, a defensive back from Colgate. His comment appeared in an NCAA article revealing why college players liked the game.

"It brings people of every culture and race into a unified piece," said Horton. "It inspires the idea of dependence and mutual respect among individuals. And, above all, it helps them realize their own capacities and potentials."

Yes, it also helps people realize their potential. There are so many who can't cope with life's problems, who panic if anything unusual occurs. You would have to say that our 1969 team, which won four times in the last three minutes, learned a big lesson: No matter what the situation looks like, there is a chance for victory. Now, whether that is victory in a football game or persevering to discover a cure for cancer, a man must learn to keep trying.

Football teaches mental and physical discipline. A boy finds out it takes concentrated effort to reach any goal. You've got to get up when you don't want to, run when you don't want to, give up food and drink, ignore pain and learn to play within the rules. Many youngsters have very little discipline—and that's too bad.

Does a player lose his independence? No, because we also want him mentally disciplined enough to act on his own. You can't become a robot in football under any circumstances. Defenses and offenses change too quickly. If a play is called and we audibilize to another one, each player is on his own. He's been told what to do, but that doesn't mean he will. He's under the stress of having to react and make the right decision. And he has to think quickly to make it. Football is more individualistic than people realize.

It isn't just the playing that's important to a young man; it's the whole environment that's educational. It's seeing other areas of the country, meeting other people, learning to talk to newspapermen and fans, speaking at banquets; in short, exposing yourself to a variety of people and conditions.

That's why I disagree with coaches who shield their players. The kids should meet as many people as possible. They should learn to communicate.

Football isn't a cure-all. There are other ways to learn these values, and I've seen many young men football didn't do much for. But for the most part it's helped the great majority.

The people who gripe about athletic scholarships don't realize what a player gives up to get one. Are they the best scholarships on campus? Hell, no. In reality they're among the poorest. Not only must the players work hard, but they must come back to campus a month before school is in session. Many of them give up lucrative summer jobs, blowing $500 or $600.

And, according to NCAA rules, students on athletic scholarships can't work for supplemental income during the school year. No rule prohibits a student on an academic scholarship from holding a job.

College students often complain because faculty members won't get close to them, but when coaches get involved with their players, they're criticized for pampering athletes. For a decade everyone in universities has heard about the "publish or perish" rule, which forces professors to spend many of their nonteaching hours researching and writing. Thus, they can't properly counsel their students. But the athletic departments do the best college counseling jobs in America.

Faculty members complain that they've got too many students to see them all. And they've got a point. If you lecture to 500 or 1,000 students, how many can you talk to in a week? Or a month? Even if you're not writing, the sheer weight of numbers is overpowering. But we're never too busy to see an athlete. Our student-teacher ratio is about 9 to 1, which is excellent. My assistants check the players' academic progress at least once a week.

We've discovered that the failure and dropout rates for football players at USC are actually lower than the university overall. They should be, because we check on them all the time. They're more organized, so they produce better than the average student.

In one four-year study made at USC in the mid-1960's, the all-university grade point average for men was 2.51. For football players it was 2.55.

The average number of USC students who graduate in four years is 51 percent, which is in line with the national average. This figure includes those who drop out for all reasons: academic, financial, emotional, marital and so forth, and also those who stretch their education over a longer period. The football players' average for graduation in four years is 71 percent.

USC's number of students who graduate in five years rises to just over 70 percent. For football players it's 81 percent.

Of course, the football staff realizes our job is to win and make the Rose Bowl. We're primarily concerned with teaching football. It's getting our players through college and they have a responsibility to it. But win or lose, they have to be in class on Monday.

We're always preaching to them to be good students.

You're here to get an education and you're a damn fool if you don't. We lay it on the line. You're getting paid an education to play football, and if you don't want it, you're crazy.

I don't know of anybody with any intelligence who spends three or four years on a college campus and isn't a little better off when he gets out. All the courses thrown at you may strike a spark that will fire now, or maybe even five years later.

Warren Stephenson, a linebacker who played for us in 1960 and 1961, was not a very good student when he came from high school, but at USC Warren found himself. A year ago he got his Ph.D. I've seen this sudden inspiration many times, both at USC and Oregon. A player fools around for a couple of years, not taking his education seriously, and then you look up in his junior year, and he's running around carrying a briefcase. Just like that, he's a tremendous student. Would he have done this if not given the opportunity?

I don't know of a greater rebuff to the charge of exploitation. Can anyone put a value on this chance to get an education?

Athletes miss more school being on the baseball or basketball teams than they do playing football. But football players have always been accused of being reluctant to hit the books. The 1972 Football Register revealed that 60 percent of the pro football players had not completed college. People said, "I told you so."

I admit that many players who go into pro football don't complete their education as quickly, because they take their bonus money and drop out of school. Chances are they've never seen that much cash before. But most of our players who became pros either picked up their degrees on time or came back to get them—young men like Mike Garrett, Ron Yary, Clarence Davis, Marlin

McKeever and Ron Mix. Many of them, such as Willie Brown, Ben Wilson and Gary Kirner, earned master's degrees.

O. J. Simpson is occasionally cited as an example of a player who didn't graduate. O.J. is maybe 10 units short. He quit school after signing a contract with an automobile manufacturer and went on the road to do advertisements. It would have cost him $100,000 to stay and get a degree. But he can come back at any time and get it. However, he may never need one. No one has proven to me the only reason you go to college is to get a degree. You go to get educated. So if you're nine or ten or 15 units short, what does that mean? It means you don't have a piece of paper.

Still, the critics never talk about the players who use their money from pro football to come back and finish their education or finance graduate school.

College administrators have complained that we're just a farm system for the pros. But less than 3 percent of all college players turn professional. How can anyone call that a farm system? In 1972 we had 30 ex-Trojans playing in the NFL, including some who had competed as long ago as 1960. That's 30 from 12 seasons, or an average of two and a half per year.

Obviously, in some years we may send six or seven players into pro football. But colleges train students for careers in business. Doesn't pro football qualify as a business? It's a big part of our economy and tremendous entertainment for millions. Why should schools only be interested in graduating engineers and dentists?

Besides, people talk about a player going into pro football as if his life ended, as if he'll never do anything else. Even most of the pros leave the game in the end and move into some other field.

But that still leaves over 97 percent of the college players who go into some other profession.

"A minority of college players compete with one eye on the pros," says former USC All-American and All-Pro Ron Mix. "But for the overwhelming majority, college is a place for an athlete to get an education and some attention. Most play football for personal pleasure and attention."

Pete Adams, our 1972 All-American tackle who now plays for Cleveland, agrees.

"For a long time I believed I had pro potential, but I didn't exactly point for the pros," Pete told an interviewer last year. "I never felt I was on a pro farm at USC. Most college players are in it for the pleasure they get out of football, and that included me. I wouldn't play football, college or pro, if I didn't like it.

"After my years at USC I certainly don't feel exploited either. Football uses you, but you use football, too. In 1972 I wasn't thinking much about pro football or being exploited. I was just thinking about the next game. I wanted to win them all."

Some university officials have contended that as long as major college football exists and does send dozens of young men into the pros each year, the pros should help pay the collegiate costs. I disagree. I see no reason for pro sponsorship, because we're not a real farm system. Besides, people who give money sooner or later demand control.

It's also been asserted that coaches are indifferent to their players after their last game. "As soon as they get through with them," goes the refrain, "they forget them." I don't know of many coaches who do that.

I feel that any time we can help our ex-players in any way, we should try and do it. We tell them all to come back—that USC is their second home. I don't believe in sending a young man on his way and forgetting him. So if they ask us, we find them jobs or give them recommendations for others. Many want to be coaches themselves, and when we hear of high school openings, we'll call a likely candidate and offer to recommend him and set up an interview with the principal.

Although we help our players in and out of school, I don't believe their status as football players entitles them to any special privileges on campus. Each one should be an integral part of the student body. I think the majority of ours are.

By far the greatest criticism of football, however—and much of it comes from our own ranks—is that it costs too much. Very few people say, "I'm against intercollegiate athletics." They say, "I'm against football."

I once asked a group of NCAA representatives, "Why do you spend 99 percent of your time complaining about football?" Because of the costs, they answered. It's an unfair criticism.

"If you had three restaurants and two were losing money," I said, "would you harass the one that was keeping you in business?"

I want to make sure athletic administrators see that point. Why undermine the one sport that holds the others up? If all we care about is showing a bigger profit, then let's cut out the smaller sports that have no profit. I wouldn't want to do that, because I like all sports and believe in a well-rounded program, but eventually that will be the answer if costs keep shooting up. If you ran out of money, logically you would only keep the restaurant open that was making it.

Football could survive at USC very well with crowds of only 25,000 a game, but it couldn't run the rest of the athletic program, which is what it's asked to do. As athletic director, which I've been since 1971, I'm often accused of favoring football—and that's both right and wrong. I like all sports and will help the other coaches as much as I can, but if we're going to have a total athletic program, we better have a successful football program. The Coliseum, with a capacity for 94,000 people, stands across the street from our campus. That represents a lot of dollars. And the additional revenue from television can be enormous.

Frank Broyles of Arkansas said it best: "Football has always been the college whipping boy, but it's also the sport that does all the giving."

The phrase "rising cost of athletics" is phony anyway. It leads people to assume we're spending wildly.

You know what's creating the rising cost? Tuition and room and board. When I was at Oregon the tuition for an out-of-state student was about $350 a year. Now it's $1,900. Figure 40 players from out of state at $350 each in 1955 and then plan on the same 40 at $1,900 today. That'll give you a clear picture of where the rising cost of athletics lies. One total is $14,000. The other is $76,000.

Food prices have ballooned too, and not only housewives feel the pinch. At universities, this has caused room and board to skyrocket. Between 1972 and 1973 our dormitory food bill went up $110 per athlete per year. With about 200 athletes in all sports, that's an increase of $22,000 in that one item alone.

Other costs, besides tuition and room and board, are jumping too, but we've gotten very tight-fisted on those. There are ways to economize. For example, by percentage, we're not spending nearly as much money for equipment as we once did, because we don't buy as much as we did in 1950 or 1960. USC spent $23,000 for equipment in 1960, and prices have doubled since. But in 1973 we spent only $26,000. We don't need stacks of extra pants, shoes, jerseys and tackling dummies.

We don't always travel first class. We don't always stay at the best hotels. We have fewer players on scholarships than USC did before I came. The most I've ever had, freshmen through seniors, is 91. The NCAA rule now limits schools to 105. Before, some of them had as many as 130.

I admit we have one advantage over an Arkansas or Nebraska, because we're in a densely populated area, which cuts our recruiting costs to a tenth of what some might be. That's because we don't travel as much.

But no matter how far you have to travel, I don't believe you need to recruit more than 16 or 20 players a year—if you're right on those 16 or 20. If you get 20 good ones a year, that's a total of 80. If you can't win with 80 players, you can't win.

We don't have athletic dorms either. Freshmen are required to live in the regular school dormitories, but the others stay in apartments. Older players still draw their room and board allotment, but that doesn't require building fancy new dorms. Players win games, not dormitories.

I've heard about all I can stand, too, from coaches who say they can't make money because the pros draw all the people. To hell with that idea. Whoever went to the University of the Rams? What about your alumni?

Several years ago we drew something like 31,000 at Stanford, and John Ralston, the coach, came over to me and said, "We just can't do anything to get the people out."

"Why can't you?" I said.

"Well, you know, we have the Oakland Raiders and San Francisco 49ers right next door."

"John," I said, "the Raiders and 49ers have nothing

to do with your attendance. If you have a good team and publicize your stars like college coaches should, you'll draw a lot of people."

Stanford got Jim Plunkett and a group of other excellent players, started to win, and the last three times we've played up there, the crowd has been between 80,-000 and 90,000 people.

Pro ball won't run anyone out of town. If we're winning, it doesn't hurt us when the Rams are successful. There's just more interest in football.

The pros have one big advantage: identification. Everybody knows about Joe Namath. Even so, we can do the same thing with O. J. Simpson, Mike Garrett or Anthony Davis. Before, during and after the season I make a point of publicizing my players. I talk about how good they are. Why should anyone come out and watch, if you say you're going to have a miserable team? Coaches who are eternal pessimists are just trying to convince people that they're geniuses. When they win they hope fans will say, "Boy, he must be some smart coach to win without any talent."

I've also heard the argument that one-platoon football is cheaper, but nobody's ever proven that. When USC had one-platoon football in the early 1950's, there were more people on scholarships than there are now. When the big schools went to one-platoon football, you know what the small schools did? They stayed two-platoon. All the time we were playing our one-platoon game, schools like Lewis and Clark were playing two-platoon. They don't have five cents. If two-platoon football is so damn expensive, why didn't they switch?

And a reversion to one-platoon would be a terrible alternative. All it will do is make the game less enjoyable to watch, which *would* make it difficult to compete with the pros.

Some oldtimer told me once that playing both offense

and defense develops more character in kids. That's ridiculous. For one thing, less of them will get to play. So how about the character of the long line sitting on the bench?

The idea is absurd, anyway. I don't see how we'll teach an offensive player character by forcing him to learn to tackle. Some great people never tackled anyone. Look at George Washington.

I laugh when I hear the oldtimers brag about being tough enough to go both ways. They were smaller, slower and loafed twice as much. The game was completely different.

But in all this clamor about football's cost, no one talks about its positive monetary effect. Our fund raisers tell me endowments for the whole university go up when we win. There can't be a better rallying point for a university than football. It draws the alumni back to see what's going on. Why do they always have homecoming during football season? There's not a lot of people who get up in the morning and think about dropping down to their old campus. But football gets them. And then maybe they'll walk over and visit the school of journalism or the school of dentistry and wind up giving money.

Some of these faculty people who are against football say they'd get just as many people without a football game. I'd like to see them do it.

And if we're on television, and the screen shows the president and all the buildings, alumni around the country can look and say, "Hey, that's my school." Think how much that's worth.

A major way for schools to make more money is by sensible scheduling. In our case, I did some financial research shortly after becoming athletic director and made a startling discovery:

USC would be better off as an independent. With our current schedules, we're being robbed of a lot of money by staying in the Pacific-8.

When our alumni see these figures, they'll think it's a scandal. When we play certain conference schools, in their stadium every other year, we lose a fortune. That's because the league is all wrong, populationwise. It's too heavy in the south—in California.

For each game during the year we split gate receipts 50-50. When we played Oregon in Eugene in 1968, 1970 and 1972, we took home $34,000, $39,000 and $37,000 as our share. When we played in the Coliseum in 1971, Oregon made $95,000.

The same disparity is true of Washington State and Oregon State, which don't draw very much at home either. In 1968, Oregon State made $91,500 in Los Angeles. The next year we flew back from Corvallis with $43,000. In both 1970 and 1972, Oregon State pocketed $105,000 in the Coliseum.

Washington State made $85,000 and $96,000 off our games in Los Angeles in 1969 and 1971. In 1970 we each grossed $19,000 at Spokane. That barely paid our expenses for the game.

Finally we switched our game with Washington State from Spokane to Seattle in 1972 and increased both schools' revenue to $79,000. But there's no guarantee Washington State will play us in Seattle every time we go north.

Stadiums and populations are not only smaller in the north, but the weather is worse, too. And there are other diversions. In 1973 our defending national champions, working on a 20-game unbeaten streak, drew 21,000 people in Corvallis for Oregon State. It was the first day of deer-hunting season.

So we go out and recruit good players and spend a

long time coaching them, hustle crowds so we can sell 50,000 season tickets, and these universities come down and take half of our work. No matter how badly they do, we get half of their work, and they get half of ours.

My belief is that we should wipe out our league's round-robin schedule and write new contracts. We'll tell those three Northwest schools we'll play you three times in Los Angeles for every game at your place. Or, if you want to keep the schedule on a home-and-home basis, you take all the money when you play at home, and we'll keep all the money when we play at home.

Here we are at USC, a private university scrambling for more money, and then I discover that in one Coliseum game with Oregon we make $95,000, and it takes three games up there to make $110,000. That's a lot of money to blow. Half the time we can't even give our coaches raises, while we're turning away hundreds of thousands of dollars because of an outdated tradition that is mutually destructive.

The presidents of those northern schools talk about how much football is costing them, and yet they're refusing hundreds of thousands of dollars, too, by not playing us in Los Angeles. They say their students want to see our team, or their coaches would rather play at home. Well, are they worried about money or aren't they?

By staying in the league USC also loses a tremendous amount of money on television games—not only on conference games, but also on nonconference games, such as against Notre Dame. That's because we must share television receipts with conference members.

When we play Notre Dame on national TV, the first 6 percent goes to the NCAA, which is standard. Of the remaining amount, a staggering 50 percent goes to Notre Dame. We get four-tenths of the other 50 percent and one of eight shares of the other six-tenths.

Notre Dame made $203,000 from television on our 1972 game, just because they're independent. They had a better day than Anthony Davis with his six touchdowns. Our TV share, after splitting with league members, was $96,000. When you add gate receipts, that was a $426,000 game for the Irish. Not counting concessions, which every home team keeps, we netted $319,000. We lost $107,000 in television money in one day by being in the Pacific-8.

Lest you get the wrong idea, I must interject here that it's not greed that makes us envious of Notre Dame. It's the cold reality of our situation. The money made from football may sound like a small fortune, but you must remember it has to support all the other sports we have that generate little or no income. Sports like track, baseball, swimming, golf, water polo, tennis, rugby and soccer. All of them have travel, medical, food and equipment expenses, and most award scholarships.

Compared with independent schools, we also lose money on bowl games. The Rose Bowl has the richest television contract of all the holiday classics. We've gone six of the last eight times, yet the conference shares equally. Off the top in 1973 we got $90,000 for expenses, but it cost us more than that to get ready for the game. Our game share was $162,000. The other seven schools did nothing all December and picked up the same $162,000.

Notre Dame has made about $400,000 in three of its four recent bowl appearances. Independent Penn State took home $435,000 from the 1972 Cotton Bowl. Even allowing for their expenses, those schools are still clearing a lot more than we do.

Everyone tells me it's so important for us to have the league. I don't believe it. We don't need it for football and we don't need it for basketball. And there are plenty of California schools for teams in the minor sports to play. They play them now. USC is better off independent.

Eventually, it's going to get so costly that something will have to be done. If we keep the Pacific-8 intact, the football schedules will have to be changed. The way the rules are written is just another example of collegiate stupidity. We complain about the consumption of money —and then throw away a chance to earn more.

So as a football coach I never want to play the easiest teams to beat. We want to play the teams that draw the best, both in Los Angeles and on the road.

In recent years many people have lobbied for a collegiate national championship game, similar to the Super Bowl. But I don't believe a playoff system is feasible. The Super Bowl doesn't give the pros a true champion either, because every team doesn't have the same schedule. If college football tried a playoff system, a team could lose all its nonconference games and still go to the playoffs because it had a good league record. What if it was a weak league?

To me, the bowl games have created much more interest than the NCAA basketball tournament. They've done a lot for college football. They're also held over the Christmas holidays when the players are out of class, and the whole atmosphere can be tremendously enjoyable for the kids.

But a playoff schedule would drag on through at least three more games, running the total to 14. I think faculty members would take a fairly dim view of this, because they're screaming overemphasis now when we're playing 11 or 12.

A playoff system would also kill the bowls. If we held them after the playoffs they'd be meaningless. It would be impossible to use all of them in the playoff structure, and even if we kept all the major ones, we could no longer retain the equality among them.

Besides, with a national playoff there would only be one winner at the end of the season. Everybody else is a loser. With all the bowls, several good teams can finish the season on an upbeat note.

The Super Bowl usually winds up being a dull game anyway. The two teams got there by playing great defense, so it will logically be low-scoring, and it has been.

But if the current bowls are good, teams should be allowed to compete in them. I object to the exclusiveness of our Rose Bowl contract. It allows just one team in the Pac-8 and Big Ten to compete after the season— and only in the Rose Bowl. It's a crime that an excellent second-best team, or in some cases, a co-champion, can't go to another bowl.

Michigan lost only one game out of 22 in 1972 and 1973 and sat home on New Year's Day both times. In 1969 and 1973 UCLA finished with 8-1-1 and 9-2 records and went nowhere. In 1972, if we had lost to UCLA, we could have finished with a 10-1 record, been national champion and still not gone to a bowl.

Because the Rose Bowl contract is the richest of all the bowl contracts, we've been worried about television trimming the money if the pact were no longer exclusive. But nobody actually knows what we would lose or gain.

My feeling has always been that the games are for the people who play in them. The youngsters who play have a right to a reward, and in college football it's a bowl. If we had to take a little less money from the Rose Bowl to let other teams and players share in the fun, it would be worth it.

If more of our teams went to bowls, I think it would also help the overall recruiting in the league and make it stronger. This appears to have been proven in the Big Eight, where several teams have gone to bowls in recent years. Many people now consider that the strongest league.

There are an awful lot of bowls and all-star games, but some of the money is donated to charity, and I know of no easier way to raise it. This is one of the side benefits of football, as exemplified by the Shrine East-West Game in San Francisco every December or the College All-Star Game every summer. Anyone who visits the Shriners' hospitals will get a graphic example of the good football has done.

How young should a boy play organized football? When I was running around in West Virginia we were never organized, and we probably had more fun than many of the kids today who play Pop Warner football. I'm not opposed to Pop Warner ball, but it's important that the coaching is good enough to make sure that proper techniques are taught for safety, and also important that all young players are allowed to occasionally handle the ball.

That is why I've always liked flag football, because everybody can be a star. Let them all run, catch and pass. They'll enjoy it more, improve their coordination and determine exactly what ability they really have.

There are some outstanding Pop Warner coaches, just as there are some outstanding Little League coaches. But there are others who not only can't teach, but don't believe in allowing youngsters to enjoy themselves. Winning becomes everything. Winning should not be everything for an eight- or ten-year-old boy.

Because of the chance of injury, I can't emphasize strongly enough that correct techniques must be taught. Without them, it can be dangerous for boys to play tackle much younger than 14 or 15, because bones and muscles aren't fully developed—particularly neck muscles—and head and neck injuries are the kind we worry about most in football.

Of course, you can break arms and legs doing anything. More people are hurt skiing than by playing football.

College football is exciting because it changes so fast, but it's always been a policy of mine never to discuss upcoming trends. Every time I read a coach's prediction, it turns out just the opposite. Three or four years ago, Ara Parseghian said we were going to see much less scoring. We promptly had an offensive explosion.

I've noticed, however, that a new rule allows girls to play in California high schools, and some of them are doing it. This has piqued my curiosity. I don't think that's all bad. If we ever lose heavily, I'd rather play girls, too. It's not a hell of a lot of fun losing with a bunch of guys.

EPILOGUE

"I don't mind driving the freeways to work"

As LONG AS I MAINTAIN my enthusiasm I want to continue in coaching. I've spent the happiest days of my life on the USC campus, in fact, nearly one-third of it. In 1973 I signed a new contract as coach and athletic director that runs for 15 years. When that contract expires in 1988, I'll be 65.

If you catch me at the end of a season I might tell you I'm quitting tomorrow, but coaches can't be held accountable for what they say at the ends of seasons. We're all tired then. If we've had a great season, we figure we can give up on a winner. If we've had a losing season, we're depressed and frustrated.

I've only been approached for a job by one other school, and that was through my closest friend in coaching. I would never have left to go to another school anyway.

But one night a few years ago I received a surprise phone call from Bear Bryant. He told me the Miami Dolphins had made him a fantastic offer to become head coach. This was before the Dolphins hired Don Shula, and Paul said he was seriously considering the offer.

However, he was worried about finding an acceptable replacement—one whom Alabama's board of trustees would be happy to hire. Paul not only has coached many years for Alabama, but he also played for the Tide, and he said he wanted to leave them with a good coach.

"John," he said in his mumbling phone voice, "how would you like to be the new coach at Alabama?"

"Paul," I said, "why would I want to leave USC to go to Alabama?"

"John, just think of it. You wouldn't have to drive the freeways to work."

"Paul," I answered, "I don't mind driving the freeways to work."

Bryant's reasoning was way out, but his offer was serious. I think he approached Darrell Royal of Texas, too, and maybe one other coach. I really think the fact he couldn't get a suitable replacement was one of the reasons he stayed at Alabama.

But if I were going to leave USC I would have gone into pro football and made two or three or four times as much money as I could in college. Just after we won the national championship in 1972, the New England Patriots offered me a $1.5 million, ten-year contract as coach and general manager. I was tempted, although I don't think any coach or ball player is worth that much money. It was my sixth pro offer.

But I like the atmosphere of a university. I always thought it would be beneficial to raise my children in this environment, and I think it has been. Over the years my sons have spent most of the football seasons at our practices and in our locker rooms. When I was an assistant at Oregon, Johnny used to walk over to campus with me almost every day.

I'll admit that when a professional team comes around and offers so much more money than you'll ever have the capability of earning and you have a family, you must think about it. I have been flattered by the six offers I've received and always considered them carefully. Each time Corky said, "Do what you think is best." New England even offered us a chauffeur to drive her through the snow.

I have many friends in pro football, several with the Rams, who offered me their job three times—in 1965, 1968 and 1970. Each time I came fairly close, but then I'd say, ah, the hell with it.

I came closest the last time, but a discouraging factor was the failing health of owner Dan Reeves. I really liked Danny, and his 1970 offer was for 15 years, beginning at $90,000 a year. But he was so sick I didn't feel he could continue as owner much longer.

If he died, I assumed the organization would be sold and I'd be stuck with a contract owned by a group of people who had not hired me. I don't like arrangements like that. When Reeves died later, the Rams were sold.

But even if the situation had been perfect, I would still have weighed my great university and position and a career I loved against an unknown—all for money. If I didn't enjoy pro football, all I'd be doing is working for money. I did that when I was a boy and didn't like it.

As I said before, when I wake up in the morning I eagerly look forward to going to work. I doubt that most people do. And after all, life is too short not to do what you really enjoy.

JOHN MC KAY

John McKay, a native of West Virginia, has been coach of the University of Southern California Trojans since 1960. Now 51, McKay is at the peak of his career. He has produced three national champions, seven Rose Bowl teams, three squads that went unbeaten, and Heisman Trophy winners Mike Garrett and O. J. Simpson. Moreover, he has won the friendship and respect of such adversaries as Paul "Bear" Bryant of the University of Alabama and Ara Parseghian of Notre Dame.

JIM PERRY

Jim Perry first became acquainted with Coach McKay in 1962 as a student-newspaper reporter for the *Daily Trojan*. After graduation from the University of Southern California in 1964, he became a UPI staff writer. In 1966–67, as Assistant Sports Information Director at USC, he became reacquainted with McKay. He then joined the *Los Angeles Herald-Examiner* as a staff writer, where he covered the Trojans with insight and zeal. After six years as a reporter, Perry has returned to his alma mater as the Sports Information Director. He says his wife, Cathy, inspired him to write this book.